GARDEN GOURMET

THE
DALLAS ARBORETUM
COOKBOOK

The Dallas Arboretum and Botanical Garden

Dallas, Texas

The Garden Gourmet
The Dallas Arboretum and Botanical Garden
8617 Garland Road
Dallas, Texas 75218
(214) 327-8263   FAX (214) 324-9801

All proceeds from the sale of *The Garden Gourmet* will go toward the restoration
of the historic DeGolyer House.

Photography courtesy: Alex Minor, minor Creations, Dallas, Texas
Watercolor Cover, courtesy of: Brandy Redd Smith
Floral Arrangements, courtesy of: Gunter's, Richardson, Texas
Food Design: Lynda Sanders
Typography: Anita Stumbo

Printed and bound in the USA by
Taylor Publishing Company, Dallas, Texas

W. Jay Love, Coordinator

ISBN: 0-9640249-0-X

Contents

Thank you to the following contributors

DOGWOOD CIRCLE

Mrs. Henry P. Shotland and Family
Mrs. Ralph Wilkinson
William Cameron & Co.

CRAPE MYRTLE CIRCLE

Anonymous
Beulah Holman
Patricia Yanigan-Eigen
Mill Daffron

FLOWERING PEACH CIRCLE

Richard L. Grandjean, M.D.
Mr. and Mrs. Charles H. Crowe
June and Jane Milley
Lydia Chandler
Mr. and Mrs. John S. Ward
Jennifer Freeman, M.D.
Mary G. Everett
Gary and Stella Klein
Sally Junkins
Carl J. Pruitt
Carol Singer
Kenneth and DyAnna Giltner
Richard and Diane Jeffrey
Lyle Ozmun
Mayor and Mrs. Steve Bartlett
Louise Suggs
Marilyn Thomas
Jack F. and Patricia B. Gorman
Gordon and Julia O'Roark
Joe Ring / Metro Factors, Inc.

Svend and Neva Muller
Judge and Mrs. James A. Baker
Congressman and Mrs. Sam Johnson
Greta Rees
Orien Woolf
June M. Driggers
Martha Barnes Weisend
White Rock Republicans Women
Nick and Lynda Sanders
Anna Bradberry
Vitality Magazine, Inc.
Lon and Judy Williams
Dr. Edwin and Natalie Ornish
Mrs. Ben P. Denman
Renee Cottrell-Brown

THE DALLAS ARBORETUM AND BOTANICAL GARDEN

The Dallas Arboretum and Botanical Society, Inc. had a prophetic beginning. Everette Lee DeGolyer, a petroleum geologist who is recognized as the founder of applied petroleum geophysics, suggested an arboretum for Dallas and chaired a committee to find a land site. Mr. DeGolyer's vision caught the imagination of his family and others and now fifty years later, his concept for a botanical preserve for Dallas is a reality on the very land he once owned.

In 1974, The Dallas Arboretum and Botanical Society, Inc. was formed as a non-profit organization dedicated to locate, develop and operate a public botanic garden within the City of Dallas. By 1980, the Society had raised over one million dollars and purchased the 22-acre Camp Estate adjacent to the original 44-acre DeGolyer Estate. In 1982, the City of Dallas and the Society signed a contract creating an arboretum and botanical garden on the combined 66 acres of the DeGolyer and Camp properties.

Since that time, The Arboretum has designed, constructed and opened five major gardens: the Lay Ornamental Garden, a contemporary Texas interpretation of an English-style perennial garden with innovative water features; the Margaret Elizabeth Jonsson Garden, 5.4 acres featuring over 2,500 varieties of azaleas; the Palmer Fern Dell, with a unique fog system for sub-tropical plants; the Main Public Entry and Arrival Garden which provides a warm welcome for visitors; and the Lyda Bunker Hunt Paseo de Flores, a ¼-mile linear garden and pedestrian walkway connecting the DeGolyer and Camp Estates.

The Society also restored the formal garden originally built with the DeGolyer House and enhanced the DeGolyer Oval Garden. The latest projects include the Garland Road Enhancement and Crape Myrtle Allee Enhancement.

The Dallas Arboretum has the unique distinction of having two historic homes on the grounds. The DeGolyer House, named Rancho Encinal for the numerous oak trees, was the home of Everette and Nell Goodrich DeGolyer. The Spanish Colonial Revival home was designed by California architects, Denman Scott and Burton Schutt. The home, completed in early 1940, has 21,000 square feet, including servants' quarters and garage.

Everette DeGolyer, know to his friends as "De" or "Mr. De," liked to refer to the house as "a California architect's notion of what a Texas oilman would want in attempting to duplicate a Mexican hacienda on the outskirts of a big modern American city."

The DeGolyers had three daughters and a son. The daughters were already married and the son was entering college when the house was built, so we are told it was built for three reasons; Mr. De's love of books, Mrs. DeGolyer's love of gardening, and their mutual love of entertaining.

The library, designed to house his extensive book collections, has over 1,700 square feet. There were extensive formal English style gardens, plus a vegetable garden, to satisfy Nell's love of gardening, and there were many large family gatherings as well as large parties with distinguished guest lists.

Mr. DeGolyer's four major book collections are now in three major universities. His first editions were given to the University of Texas. He built a special "History of Science" collection for the University of Oklahoma, reputed to be one of the finest in the country. His two largest collections, one on Texas and the Southwest and his working collection on geology are in the DeGolyer Library at Southern Methodist University.

Mr. De was involved in various petroleum businesses. He was a founder of Core Laboratories and founded his own company, DeGolyer and MacNaughton, reputed to be the foremost petroleum consulting firm in the world. He was an investor in a small company, Geophysical Services, Inc. He encouraged J.C. Karcher, the original owner to work in seismograph research and Karcher's invention of the reflection seismograph revolutionized the oil business. GSI later became Texas Instruments.

The DeGolyer House is on the National Register of Historic Homes and in 1993 was awarded a Texas Historic Landmark designation. It is open daily for guided tours.

The Camp House, built for Alex and Roberta Coke Camp, was designed by John Staub and was completed in 1938. The house is a combination of Latin Colonial, English Regency and Art Deco styles, combined very harmoniously. It is one-room deep throughout, with all living and bedrooms obtaining three or four exposures. Alex Camp died about the time the house was completed and Roberta did little entertaining here. However, she remained very active in Dallas society and numerous philanthropic activities.

The Camp House is currently used as administrative offices for the Dallas Arboretum and Botanical Society. It is not open for public tours, but is a favorite spot for weddings and receptions on weekends and evenings.

More than 250,000 visitors tour The Dallas Arboretum every year, coming from all over the world. Special events highlight every season such as Dallas Blooms, a spectacular spring display of thousands of blooming tulips, pansies, azaleas and more. Autumn at the Arboretum is the showplace for fall color with thousands of colorful chrysanthemums blazing throughout the gardens, and Christmas at the Arboretum celebrates the holiday as the DeGolyer House is trimmed with festive decorations by Dallas' top designers.

Whatever the season, there is always something to enjoy on these beautiful grounds overlooking scenic White Rock Lake, just minutes away from downtown Dallas.

Information compiled by Diane Jeffrey

The quatrefoil at the top of each page is stylized from the architectural feature on the front of the DeGolyer Estate framing the front door. The quatrefoil is a conventionalized representation of a flower with four petals.

Cookbook Chairman	Stella Klein	
Co-Chairman	Lynda Sanders	
Secretary	Ruth Barnard	
Treasurer	DyAnna Giltner	
Data Entry	Virginia Salter	Sue Smith
Recipe Testing Chairman	Pam Easter	
Testing Committee	JoAnna Almgren	Stella Klein
	Ruth Barnard	Lucy Martin
	Ann Boecher	Virginia Salter
	Kala Casebolt	Lynda Sanders
	Noreen Collins	Helen Tieber
	Peggy Dawson	Anne Walker
	Dorothy Jones	Jan Workman
Recipe Coordinator	Pam Easter	
Proof-Readers Chairman	Neva Muller	
Proof-Reading Committee	Jeanne Barnes	Margot Winspear
	Anna Bradberry	
Finance Chairman	Helen Tieber	
Finance Committee	Barbara Adamson	Martha Weisend
Marketing Chairman	Pat Yanigan-Eigen	
Marketing Committee	Ruth Miller	Jack Pruitt
Historical Consultant	Diane Jeffrey	
Arboretum Staff Coordinators	Lydia Chandler	Jill Magnuson
	Lisa Jones	Suzanne Townsend
	Nancy Howell	

The Garden Gourmet, Dallas Arboretum Cookbook is dedicated to the Docents of The DeGolyer House for reviving the idea of a cookbook started by Susan Morris in 1990. This book is in her memory.

Special thanks to Stella Klein, whose smiling face has been a source of joy. This project could not have been accomplished without her spirit, patience, confidence, and her endless enthusiasm. Thanks for staying on top of so many details and for sharing the vision.

Our sincere appreciation to all who submitted the hundreds of recipes to this committee. We were unable to incorporate all of these recipes due to similarity or lack of space.

Our appreciation goes to all the people who committed their efforts and talents in creating a cookbook of quality and excellence, in keeping with the standards of The Dallas Arboretum.

We Thank You

APPETIZERS

— ■ —

GARDEN GOURMET COOKBOOK

ASPARAGUS ROLL-UPS

1 package cream cheese
1 package blue cheese
½ cup margarine, melted

1 egg
1 loaf white bread
1 to 2 cans asparagus spears

Drain asparagus. Count spears and pull out same number of bread slices. Remove crusts and roll thin with rolling pin. Soften cream cheese and crumbled blue cheese in microwave. Add slighly beaten egg and stir until blended. Spread on bread slices and place one asparagus on long edge of bread slice. Roll up and cut into thirds. Dip in margarine and bake on greased cookie sheet at 375 degrees for 15 to 20 minutes.

Lynda Sanders

ARTICHOKE SQUARES

1 onion, finely chopped
1 clove garlic or ⅛ teaspoon
    garlic powder
2 tablespoons margarine
4 eggs, beaten
¼ cup fine bread crumbs
    Salt and pepper to taste

½ teaspoon oregano
¼ teaspoon Tabasco
2 cups sharp cheddar cheese, grated
5 tablespoons fresh parsley, minced
1 8½-ounce can artichoke hearts,
    drained, rinsed and chopped

Sauté onion (and clove garlic, if using) in butter or margarine until limp. Remove from heat. Combine beaten eggs, crumbs, salt, pepper, oregano and Tabasco. Fold in cheese, parsley and artichokes; add onion and garlic. Stir. Place in a greased 9-inch square pan. Bake for 30 minutes in 325 degree oven. Doubled recipe may be baked in a 9×13-inch pan. May be served hot or cold.

Louise Suggs

ARTICHOKE/BACON APPETIZERS

1 16-ounce can water packed
   artichoke hearts

5 to 6 slices bacon
   Dijon mustard

Cut artichoke hearts in half and set aside. Cut bacon slices in thirds and spread with mustard. Wrap bacon (mustard side in) around artichoke half and secure with a toothpick. Place on the rack of a broiler pan and bake at 400 degrees until bacon is to desired doneness (20 to 30 minutes). Drain for a few minutes on paper towels and serve on a warmed platter or tray. Makes about 16 pieces which will serve 4 to 5 people.

Martha Baker

MARINATED MUSHROOMS

1 pound mushrooms
¾ cup olive oil
3 tablespoons tarragon vinegar
½ teaspoon salt

Freshly ground black pepper
2 teaspoons minced parsley
½ teaspoon minced fresh or dried Tarragon

Wash mushrooms and slice lengthwise through stem and cap. Combine other ingredients and mix well with mushrooms. Let stand in glass bowl 5 to 6 hours at room temperature; do not chill. Serve with cocktail picks as an appetizer or add to tossed salad.

Willard Baker

SPINACH NUGGETS

6 eggs, well beaten
2 10-ounce packages frozen
   chopped spinach
3 cups herb seasoned stuffing mix
1 large onion, finely chopped

¾ cup margarine
½ cup Parmesan cheese, grated
1 teaspoon pepper
1½ teaspoons garlic salt
½ teaspoon thyme

Cook spinach as package directs; drain *very* well. Add stuffing mix to well beaten eggs. Let stand 5 to 10 minutes or until stuffing softens. Add spinach and remaining ingredients to stuffing mixture. Shape into ¾-inch balls and place on foil lined cookie sheet. Bake at 325 degrees for 15 to 20 minutes. Serve warm or at room temperature. Can be frozen after cooking and cooled. Reheat in microwave. Makes 11 dozen.

Lanette Sprott

STUFFED JALAPEÑO PEPPERS

4 large jalapeño peppers, with stems
1 egg
1/4 pound crab meat, minced
1 pound processed cheese
1/4 cup cracker meal (or 6 to 8 saltines, finely crushed)

1 tablespoon onion, grated
1/4 teaspoon salt
1/8 teaspoon pepper
Dash Worcestershire sauce
Lemon slices

Parboil peppers until crisp tender, or steam in microwave. Split peppers and remove seeds. Stuff cavity with cheese; close pepper. Mix egg, onion, crackers and seasoning together. Add crab meat to mixture and mix all together. If too dry, add a little milk. If too moist, add cracker crumbs. Mold crab/cracker mixture around peppers. Deep fry in hot oil until golden brown. This can be a hot taste, depending on the heat in the peppers . . . have water handy! Serve with a red seafood sauce made of catsup, lemon juice and horseradish too taste. Garnish with a slice of lemon and parsley. Shrimp or fish can be substituted for crabmeat. Serves 4.

Barbara Lake

ASPARAGUS APPETIZER

1 can asparagus spears
1 loaf sandwich bread
8 ounces cream cheese
1 tablespoon mayonnaise

1 egg, beaten
1/2 cup butter, melted (for dipping)
Parmesan cheese for rolling

Cut crust from bread and roll each slice flat. Spread with mixture of cream cheese, mayonnaise and egg. Place one asparagus spear on bread slice and roll up firmly. Cut into thirds. Dip in melted butter and roll in Parmesan cheese. Bake at 350 degrees for 15 minutes. May be frozen before cooking.

Sunny Krutz

MEAT ROLL-UPS

1 large jar chipped beef
8 ounces cream cheese

1/3 cup Parmesan cheese
1 tablespoon horseradish

Combine last 3 ingredients and spread on each chipped beef slice. Roll and refrigerate overnight. Serves 8.

LaVera Gardner

ASPARAGUS SANDWICHES

1 large loaf sandwich bread, very
   fresh and soft

2 15- to 16-ounce cans asparagus spears
   Mayonnaise to cover bread

Trim crust from bread. Lay the trimmed slices on a flat surface and flatten with a rolling pin. Cover each slice with mayonnaise. Drain the asparagus. Handle gently so the tops stay on. Place one spear on each slice of bread diagonally. Fold two side corners together to form a blanket. Place rolled sandwiches in a plastic storage container, fold side down. Let the sandwiches sit for 3 to 4 hours before serving, folded side up. Sandwiches can be made a day ahead. Serve on a salad plate or as tea sandwiches, or for appetizers. Can be cut in half for bite size food.

Virginia Duncan

HOLIDAY SANDWICHES

1 3-ounce package cream cheese,
   softened
¼ cup pecans, finely chopped
¼ cup dates, chopped

¼ cup crushed pineapple, well drained
16 slices wheat, white or green/red
   (for Christmas) sandwich bread

Combine first 4 ingredients and set aside. With a tree-shaped 3½-inch cookie cutter (or other holiday shape), cut 32 Christmas trees from bread slices. Spread about 1½ teaspoons filling on half of trees; top with remaining trees. Optionally, decorate trees with cut-up maraschino cherries or your choice of decoration.

Anne Boecher

PICKLE SANDWICH

1 large loaf of sandwich bread,
    white or wheat (the fresher the better)

8 medium size dill pickles
Filling

Take 3 bread slices and trim off crusts. Overlap the 3 trimmed bread slices about ½-inch and roll with a rolling pin until very flat and the overlapping ends stick together. Repeat with remainder of loaf. There should be a total of 8.

Filling:

8 ounces cream cheese
Seasonings to taste

1 8-ounce carton small curd cottage
    cheese (light, if you prefer)
Mayonnaise to taste

Combine filling ingredients by hand or in blender. Spread filling on the flattened bread. Put the pickle on one end and roll the bread (spread with the filling) around it. Place the rolls side by side in a pan and chill at least 4 hours. They can be prepared a day before serving. When ready to serve, slice the rolls with a sharp knife. Each roll should yield 6 or 7 slices. (Suggested seasonings: Spice Islands Beau Monde, garlic powder, paprika, pepper.)

D'Maris Crowe

SWEET ONION & HERBED MAYONNAISE SANDWICH

¾ cup reduced-calorie mayonnaise
3 tablespoons dill, finely chopped
3 tablespoons finely chopped
    tarragon or parsley
2 teaspoons orange zest, finely grated

18 slices soft-white or egg-style bread
    (about 3½-inch square)
Sweet onion, sliced very thin
    (Vidalia, Maui or red)
Additional chopped herbs (optional)

In a small bowl, mix mayonnaise, dill, tarragon (or parsley) and orange zest. Remove bread crusts and spread one side of each slice with 2 teaspoons of the herbed mayonnaise mixture. Cover 9 slices of bread with onion; top with remaining 9 slices. Cut each sandwich into 2 circles with a 1½-inch round cookie cutter. Lightly spread remaining mayonnasie around outside edge of sandwiches and roll in additional chopped herbs to decorate. Yield: 18 sandwiches.

Note: Use equal parts light mayonnaise and light cream cheese. Herbs may be added "to taste." Spread on thin white or wheat bread.

Louise Suggs

ALMOND HAM ROLL-UPS

1 8-ounce package cream cheese	¼ teaspoon dry mustard
2 tablespoons mayonnaise or	¼ teaspoon paprika
salad dressing	1 to 2 tablespoons finely chopped
1 teaspoon instant minced onion	almonds, toasted
⅛ teaspoon hot sauce	⅛ teaspoon pepper
1 teaspoon Worcestershire sauce	1 12-ounce package thinly sliced ham

Soften cream cheese. Combine all but ham. Stir until blended. Put 1 tablespoon of mixture on each ham slice. Roll up and cut into pieces. Freeze up to 1 month; thaw 1 hour before serving. Makes 5 dozen.

Doris Constant

TORTILLA ROLL-UPS

4 large flour tortillas	1 9-ounce can bean dip
1 2½-ounce can ripe chopped olives	1 8-ounce container light pasteurized
1 4-ounce can chopped green chilies	cream cheese

Spread cream cheese on tortilla, then spread bean dip. Sprinkle ripe olives and green chilies on top. Roll and slice in one inch pieces. Chill before serving. Can be served with picante sauce.

Marjorie Weber

CANAPES AU ROQUEFORT

24 small slices rye bread or toast	2 tablespoons cream
7 ounces Roquefort cheese	2 tablespoons ground almonds
12 ounces cream cheese	24 walnut halves

In a bowl, crush the cream cheese and mix with the Roque-fort, cream and almonds. Spread this mixture on the slices of rye bread. Decorate with walnut halves.

Cookbook Committee

MEXICAN FUDGE

6 *eggs, beaten*
1 *pound cheddar cheese, grated*

1 *4-ounce can chopped jalapeños*
Black olives

Lightly grease an 8×8-inch Pyrex dish. Drain jalapenos and spread over bottom of dish. Mix cheese and eggs and pour over jalapeños. Slice olives and place on top of cheese mixture. Bake 30 minutes at 350 degrees. Cool slightly and cut into small squares with olive slice centered on top of each square.

B. Copeland

PEPPER SNACKS

1 *3-ounce package cream cheese,*
 softened
½ *cup cheddar cheese, shredded*
2 *tablespoons chopped green chiles*

2 *tablespoons chopped ripe olives*
1 *teaspoon instant minced onion*
5 *drops hot pepper sauce*
1 *can quick crescent dinner rolls*

In small mixing bowl, combine all but dinner rolls and blend well. Separate crescent dough into rectangles. Press perforation to seal. Spread mixture onto 4 rectangles. Starting along long side, roll up each rectangle jelly roll style. Cut each roll into 10 slices, and place cut side down on greased cookie sheets. Bake at 375 degrees for 12 to 15 minute, until golden brown. Serve hot. Can be reheated uncovered on a cookie sheet at 400 degrees for 5 minutes. To make ahead, prepare, cover and refrigerate for 2 to 3 hours. Bake as directed.

Zelma Klingman

HOT CHEESE PUFFS

1 *loaf French bread*
1 *pound sharp cheddar cheese*
6 *ounces cream cheese*

1 *cup margarine*
4 *egg whites, stiffly beaten*

Cut French bread into 1-inch cubes after removing crust. In double boiler, melt cheeses and margarine, stirring frequently. When cheese is completely melted and blended, fold in egg whites. Cheese should be off heat when egg whites are added. Dip bread cubes into cheese mixture, coating thoroughly. Freeze on wax paper covered cookie sheet 1 to 2 hours. Store in plastic bag until ready to use (up to 3 months). When ready to use, bake at 400 degrees for 10 to 12 minutes. Serve immediately.

Renee Morris

HAM PUFFS

1 8-ounce package cream cheese,
　softened
1 egg yolk
1 teaspoon baking powder

Thin sliced bread
Mayonnaise
1 4½-ounce can deviled ham
Paprika

Combine cream cheese, egg yolk and baking powder. Mix until blended and smooth. Then cut four small rounds from each slice of bread. (A shot glass makes a good cutter.) Spread each round with mayonnaise, then a thin layer of deviled ham. Spoon cheese mixture on the ham and sprinkle with paprika. Can be frozen at this point. To serve, put in 375 degree oven for 10 to 15 minutes.

Anne S. Boecher

TUNA PUFFS

Puffs:
　½ cup water
　½ cup butter
　　Dash of salt

½ cup flour
2 eggs

Filling:
　2 6½-ounce cans tuna
　1 cup celery, chopped fine
　2 tablespoons onion, chopped
　　Dash of salt

2 tablespoons sweet pickles, chopped
4 ounces cream cheese
2 tablespoons mayonnaise

Puffs: Combine water, butter and salt in saucepan and bring to a boil. Add flour all at one time and stir vigorously until mixture forms a ball and leaves the side of the pan. Remove from heat. Add eggs one at a time. Beat until satiny. Drop by teaspoon onto a cookie sheet. Bake at 400 degrees for 30 minutes, or until puffs are golden.

Filling: Drain and flake tuna. Combine with celery, onion, pickle, cream cheese and mayonnaise, and salt. Mix thoroughly. Cut tops from puff shells. Fill each with approximately 2 teaspoons of salad. (Or fill with any of your favorite salad fillings such as ham or chicken.) Makes about 50 hors d'oeuvres.

Stella Klein

SHRIMP TOAST

1 pound jumbo raw shrimp	1 tablespoon cornstarch
1 can water chestnuts	1/2 teaspoon MSG
1/4 medium onion	1 egg
1 teaspoon salt	12 slices thin bread
1 teaspoon sugar	Plain bread crumbs

Finely chop shrimp, water chestnuts and onion. Add salt, sugar, cornstarch, MSG, and egg. Mix well. Remove crusts from bread and cut in fourths, crosswise. Spread mixture on bread, sprinkle with crumbs. Fry, shrimp side down in about one inch of vegetable oil until lightly golden. Serve hot. Makes 48 pieces. Can be frozen and thawed. Reheat in 350 degree oven.

Carole Cohen

SUMMER PIZZA

2 large rolls of crescent dough	1 cucumber, chopped
2 8-ounce packages cream cheese	5 green onions, chopped
1/3 cup salad dressing	1 tomato, chopped
1 green pepper, chopped.	Dill weed

Unroll crescent dough and lay on a 9×13-inch cookie sheet. Bake until golden brown, about 10 minutes. (Use oven temperature shown on dough can.) Mix softened cream cheese and salad dressing together and spread on crust. Top with vegetables, then sprinkle with dill weed.

Joy Newton

VEGETABLE BARS

2 cans refrigerated crescent rolls
2 8-ounce packages cream cheese
1 cup mayonnaise
1 egg
1 package ranch style dry dressing mix

½ cup shredded carrots
½ cup finely chopped broccoli
½ cup finely chopped cauliflower
8 ounces finely shredded cheddar cheese

Flatten crescent rolls on a large cookie sheet. Beat the egg and brush over flattened crescent rolls before baking. Bake at 375 degrees for 12 minutes. Cool. Mix the cream cheese, mayonnaise and dressing mix, and spread on the crescent rolls. Sprinkle the vegetables over the cream cheese in the order listed. Very lightly press the vegetables into the cream cheese mixture. Sprinkle cheese over the vegetables and refrigerate. Can be made a day before serving.

Note: ½ cup chopped red bell pepper and 2 tablespoons chopped onion may also be added to vegetable topping.

Linda Farabee and Pauline Ellis

BABY BRIE WITH SUN-DRIED TOMATOES

1 pound baby brie
½ cup oil-soaked sun-dried tomatoes

¼ cup chopped parsley
20 slices French bread

Preheat oven to 350 degrees. Drain tomatoes, reserving oil. Chop tomatoes finely and combine with chopped parsley. Slice brie in half. Slice each half into 10 wedges. Place each slice of brie on a piece of bread that has been brushed with the reserved oil from tomatoes. Top with 1 teaspoon of the tomato mixture. Place on cookie sheet and bake 5 to 7 minutes. Serve immediately.

Janet Trlica

BEORGE

1 package phyllo pastry sheets
1 cup margarine, melted

1 pound Muenster cheese, grated
2 eggs

Mix cheese and eggs. Lay out 3 pastry layers, brushing margarine between layers. Cut into 5 strips. Place 2 tablespoons cheese/egg mix onto end of each strip. Fold into triangle, buttering when folding. Place on a cookie sheet. Bake at 350 degrees, 15 to 20 minutes. Can be frozen. Serves 25. (Egg roll wrappers may be folded in this manner, using flour/water paste to seal.)

Carol Russell

BAKED CHEESE IN PASTRY

1 package refrigerated flaky biscuits
  (or pastry dough)
1 7- to 10-ounces Gouda cheese
  (round or slab)

3 or 4 scallions, minced
1 egg yolk, beaten
  Butter

Preheat oven to 350 degrees. Remove pastry or biscuit dough from cylinder. With fingers divide dough into 2 parts. Pat each part into a circle and place one circle on a foil covered cookie sheet. Put cheese in center of circle. Sprinkle minced scallions over cheese. Place other circle of dough over cheese. Crimp edges to seal cheese in dough. Trim off a little dough to make leaves or other decoration. Dot with butter and then brush with egg yolk. Bake 30 to 45 minutes or until browned. Serve with chilled grapes.

Peggy Dawson

CAVIAR PIE

6 hard-boiled eggs
8 tablespoons butter, melted
6 small white onions, chopped

3 4-ounce jars lumpfish caviar
1 16-ounce carton sour cream

Put eggs through a sieve or chop in food processor for 20 seconds. Place in 8¼-inch Pyrex cake pan. Stir in melted butter. Cover and refrigerate for one hour. Spread chopped onions on top of eggs. Layer caviar on onions and top with sour cream. Serve with white wafer crackers.

Barbara Bigham

SALAMI EGG MOUSSE CORNETS

24 thin slices salami
5 hard cooked eggs, chopped
3 ounces cream cheese, softened
1 teaspoon chopped parsley

¼ cup soft butter
Salt and pepper to taste
Worcestershire sauce to taste

Mix eggs, cream cheese, butter, parsley and spices to a smooth paste. Place in pastry bag. Fold salami slices in half, then form into cone shapes. Press mixture into cones. Can be decorated with small dill pickle slices. If needed, hold with toothpicks.

Virginia Salter

EGG~PEANUT SPREAD

6 boiled eggs, finely chopped
½ cup roasted peanuts, finely chopped
2 tablespoons pimiento, finely chopped
2 tablespoons olives, finely chopped
1 tablespoon chives, finely chopped

½ teaspoon salt
¼ cup mayonnaise
¼ cup milk
¼ teaspoon Worcestershire sauce

Combine all finely chopped ingredients and salt. Mix mayonnaise, milk, and Worcestershire together and blend in the egg mixture. Serve with crackers and potato chips. Yield: 2 cups.

Greta Rees

PECAN STUFFED EGGS

6 hard cooked eggs
¾ cup mayonnaise
½ cup chopped pecans
1 teaspoon onion, grated
1 teaspoon vinegar

½ teaspoon dry mustard
½ teaspoon salt
½ teaspoon minced parsley
Fresh parsley or dill sprigs for garnish

Cut eggs lengthwise. Remove yolks and place in bowl. Mash and combine with remaining ingredients (except garnish). Put yolk mixture back into whites and garnish with parsley or dill.

Virginia Salter

BAKED ARTICHOKE DIP

1 to 2 cans artichoke hearts
1 cup mayonnasie
1 tablespoon olive oil

1 cup Parmesan cheese
Fresh dill, chopped
Ground black pepper

Place olive oil in pie plate. Mix artichoke hearts, mayonnaise and Parmesan cheese. Place mixture in pie plate. Add dill and pepper. Bake at 350 degrees for 20 to 30 minutes. Serve warm with crackers.

Julie Hogg

HOT ARTICHOKE DIP

1 large can artichokes, drained
    and chopped
1 cup mayonnaise

1 garlic clove, chopped
½ cup grated Parmesan cheese
Salt and pepper to taste

Add mayonnaise to drained artichokes, garlic, cheese and seasonings and mix together. Pour into crock and bake at 350 degrees until top browns (about 30 minutes). Serve with assorted vegetables (cucumber, cauliflower, carrots, etc.).

Janet Buttimer

ARTICHOKE DIP

2 cans artichoke hearts, drained
1 cup mayonnaise
1 cup sour cream

4 green onions
1 7¾-ounce can spinach
3 cups grated Swiss cheese

Chop up artichoke hearts and spinach and green onions, very fine. Combine with the mayonnaise, sour cream and cheese. Bake at 350 degrees for 20 minutes or until golden brown on top. Serve with corn chips. Serves 16.

Noreen Collins

CAROL LAMMERS' BLACK-EYED PEA DIP

2 cans black-eyed peas, drained
5 jalapeños, chopped
1 tablespoon jalapeño juice
½ medium onion, chopped

1 clove garlic, minced
½ pound extra sharp cheddar cheese
½ cup margarine

Combine peas, peppers, juice, onion and garlic in a food processor. Whirl until smooth. Heat cheese and margarine in microwave until cheese melts. Combine with pea mixture. Serve in a chafing dish to keep warm, with tortilla chips.

Meri Ann Lawson

VEGETABLE DIP

2 to 3 cups thick white sauce
2 pounds cheddar cheese, grated
1 8-ounce jar Cheese Whiz
⅓ cup beer

Dash garlic powder
2 to 3 dashes Tabasco sauce
1 tablespoon mustard

Prepare white sauce and stir in cheese. Blend over medium heat. Add Cheese Whiz, beer, garlic powder, Tabasco, and mustard. Cook 5 minutes.

Carol Russell

CURRY DIP WITH RAW VEGETABLES

½ cup mayonnaise
1 cup sour cream
2 tablespoons fresh lemon juice
Salt and pepper to taste
1 teaspoon curry powder
½ teaspoon paprika

2 tablespoons fresh parsley, minced
½ teaspoon dried tarragon, crushed
1 tablespoon grated onion
2 teaspoons prepared mustard
1 tablespoon minced chives
Several dashes Tabasco sauce

Combine all ingredients, check seasonings and chill overnight. Serve with assorted raw vegetables. This dip improves each day.

Robbie Foster

HOT CRAB DIP

1 8-ounce package cream cheese,
  softened
1 8-ounce package Neufchatel
  cheese, softened
¼ to ½ teaspoon garlic powder (to taste)

2 6- to 7-ounce cans crabmeat, undrained
½ cup onion, chopped (see note)
2 scant tablespoons lemon juice
  Black pepper
  Paprika

Mix all ingredients together and pour into baking dish. Bake at 350 degrees until it bubbles, about 30 minutes. Serve with crackers. (May be made 24 hours ahead before baking. Can then substitute 2 tablespoons dried minced onion for chopped onion. Refrigerate. If cold, may take 45 to 50 minutes to heat.)

Dedicated to Debra Smith

SHRIMP DIP

1 cup shrimp
¼ cup mayonnaise
2 teaspoons grated onion
1 3-ounce package cream cheese

1 teaspoon lemon juice
1 tablespoon Worcestershire sauce
  Salt and pepper to taste
  Dash paprika

Soften cream cheese. Thoroughly mix with other ingredients. Serve with your favorite crackers.

Martha Weisend

SPINACH DIP

2 cups sour cream
1 cup mayonnaise
1 package leek soup mix
1 10-ounce package frozen
  spinach, drained, chopped

1 teaspoon parsley, chopped
1 teaspoon dill
½ cup green onion, chopped
  Garlic to taste

Combine all ingredients, stirring thoroughly.

Doris Johnson

BACON-HORSERADISH DIP

1 8-ounce package cream cheese
2 tablespoons prepared horseradish
1 cup sour cream
3 tablespoons chives, finely cut

8 strips bacon, cooked crisp
Dash of garlic salt
Dash of red pepper

Soften cream cheese at room temperature. Blend with horseradish, sour cream and chives. Crumble bacon and add to mixture. Season with garlic salt and pepper. (If desired, put in only one-half the bacon and then sprinkle the rest of bacon on top of dip.)

Pauline Ellis

CUCUMBER DIP

1 cucumber
1 small onion, grated
1 8-ounce package cream cheese

1 teaspoon Worcestershire sauce
1 tablespoon sour cream
Salt and pepper

Soften cream cheese. Grate cucumber with skin; squeeze out all water. Add cucumber and onion to cheese. Add Worcestershire, sour cream, salt and pepper. Chill until firm. Serve with crudites and assorted crackers or bread sticks.

Carole Cohen

MEXICAN CORN DIP

3 12-ounce cans Mexican corn, drained
1 can chopped green chilies
1 or 2 whole mild jalapeños, seeded and chopped

10 ounces sharp cheddar cheese, shredded
6 thin green onions, chopped
1 cup sour cream
¾ cup mayonnaise

Mix all ingredients and serve with chips. This recipe makes a large amount.

Carol Laquey

WATER CHESTNUT DIP

1 8-ounce carton sour cream
1 cup mayonnaise
1 8-ounce can water chestnuts,
   drained and chopped

2 tablespoons soy sauce
1/2 cup chopped parsley
3 green onions, chopped
2 or 3 drops Tabasco sauce

Mix ingredients well and refrigerate at least 4 to 5 hours before serving. Makes 3 cups of dip.

Robert Ruth

MADALYNNE'S HERBED CHEESE

12 ounces small curd cottage cheese
 8 ounces cream cheese
1/4 cup chopped parsley
1/4 cup chopped chive tops
 2 large cloves garlic, chopped

1 teaspoon fresh basil leaves, chopped or
   1/2 teaspoon dried basil
1/2 teaspoon dried thyme
1/4 teaspoon onion salt
1/4 teaspoon fine herbs

Combine all ingredients in food processor and process until smooth and creamy. Line small covered dish with cheese cloth or clean thin cloth. Fill bowl with cheese mixture. Twist top of cloth. Cover with lid and chill to let ripen at least 24 hours. Keeps well several weeks. Serve with crackers.

Madalynne Callahan

MOCK BOURSIN

1 cup butter
1/2 teaspoon salt
 2 8-ounce packages cream cheese
1/2 teaspoon garlic salt
1/4 teaspoon thyme

1/4 teaspoon basil
1/4 teaspoon marjoram
1/4 teaspoon dill weed
1/4 teaspoon ground pepper

Mix well. Chill for several hours. Serve with assorted crackers.

Carol Russell

CHEESE ROLL

2 pound package Velveeta cheese,
 at room temperature
¾ cup pecans, finely chopped
1 small onion, finely chopped

8 ounces cream cheese,
 at room temperature
1 2-ounce jar pimiento
¼ to ½ cup jalapeño pepper, chopped

Line cookie sheet with waxed paper. Roll out soft Velveeta cheese. Top with thin layer of cream cheese. Sprinkle on remaining ingredients. Gently roll cheese. Garnish with finely chopped pecans and parsley. This is very different from most cheese logs or cheese balls. It's delicious and colorful.

Sue Scott

PINEAPPLE CHEESE BALL

1 8-ounce cream cheese, softened
½ cup crushed pineapple, drained
1 cup pecans, chopped
1½ teaspoons seasoned salt

2 tablespoons green pepper,
 finely chopped
1 tablespoon purple onion, minced

Combine cheese and pineapple in bowl and beat at medium speed until well blended. Add pecans, green pepper, onion and salt. Blend well. Cover and chill at least 1 hour.

Eleanore Nelson

APPLE DATE SPREAD

1 8-ounce package cream cheese, softened
¼ cup milk
1½ cups pecans, coarsely chopped

1 cup apples, unpeeled, coarsely chopped
 (use tart, fresh apples such as Granny Smith)
¾ cup chopped dates

Combine cream cheese and milk until smooth. Stir in pecans, apples, and dates. Refrigerate until flavors blend (overnight). Remove from refrigerator shortly before serving to allow mixture to be more spreadable. Serve with crackers.

Dedicated to Bob Brackman

CRAB CHEESE APPETIZER

1 8-ounce package cream cheese
2 tablespoons horseradish
1 tablespoon lemon juice

1 cup crab meat, well drained
1 bottle cocktail sauce

Soften cream cheese. Add horseradish, then lemon juice. Press into serving dish. Top with crabmeat and drizzle with cocktail sauce. Serve with crackers.

Kathleen Flessner

HOT CRAB HORS D'OEUVRES

1 pound lump crab (you may use
  "snow crab" if you wish)
1 8-ounce and 1 3-ounce
  package cream cheese

Lemon pepper to taste
Seasoning salt to taste
Picante sauce to taste

Soften the cream cheese and add all the above ingredients. Heat in a double boiler and serve on round crackers. Can be served in a small chafing dish with crackers around it. Serves 4 to 6.

Annette Strauss

SALMON BALL

1 large can pink salmon, drained
  and boned
8 ounces cream cheese
1 tablespoon lemon juice

2 tablespoons onion, finely chopped
1 teaspoon salt
½ cup pecans, chopped
3 tablespoons chives, chopped

Mix first 5 ingredients well. Form into 1 large or 2 smaller balls. Wrap in wax paper and chill for at least 3 hours. Roll in pecans and chives. Can be wrapped and frozen. Serve with crackers.

Cal Small

MOCHA PUNCH

1 gallon regular coffee (brewed)   1 gallon of vanilla ice cream
2 cups sugar   1 pint whipping cream, whipped

Add sugar to hot coffee and let cool. Add whipped cream, spoon in ice cream that has been chopped up in chunks before serving time. Serves 40 or 50.

Dedicated to Ruth Potter

HOPE'S COFFEE PUNCH

2 cups instant coffee powder   1 gallon milk
2 cups sugar   1 gallon vanilla ice cream, softened
3 cups water   Vanilla to taste

Heat water and dissolve coffee and sugar. Cool. Combine with remaining ingredients in punch bowl. Makes 50 ½-cup servings.

Frances Collins

SPICED MINT TEA

1½ cups of sugar   ¾ cup orange juice
2½ cups water   1 cup lemon juice
1 cup mint leaves   3 cups strong tea

Bring mixture of sugar and water to a boil and cook 5 minutes. Add mint and juices. Steep 1 hour. Strain and add tea. Serve well chilled over crushed ice. Serves 8.

Billy McSpedden

DeGOLYER ALMOND TEA PUNCH

3 regular tea bags   ½ cup lemon juice
6 cups water (divided use)   2 teaspoons almond extract
1 cup sugar   1 teaspoon vanilla extract

Steep tea bags in 2 cups boiling water. Remove bags and set aside. Mix sugar and 4 cups of water; boil until sugar is dissolved. Combine tea and sugared water with remaining ingredients. Serve hot or cold.

Lydia Chandler

READY-TO-DRINK ICED TEA

3 quarts medium strength tea
   (use 2 family-size tea bags)
½ cup sugar

1 quart ginger ale
1 12-ounce can frozen lemonade
   concentrate, thawed

Combine tea, sugar and lemonade concentrate. Just before serving, stir in ginger ale. Pour over ice in glasses. Serves 10.

Greta Rees

FRENCH MINT TEA

6 cups water
2 cups sugar
   Lemon rind
1½ teaspoons vanilla
1½ teaspoons almond extract

3 lemons, juiced
4 tea bags
4 cups boiling water
2 46-ounce cans pineapple juice

Boil 6 cups water, sugar and lemon rind for 5 minutes. Remove rinds. Add vanilla, almond flavoring and lemon juice. Steep tea bags in 4 cups boiling water. Add to spice mixture and add pineapple juice. Chill.

Lynda Sanders

STRAWBERRY TEA PUNCH

1½ quarts boiling water
3 family size tea bags
½ cup sugar

1 6-ounce can frozen lemonade
   concentrate, thawed
1 10-ounce package frozen
   strawberrries, thawed

In pitcher, pour boiling water over tea bags. Brew for 4 minutes. Remove tea bags and stir in sugar, lemonade, and strawberries. Serve over ice in iced tea glasses. Can also be served in punch bowl for an excellent party punch. Serves 8 to 10.

Debbie (Mrs. John) Carona

QUICKIE TEA

1 tablespoon instant tea
1 tub lemonade flavor sugar free
    Crystal Light
2 6-ounce cans pineapple juice

2 quarts water
1 teaspoon almond extract
1 teaspoon vanilla

Combine all ingredients and shake well. Serve over ice. Garnish with fresh mint sprig. (Takes 5 minutes.)

Doris Anton

SUMMER COOLER

⅓ cup grenadine syrup
1 6-ounce can frozen lemonade

1 teaspoon almond flavoring
2 quarts iced tea

Add lemonade to syrup. Stir in flavoring and tea. Garnish with lemon slices and cherries. Great for ladies' luncheon.

Martha Weisend

PRECEPT PUNCH

2½ cups water
2 cups brown sugar
   Mint leaves

1 6-ounce can frozen lemonade
    concentrate, thawed
1 6-ounce can frozen orange juice
    concentrate, thawed

Bring the above ingredients (except mint) to a boil. Pour over freshly washed mint. Let steep until cool. Mix one part syrup with two parts of Perrier. Serve over ice.

Annette Banks

SUNSHINE SHAKE

2 quarts orange juice
1 cup instant nonfat dry milk
2 teaspoons sugar

2 8½-ounce cans crushed pineapple,
    undrained
4 bananas, sliced

Combine all ingredients in electric blender and blend until smooth. Chill thoroughly before serving. Needs to be stirred before pouring. Serves 8.

Greta Rees

APRICOT NECTAR PUNCH

3 cups water
2 regular size tea bags
10 whole cloves
2 2-inch cinnamon sticks

2 12-ounce cans apricot nectar
½ to ¾ cup sugar
¼ to ⅓ cup lemon juice

Bring water to a boil. Add tea bags and steep for 5 minutes. Remove tea bags, add spices, bring to a boil again. Add remaining ingredients. Remove spices prior to serving. Serve hot or cold. For variety, substitute any Kern's fruit nectars for the apricot nectar.

Ruth Barnard

FROZEN PUNCH

1 46-ounce can pineapple juice
1 12-ounce can frozen lemonade
  concentrate, thawed

3 cups apple cider or juice
2 bottles ginger ale
1½ cups sugar

Mix fruit juices and sugar; freeze in plastic containers. About 1 hour before using, set out to thaw. It needs to be "mushy." Add ginger ale at the last minute. Freezer containers should be 1 to 2 quarts, since it takes a while to thaw. On a hot day you cannot have too much of this punch. Very refreshing! Makes 25 cups.

Glenna Clayton

HOT APPLE CIDER

1 gallon apple cider
1 6-ounce can lemonade
1 teaspoon cinnamon
1 cup red hots

1 6-ounce can frozen orange juice
½ teaspoon nutmeg
3 teaspoons allspice

Mix cider, orange juice and lemon juice in crock pot. Put spices in cheese cloth bag and add to cider. Bring to boil and simmer several minutes. Turn to low to keep hot. Add red hots. Remove bag of spices.

Karen Bradshaw

WASSAIL

2 quarts apple cider
2 cups orange juice
Juice from 2 (#2) cans of
    pineapple juice

1 cup lemon juice
1 stick whole cinnamon
1 teaspoon whole cloves
    Sugar or honey to taste

Combine ingredients and bring to simmer. Serve hot.

Dedicated to Larry Armstrong

HOLIDAY EGGNOG

Make ahead one week!

4 eggs, separated
¾ cup bourbon
⅛ cup brandy

2 cups whipping cream
¾ cup sugar
2 cups half-and-half

With mixer, beat egg whites until stiff and set aside. Beat egg yolks and stir in bourbon, brandy, and whipping cream (not whipped). Fold in egg whites. Add sugar and half-and-half, stirring well. Refrigerate for 1 week before serving. Tastes better if prepared ahead. Makes 12 four-ounce servings. May be doubled to make about 1 gallon.

Suzanne Betterley

HOLIDAY NOG

6 eggs
¼ cup sugar
¼ teaspoon cinnamon
¼ teaspoon cardamon
¼ teaspoon ground cloves
    Nutmeg

1 quart vanilla ice cream (softened)
6 cups orange juice
¼ cup lemon juice
    Ice ring with orange and lemon slices
      (optional)
1 quart ginger ale

Beat eggs on low speed, adding sugar and spices until dissolved. Gradually add ice cream and juices. Cover and chill. Just before serving, pour into large bowl and stir in ginger ale. Sprinkle with nutmeg and add ice ring.

Kathleen Flessner

SANGRIA

1 25.4-ounce bottle Burgundy or
    other dry red wine, chilled
½ cup of sugar
1 orange, thinly sliced

1 lemon, thinly sliced
1 10-ounce bottle club soda, chilled

Combine first 4 ingredients in a large pitcher, stirring to dissolve sugar. Add club soda just before serving. Serve over ice. Yield: about 1 quart.

Dorothy Jones

CLASSIC SANGRIA FOR A CROWD

4 large oranges
5 lemons
2 limes

3 pounds granulated sugar
2½ quarts water

Cut all the fruit into thick slices and wedges. In large sauce pan with the amount of water indicated, slow-boil half of the fruit, adding the sugar gradually as it dissolves. Simmer and stir solution continuously until saturated with sugar and syrup. Stop simmering when bitter taste from rind begins. Mash and squeeze the remaining pieces of fruit (less rind) in the hot syrup and let stand. Chill the base before using. Will keep refrigerated indefinitely in a tightly sealed jar. Makes base for approximately 8 pitchers (64 servings).

To make one pitcher (8 servings) of sangria, combine:

5 ounces sangria base (above)
1 fifth Torres Sangre de Toro
1 large orange, thinly sliced

3 lemons, thinly sliced
1 fresh peach, thinly cubed
4 ounces soda water

Serve in large wine glasses in which have been placed 2 or 3 ice cubes and 2 very thin slices of orange and lemon.

Ruth Barnard

PINEAPPLE CONVERSATION PUNCH

1 bottle dry white wine
1 bottle dry vermouth
2 bottles light champagne

6 12-ounce cans pineapple chunks
2 bottles maraschino cherries

Drain juice off pineapple and cherries; place fruit in large bowl. Marinate in wine and vermouth for 12 to 24 hours. Pour mixture and champagne over an ice ring when ready to serve.

Dedicated to Frank Thomas

CHAMPAGNE PUNCH

2 cups sugar
2 cups water
2 cups apricot nectar
Juice of 6 lemons
2 fifths champagne

1 6-ounce can frozen orange juice
2 12-ounce cans frozen apple juice
2 cups pineapple juice
2 12-ounce bottles ginger ale

Boil sugar and water for 1 minute; cool. Add juices and freeze in a Bundt pan or similar mold. Thaw 1 to 1½ hours before serving. Add cold ginger ale and champagne. Serve over block of ice in punch bowl or substitute frozen ring mold of punch juice. (For non-alcoholic punch, use all ginger ale.)

Pat Marshall

MARGARITAS

1 12-ounce can frozen limeade
2 cans cold water or
  1 can water and 12 ice cubes

6 ounces tequila
1 ounce Cointreau

OR

1 6-ounce can frozen limeade
12 to 14 ice cubes

6 ounces tequila
3 ounces Lite beer (substitute for Cointreau)

Cover with plastic wrap in open container for easy spooning into glasses. Makes six 4-ounce drinks.

Annella Collins

POLLY'S PUNCH

1 46-ounce can pineapple juice   1 large bottle Piña Colada Mix
1 2-liter bottle Diet Sprite

Let chill. Float frozen mold made of juice on top.

Polly Richter

PINK SQUIRREL

½ jigger Creme de Almond   3 tablespoons ice cream
½ jigger Creme de Cacao

Mix ingredients. Makes 1 drink.

WHITE RUSSIAN

1 ounce Kahlua   2 ounces cream
1 ounce vodka

Mix gently and serve over ice.

RED ROOSTERS

1 6-ounce can frozen orange juice   1 pint (or less) vodka
1 quart cranberry juice   Juice of 1 lemon

Mix in plastic container. Freeze. Blend a few seconds in blender before serving. Serves 10 to 12.

VELVET PEACH

1 ounce vodka   ½ cup cling peach slices
1 ounce peach brandy   Dash vanilla extract
1 scoop vanilla ice cream

Place above ingredients in blender and mix until smooth. Pour into chilled glass and garnish with whipped cream and peach slices. Makes 1 drink.

Martha Baker

HOT WINE MIX

6 cups sugar
2 tablespoons ground cinnamon
2 tablespoons ground cloves

1 tablespoon ground allspice
¾ teaspoon ground nutmeg
Burgundy or other red wine

Combine first 5 ingredients in a bowl and mix well. Store in air tight container. Combine 2 teaspoons of the mix and ½ cup water. Bring to a boil. Reduce heat and add 1 cup of wine and heat thoroughly but do not boil. Serve with cinnamon stick. Makes 72 servings.

Joyce Kirkland

CAPPUCCINO

1 package sweet cocoa mix
1 ounce cognac

6 ounces hot coffee
Heavy cream, whipped

Mix chocolate and cognac. Add coffee, stir well, top with whipped cream. Serves 1.

Nan Spires

ORANGE JULIUS

½ cup water
½ cup milk
⅛ teaspoon vanilla

3 tablespoons sugar
¼ of a 12-ounce can frozen
   orange juice concentrate
6 to 8 ice cubes

Mix all ingredients in a blender. Blend until slushy. Serves 2.

Mary Tullie Critcher and Sara Suderman

RECEPTION PUNCH

46 ounces canned apricot nectar
46 ounces canned pineapple juice
23 ounces orange juice

1 12-ounce can frozen lemonade
1 bottle champagne
1 quart or liter bottle ginger ale

Mix first 4 ingredients. Chill. When ready to serve, pour into punch bowl and add champagne and ginger ale. For excitement, place a 3-pound block of "dry ice" in the punch to create bubbles and mists.

Julia O'Roark

BROCCOLI SOUP

1 small bunch fresh broccoli, cut up
½ medium onion
2 cups water
6 chicken bouillon cubes

4 cups milk
¾ cup flour, mixed with just enough water
   to make it runny
1 teaspoon dry mustard
2 cups mild cheddar cheese, grated

Combine broccoli, onion, water and bouillon. Bring to a boil and cook until broccoli is tender. In a larger pan bring milk to boil and thicken by slowly adding flour mixture a little at a time, stirring to prevent lumps (should be pretty thick). Add mustard, then cheese. Remove from heat and stir until cheese is just melted. Add broccoli mixture. Turn heat to lowest temperature to warm. Curdles easily if heat is too high.

Andrea Bailey

CARROT GINGER SOUP

4 tablespoons butter
6 large carrots, peeled, chopped
½ to 1 onion, chopped
2 stalks celery, chopped
2 cloves garlic, finely chopped

1 ounce (or more) ginger, finely chopped
4 quarts chicken stock (a little over a gallon)
½ cup half-and-half, or to taste
Salt and white pepper to taste

In a large saucepan, sauté carrots, onion, celery, garlic, and ginger until softened. Add stock or water. Bring to a boil and simmer until carrots are tender. Blend or purée in batches in a blender or food processor until smooth. Strain into a large pot. Heat to boiling. If desired, thicken with rice flour mixed with cold water to desired thickness. Add cream, salt and pepper just before serving. Use as a light starter to a meal.

Jeanne Slot — Chef, Banff Springs Hotel

BETTYE'S BUSY DAY SOUP

1 can minestrone soup
1 can tomatoes with green chilies
1 can tomatoes
1 pound ground round or lean beef

1 can whole corn
1 can Veg-all
1 can ranch style beans

Brown beef and add to the cans of vegetables with liquid. Let simmer approximately 1 hour.

Bettye Peterman

SPICY TOMATO CORN CHOWDER

2 10¾-ounce cans tomato soup
2 soup cans 2% milk
1 16-ounce can cream style corn
1 tablespoon sugar
¼ teaspoon curry powder

1 small onion, finely chopped
Salt and pepper to taste
⅛ teaspoon garlic salt
Liquid hot pepper sauce to taste

Combine all ingredients. Heat to just before boiling. Reduce heat and let simmer 10 to 15 minutes. Serve with your favorite salad and sesame seed hard rolls.

Jeanne Bryant

CORN CHOWDER

¼ cup onion, finely chopped
3 tablespoons butter
2 16-ounce cans creamed corn
2 10¾-ounce cans cream of
   potato soup

3 cups milk
1 tablespoon dried parsley
1 teaspoon salt
¼ teaspoon pepper.
¼ teaspoon celery seed

Sauté onion in butter until transparent. Add remaining ingredients, stirring well. Simmer 20 minutes. Flavor is enhanced by preparing a day ahead. Serves 8.

Rhonda Suderman

ROASTED CORN BISQUE

5 cups niblet corn, drained
2 cups water
5 Anaheim green chilies, chopped
5 mild *jalapeños*, minced
1 teaspoon shallots, minced
1 cup canned mild *green chilies*, chopped
½ cup bacon, cooked, crumbled
1 teaspoon cilantro, chopped
1 pinch fresh oregano
1 pinch fresh basil
1 ounce Tabasco sauce (or to taste)

2 pinches Albuquerque chili pepper
  or cayenne
2 pinches dark red chili powder
1 teaspoon sugar
1 teaspoon Worcestershire sauce
1 tablespoon chicken bouillon granules
2 teaspoons cumin
  Salt and pepper, to taste (if needed)
5 cups cream style corn
  Skim milk, if needed
  Sour cream for garnish

Spread the niblet corn on a sheet pan and bake at 350 degrees for 20 minutes. (Spray baking sheet with oil or toss corn in olive oil before baking.) To test for doneness, bite a piece. It is done when it feels slightly hard and sticks to your teeth. Sauté corn with remaining ingredients (except sweet cream corn and sour cream) over high heat for 5 minutes. Add sweet cream corn and simmer for 15 minutes. Purée the mixture until silky smooth. Thin with skim milk, if necessary. Reheat and serve. Garnish with a little sour cream or yogurt.

Karen Olsen Smith

PORTUGUESE BEAN SOUP

1 link (approximately 1 pound)
  smoked sausage
1 tablespoon margarine
1 cup onion, chopped
1 cup celery, chopped
1 can whole new potatoes or 2 to 3 cups
  potatoes, peeled and cut up

1 14½-ounce can tomatoes
1 can pinto beans, undrained
1 can kidney beans, undrained
3 to 4 cups cabbage
2 cups sliced carrots, cooked
  Salt and pepper to taste
3 cups water or broth

Cut sausage in small slices and simmer in small amount of water in a Dutch oven. Add margarine, onion and celery, and sauté. Add remaining ingredients and continue to cook just until cabbage is tender. Additional water or broth may be added as the soup will thicken as it stands. This soup is better the second day. Makes a Dutch oven full. Serves 10 to 12.

Neva Muller

CUBAN BLACK BEAN SOUP

Non-stick vegetable spray
2 cups dried black beans, washed
   and picked over
2 quarts chicken stock
2 bay leaves
1 fresh jalapeño, chopped with seeds
¼ cup olive oil

4 large onions, chopped, divided use
2 green bell peppers, stemmed, seeded,
   and chopped
4 to 6 cloves garlic, peeled and pressed
   Salt to taste
1¼ to 2 cups cooked white rice

Spray a large, heavy soup pot with nonstick spray and in it soak the beans in stock overnight.

The next day, add enough stock or water to cover the beans by 1 inch. Add the bay leaves and jalapeno. Cover the pot and bring to a boil. Turn the heat down very low and let simmer, partially covered, until the beans are tender, about 1½ to 2 hours.

Meanwhile, in a skillet, heat the oil over medium heat. Sauté 3 chopped onions and peppers until softened, about 3 minutes. Stir in the garlic and cook a few seconds more.

When the beans are tender, add the onion mixture and season with salt. Simmer 20 minutes more. Serve with rice and remaining chopped onion. Serves 6 to 8. *If jalapeño seeds are left out, soup won't be spicy at all.*

Karen Knox

BAKED POTATO SOUP

6 to 8 slices bacon, fried crisp
    reserve drippings
1 cup onions, chopped
⅔ cup flour
6 cups hot chicken broth
4 cups baked potatoes, peeled
    and diced
2 cups cream or evaporated skim milk

¼ cup parsley, chopped
1½ teaspoons garlic, minced
1½ teaspoons dried basil
1½ teaspoons salt
1½ teaspoons red pepper sauce
1½ teaspoons pepper
1 cup cheddar cheese, grated
½ cup green onion, sliced

Crumble bacon; set aside. Cook onions in drippings until transparent. Add flour, stirring to prevent lumps. Cook 3 to 5 minutes until mixture begins to turn golden. Add chicken broth, whisking to prevent lumps until liquid thickens. Reduce heat to simmer and add remaining ingredients, except cheese and green onions. Simmer 10 minutes; do not allow to boil. Add grated cheese and green onions. Heat until cheese melts. Garnish with crumbled bacon. Makes 2 quarts.

Sue Smith

LADY PRIMROSE'S SQUASH SOUP

1 medium onion, chopped
2 cloves garlic, minced
1 tablespoon margarine
½ teaspoon white pepper
    Salt to taste

2½ cups chicken stock
3 pounds winter squash, peeled,
    seeded and diced
2 cups milk, 2% or skim
    Dash nutmeg

Sauté the onions and garlic in margarine until transparent. Add rest of ingredients, except milk and nutmeg, and bring to boil for 15 minutes. Remove from heat, stir in milk and nutmeg. Puree soup in blender. Return to heat but do not boil. Serves 10.

Caroline Rose Hunt

PUMPKIN SOUP

¼ cup margarine
1 medium onion, chopped
2 large shallots, chopped
1 medium baking potato, peeled
    and chopped
3 celery ribs, chopped
2 medium carrots, chopped
¼ cup dry Madeira

6 to 7 cups chicken stock, divided
1½ teaspoons dried thyme
1 bay leaf
1 3-pound pumpkin, peeled, seeded
    and cubed or 3 cups pumpkin purée
¼ teaspoon pepper
½ cup evaporated milk
Salt to taste

In a medium saucepan, melt the margarine over low heat. Add vegetables and sauté covered until softened, stirring occasionally (about 15 minutes). Add Madeira, cook covered over low heat 5 minutes. Add 6 cups stock, herbs, and pumpkin. Partly cover. Simmer 30 minutes or until pumpkin is very soft. Purée the soup in batches in a blender until smooth. Return to pan and add milk, salt and pepper. Reheat and serve, adding more chicken stock if it is too thick. Serves 8.

Pat Norvell

COLORFUL SQUASH SOUP

1 14½-ounce can chicken broth
    plus ½ can water
3 to 4 small medium yellow squash,
    cut in ¼-inch rounds (if rounds
    are large, slice in half)

⅓ cup frozen yellow corn kernels
1 teaspoon pimiento bits
    Juice of ½ lemon
¼ teaspoon (or less) dried dill weed
    Salt and pepper to taste

Skim fat from top of broth before adding water. (Swanson's broth has ⅓ less salt than others.) Bring broth and water to boil. Add yellow squash and cook crisp tender; *do not overcook.* Add corn, pimiento, lemon juice and dill weed. Cook a few minutes longer. Season with salt and pepper. Optionally, cooked rice can be added. This soup can be frozen for later use.

Lena Vatsures

SIMPLE WHITE CONSOMMÉ

4 pounds lean meat
3 pounds beef knuckles, with bone
4 large, organically grown carrots
3 turnips (about 2½ pounds)
4 leeks, (white part), tied in a bundle
2 tablespoons coarse salt
  Bones and giblets from 2 chickens,
    previously browned and tied in cloth

2 celery stalks, without leaves
1 medium onion
1 large clove garlic
1 sprig thyme
8 quarts good water, cold
  Marrow bones, broken and previously
    browned and tied in cloth

The better the meat cut and the closer to the bone, the better the flavor. Determine best bone meat: leg, shoulder, cheek, arm blade, arm, rib, tail, hip, back leg. Tie meat with string and boil in water until bone is completely clean. Add salt and all vegetables. Simmer slowly for 5 hours. Add marrow bones and chicken bones and giblets. Do not cook stock more than 5 hours. Remove surplus fat. Strain stock through wet cheese cloth and ring out, then line the inside of a fine strainer (china cap), and strain again. Makes 6 quarts.

Randuk addition: First start bone boiled separately for 3 hours with salt, simmering and cool to sweat the bones, then add all of the above for 4 hours.

Ray Randuk

HAMBURGER BARLEY VEGETABLE SOUP

1½ pounds ground beef
6 cups water
3 beef bouillon cubes or 3 teaspoons
    instant beef bouillon
2 cups carrots, sliced
1½ cups onions, coarsely chopped
1½ cups celery, coarsely chopped
½ cup green pepper, coarsely chopped

½ cup barley
1 teaspoon salt
⅛ teaspoon pepper
2 bay leaves
¼ cup catsup
1 28-ounce can tomatoes, undrained, cut up
1 8-ounce can tomato sauce

In 5-quart Dutch oven, brown ground beef. Drain. Stir in remaining ingredients. Bring to a boil. Reduce heat; cover and simmer 1 hour or until vegetables and barley are tender. Remove bay leaves. Adjust seasoning, possibly add more pepper or garlic flavor. Makes ten 1½-cup servings.

Anne Boecher

VELVETY BRIE SOUP

1 6-ounce fully ripened Brie	1/2 cup flour
2 carrots, scraped, finely chopped	2 15-ounce cans chicken broth
3/4 cup celery, chopped	1 teaspoon thyme
1/2 cup onion, chopped	1 bay leaf
1/2 cup butter	1/2 cup skim milk or cream

Remove and discard rind from cheese. Cut into 1/2-inch cubes and set aside. Sauté vegetables in butter until tender. Sprinkle flour on vegetables and stir until well blended. Stir in chicken broth. Cook until thick and bubbly. Add thyme and bay leaf. Gradually add cheese cubes and stir until cheese is melted. Reduce heat to low, stir in milk and cook until thoroughly heated. Do not boil. Remove and discard bay leaf.

Sandra Juetten

LENTIL BURGER SOUP

1 pound lentils	1/2 cup margarine
4 quarts water	2 onions, minced
2 tablespoons salt	Seasonings of choice: garlic salt, Accent,
1 teaspoon pepper	celery salt, seasoning salt
1 tablespoon dill weed	1 to 1 1/2 pounds ground meat
1 28-ounce can tomatoes	1 cup vermicelli, broken in pieces
1 8-ounce can tomato sauce	

Simmer everything but meat and vermicelli for approximatley 1 1/2 hours. Brown meat, drain. Add meat and vermicelli to soup. Cook another 30 minutes. Flavor seems to improve with reheating. Keeps well in refrigerator and freezes well. Serves a bunch!

Pat Hill

ITALIAN SAUSAGE LENTIL SOUP

1 pound Italian sausage
1 large onion, finely chopped
1 small green pepper, finely chopped
1 medium carrot, finely chopped
2 14½-ounce cans chicken broth,
    or use your own stock
1 large garlic clove, minced

1 bay leaf
1 14½- to 16-ounce can whole tomatoes
    with liquid, coarsely chopped
1 cup water
¾ cup dry lentils
¼ cup country style or regular Dijon mustard

In a soup pot or Dutch oven, brown the sausage (remove the casing). Hot sausage has more flavor and is not hot in the soup. Remove sausage and drain on paper towels. Drain grease from pot. Crumble the sausage and return to the pot along with remaining ingredients, except mustard. Simmer, covered, 1 hour or until vegetables and lentils are tender. Stir in mustard. Remove bay leaf. Serves 6.

Marinell Price

TACO SOUP

2 pounds chicken breasts
1 onion, chopped
1 green pepper, chopped
1 can tomatoes with chilies
1 can stewed tomatoes
1 can whole kernel corn

1 can ranch style pinto beans
    with jalapeños
1 can kidney beans
1 package ranch dressing mix (dry)
1 package taco seasoning mix (dry)
2½ cups chicken broth
1 cup grated cheddar cheese

Cook chicken until tender. Cut into bite-sized pieces. Sauté onion and green pepper together in a Dutch oven; drain off grease. Add remaining ingredients. Cook for about 30 minutes on simmer. Serve with grated cheese on top.

Judy Mullikin

TORTILLA SOUP

1 small onion, chopped
2 cloves garlic, crushed
2 tablespoons oil
1 cup tomatoes, peeled and chopped, (or canned)
1 14-ounce can condensed beef bouillon
1 14-ounce can condensed chicken broth
1½ cups water
1½ cups V-8 juice
1 teaspoon ground cumin

1 teaspoon chili powder
1 teaspoon salt
⅛ teaspoon pepper
1 teaspoon Worcestershire sauce
1 tablespoon bottled steak sauce
6 tortillas, cut in ½-inch strips
¼ cup cheddar cheese, shredded (may use more)
Cooked chicken, cut in bite size pieces (optional)
1 4-ounce can chopped green chilies

Sauté onion and garlic in oil until soft. Add tomatoes, bouillon, chicken broth, water, V-8, cumin, chili powder, salt, pepper, Worcestershire and steak sauce. Bring soup to a boil; lower heat, simmer covered for 1 hour. Add tortillas and simmer 10 minutes longer. Add green chilies last 20 minutes. Add cooked chicken. Add cheese when ready to serve.

Pat Layden

TORTILLA SOUP

1 onion, chopped
2 cloves garlic, minced
1 tablespoon vegetable oil (plus
    additional for frying)
1 10½-ounce can chopped tomatoes
    with green chilies, drained
1 14½- to 16-ounce can tomatoes, puréed

3 cups chicken stock
1 teaspoon chili powder
1 teaspoon cumin
Salt to taste
4 corn tortillas, cut into ¼×1½-inch strips
1 cup diced cooked chicken (optional)
Optional garnishes: diced avocado, grated
    Monterey Jack or cheddar cheese, sour cream

In large saucepan, sauté onion and garlic in 1 tablespoon vegetable oil about 5 minutes, until onions are soft. Add tomatoes with green chilies, puréed tomatoes, chicken stock, chili powder, cumin and salt. Heat to boiling, reduce heat and simmer 20 to 30 minutes. Meanwhile, cut tortillas into thin strips and fry until crisp in ¼-inch of hot oil; drain on paper towels. Add chicken, if desired, and tortilla strips to soup and heat through, about 5 minutes. Garnish each serving with sprinkling of diced avocado, cheese and a dollop of sour cream. Makes 8 servings.

Shelby Marcus

FRENCH CHICKEN SOUP

3 chicken breasts, cut in strips
2 tablespoons vegetable oil
2 large onions, sliced in rings
2 cloves garlic, chopped
1 16-ounce can whole tomatoes
1 14-ounce can condensed chicken broth
1 cup water

1 cup dry white wine
1 tablespoon sugar
1 teaspoon dried thyme leaves
1 teaspoon salt
¼ teaspoon pepper
1 bell pepper, cut up

In big pot, heat oil and brown the chicken. Remove the chicken and stir in onions and garlic until tender; return chicken. Add tomatoes, liquid broth, water, wine, sugar, thyme, salt and pepper. Break up tomatoes. Heat to boiling and then reduce. Cover and simmer for about 1 hour. Add bell pepper, heat to boil, cover and simmer 10 minutes.

Susy Lawlis Gartman

WHITE CHILI

1 onion, chopped
1 garlic clove, chopped
1 tablespoon oil
1 teaspoon cumin
1 can white kidney beans, drained
1 can garbanzo beans, drained

1 can white corn, drained
2 cans chopped green chilies
1½ cups water and 2 teaspoons chicken
    bouillon or 1 can chicken broth
2 to 4 chicken breasts, chopped (raw)
    Monterey Jack cheese, grated

Sauté onion and garlic in oil with cumin. Add beans, corn and chilies, broth and chicken. Simmer one hour in Dutch oven or bake in casserole 1 hour at 350 degrees. Add grated cheese in each bowl when served. Serve with corn bread.

Peggy Dawson

JIM LAKE'S CHILI

3 pounds lean chili meat
12 jalapeños or any hot chilis
1 tablespoon oregano
1 tablespoon cumin
1 tablespoon salt

1 teaspoon cayenne pepper (optional)
1 teaspoon Tabasco (optional)
6 tablespoons chili powder
4 cloves garlic, minced
2 tablespoons masa triga
    (flour may be substituted)

Remove stems from peppers. Boil for 30 minutes. Grind or mash. Save water. Sear meat in heavy pot (preferably cast iron). Add mashed peppers and enough water to cover meat (use water from boiling peppers for extra hot flavor). Bring to boil; simmer for 30 minutes. Add next 7 ingredients (seasonings and garlic) to meat. Bring to boil; then simmer for 45 minutes. Add water as needed and stir. Mix 2 tablespoons of masa triga or flour to thicken. Simmer for 30 minutes. Serve with cooked rice, chopped onion, shredded cheddar cheese and beans. Serve with crackers or corn chips. Serves 8.

Jim Lake

NANCY HAMON'S CHILI

1 *large yellow onion*	2 *teaspoons cilantro*
2 *pounds lean chuck, venison, or*	1 *tablespoon marjoram*
armadillo, ground	1 *tablespoon oregano*
5 *or 6 cloves garlic*	1 *heaping tablespoon cumin*
1 *8-ounce can tomato paste*	2 *ounces chili powder*
2 *cups water*	*Salt to taste*

Pour boiling water over the garlic cloves and peel them. Slice onion. Put garlic and onion in the blender with a cup of water. Chop coarsely. In a heavy pot, brown the meat well, then add the onion-garlic mixture and the rest of the ingredients. Simmer covered for at least an hour and a half; add salt to taste. Like many similar dishes, this improves with age.

Nancy Hamon

CHARLIE CROWE'S CHILI

3 *pounds lean beef*	1 *teaspoon ground comino*
¼ *cup olive oil*	1 *teaspoon oregano or marjoram*
1 *quart water*	1 *teaspoon red pepper*
2 *bay leaves (optional)*	½ *teaspoon black pepper*
8 *dry chili pods,* or	1 *tablespoon sugar*
6 *tablespoons chili powder*	3 *tablespoons paprika*
3 *teaspoons salt*	3 *tablespoons flour*
10 *cloves garlic, finely chopped*	6 *tablespoons corn meal*

Heat olive oil in 6 quart pot. Add meat and sear over high heat, stirring constantly until gray, *not brown.* Add one quart water and cook (covered) at bubbling simmer, 1½ to 2 hours. Then add all ingredients except thickening. Simmer 30 minutes longer. Skim off any fat. Now add thickening, previously mixed in cold water. Cook 5 minutes to determine if more water is necessary (likely) for desired consistency. Stir to prevent sticking after thickening is added. (Thicken with flour, corn meal or cracker meal.) Taste for degree of hotness you prefer.

Charles Crowe

BLACK-EYED PEA SHRIMP GUMBO

2 cups water
1 medium onion, sliced
2 14- to 16-ounce cans stewed tomatoes
¼ teaspoon hot pepper sauce
2 tablespoons Cajun seasoning
2 garlic cloves, minced

¾ cup uncooked regular rice
1 10-ounce package frozen cut
   okra, thawed
2 cans black-eyed peas, drained
1 pound medium fresh shrimp,
   peeled and deveined

In a large Dutch oven, combine water, tomatoes, hot pepper sauce, Cajun seasoning, garlic and onion. Bring to boil, cover and simmer 20 minutes. Stir in rice and okra and simmer covered for an additional 15 minutes. Add shrimp and black-eyed peas, cook until heated through (about 6 minutes). Serves 8.

Sarah Diamond

OYSTER AND ARTICHOKE SOUP

½ cup butter
1 cup celery, finely chopped
½ cup green pepper, finely chopped
2 cups green onions, chopped
2 cloves garlic, crushed
3 14-ounce cans artichoke hearts,
   rinsed and drained

3 tablespoons flour
3 pints oysters, drained
9 cups chicken broth
   Seasoning salt to taste
   Medium grind black pepper, to taste
1½ tablespoons Worcestershire sauce
1 tablespoon Pickapeppa sauce

Cut oysters into thirds with scissors, and discard muscle. Sauté celery, green pepper, and green onions in butter until soft. Add garlic and artichoke hearts (remove small leaves and cut hearts into quarters). Sprinkle with flour and cook until flour is cooked, stirring constantly to avoid sticking. Add oysters, chicken broth and seasoning. Simmer at least 30 minutes, stirring occasionally to avoid sticking. Flavors blend even better after having been refrigerated a day. Serves 10. Leftover soup freezes well.

Margot Winspear

CRAB SOUP

¾ cup carrot, chopped fine
¾ cup celery, chopped fine
¾ cup onion, chopped fine
½ cup unsalted butter (or margarine)
¼ cup flour
4 cups milk
4 cups half and half
2 bay leaves

1 tablespoon ground white pepper
1 teaspoon salt
⅛ teaspoon cayenne pepper
1 teaspoon Old Bay seasoning
1 tablespoon Worcestershire sauce
2 6-ounce cans crab meat (picked over
   to remove shell)
½ pound imitation crab

Melt butter, sauté carrot, celery and onion until onion is transparent and soft. Add flour, stirring briskly for 3 minutes. Add milk and cream slowly, stirring to blend. Add bay leaves, pepper, salt, cayenne pepper and Old Bay seasoning. Blend well and add Worcestershire sauce. Bring to boiling point, quickly reduce heat and simmer, stirring, 8 to 10 minutes. Add crab and imitation crab. Cook *one* minute. Discard bay leaves. Ladle into bowls and serve.

Kaki Russell

SALMON BISQUE

¼ cup margarine or butter
¼ cup onion, chopped
¼ cup celery, chopped
¼ cup flour
3 cups milk
1 cup tomato juice

1½ teaspoons salt
1 pound can pink salmon, discard
   bones and dark skin
2 tablespoons parsley, chopped
   Lemon slices, optional

In the top pan of a double boiler, melt butter over direct heat and sauté onion and celery 5 minutes. Heat water in bottom pan of double boiler. Add flour to onion-celery mixture and cook on low heat about 1 minute. Then place over simmering water, add milk and cook until smooth and thick. Add salt and tomato juice. Drain and flake the salmon and add to soup. Heat and eat. Serves 6.

Pat Norvell

COLD AVOCADO SOUP

9 very small avocados
2 medium green onions, with tops
1/2 cup sour cream

1/2 cup milk
4 cups chicken broth (instant boullion cooled)
Salt and pepper

Combine ingredients and process in blender (do in 3 batches as blender will not hold entire amount). Serve chilled in stemmed wine glasses, with sprinkles of dill on top. This is thick. If thinner consistency is desired, thin with more chicken broth.

Martha Baker

BLENDER CUCUMBER SOUP

1 1/2 cups sour cream
1 10 3/4-ounce can cream chicken soup
1 14-ounce can chicken broth
1 cucumber, cut up
1 small onion, cut up

Dash of Tabasco
1/2 teaspoon curry powder
1/2 teaspoon Worcestershire sauce
Salt and pepper to taste

Mix ingredients in a large bowl. Put half of mixture in a blender and blend until smooth. Repeat with second half. Mix together and chill thoroughly. Serve ice cold. Serves 6.

Virginia Duncan

ZUCCHINI SOUP

1 pound zucchini
1 small onion, cut into 4 parts
1 cup chicken broth
Salt and pepper to taste

1/2 teaspoon basil
1 cup milk, divided
1/2 cup cream

Combine zucchini, onion, chicken stock and seasonings; cook and simmer for 20 minutes. Add 1/2 cup of milk and put all the above in the blender. Once blended return to pan and add remaining 1/2 cup milk and the cream. Mix well and refrigerate for a few hours. Serve cold.

Luisa Bridges

GOLDEN TOMATO-PAPAYA GAZPACHO WITH BASIL

2 pounds ripe yellow tomatoes
   (regular or cherry)
1 large (1¼ pounds) ripe papaya,
   peeled, seeded and diced
1 cup cucumber, diced
¼ cup white onion, minced

2 tablespoons white wine vinegar
2 cups regular strength chicken broth
2 tablespoons fresh basil leaves, minced
⅛ teaspoon liquid hot pepper sauce
Salt
Fresh basil sprigs

Stem small tomatoes or core large ones. Rinse and drain. Dice tomatoes. Put into a large bowl. Stir in papaya, cucumber, onion, vinegar, broth, basil and liquid pepper sauce. Add salt to taste. Cover and chill until cold, at least one hour or up to a day. Serve or transport in a chilled thermos. To enjoy cold, serve within 2 hours. Garnish with basil sprigs. Makes 10 to 12 servings.

Michael Cohen

COLD PEACH SOUP

1½ cups water
4 cloves
¾ cup sugar
1 cinnamon stick, broken
2 tablespoons cornstarch, mixed with
   ¼ cup cold water

1½ cups dry white wine
3 pounds ripe peaches
1 cup fresh, frozen, or canned
   blueberrries (optional)
1 cup heavy cream, whipped and sweetened

Pour water into a small saucepan. Add cloves, sugar, and cinnamon. Bring to a boil. Reduce heat and simmer 10 minutes. Add diluted cornstarch, whipping it into the syrup with a wire whisk. Bring syrup to a boil again. Remove from heat, stir in wine and refrigerate. Wash peaches, peel, split, seed, slice enough of the nicest ones for 2 cups and add to syrup. Puree others, add to syrup mixture. Refrigerate several hours or overnight. If desired, sprinkle with blueberries and a dollop of whipped cream. Serve cold.

Note: Peach soup is delicious served as a dessert. Serve over slices of pound cake and garnished with whipped cream.

Liz Minyard

CHEESY CORN CHOWDER

3 to 5 ears fresh sweet corn
1 small white onion, chopped
½ pound bacon
1 large potato

⅓ cup salt-free butter
¾ pound sharp cheddar cheese, grated
½ pint whipping cream
½ pint half-and-half
Salt and pepper to taste

Wash and shuck corn. With side of a sharp knife, gently cut corn off cob, scraping well to remove pulp and liquid. Set aside. Cut bacon into bite-sized pieces and brown in a Dutch oven on top of stove. When done, remove and drain on paper towel. Pour off grease, but do not scrape or wash pan. Add butter, onion and corn. Sauté until tender. Add carton of whipping cream and ¾ of the half-and-half. Microwave potato for approximately 4 to 5 minutes, or until nearly done. Do not cook completely. Peel potato and dice. Add to chowder along with salt and pepper. Continue cooking and stirring for 15 to 20 more minutes. Adjust amount of cream at this time. Remainder of half-and-half may be added if needed. Add cheddar cheese and cook 10 minutes longer or until cheese is melted and thoroughly incorporated. Ladle into bowls and top with crumbled bacon.

Lynda Sanders

LOW-FAT HEARTY TACO SOUP

1 pound extra lean ground beef
1 4-ounce can chopped green chilies
1 package taco seasoning mix
1 can hominy, with liquid
1 can pinto beans, with liquid
1 can kidney beans with liquid

3 cans stewed tomatoes
1 onion, chopped
1 teaspoon salt
1 package ranch dressing mix
1½ to 2 cups water

Brown hamburger meat. Add onion and cook until clear. Add remaining ingredients and simmer for 60 minutes. Freezes well. Approximately .5 grams fat and 160 calories per cup.

Tina Lewis

My Favorite Soup

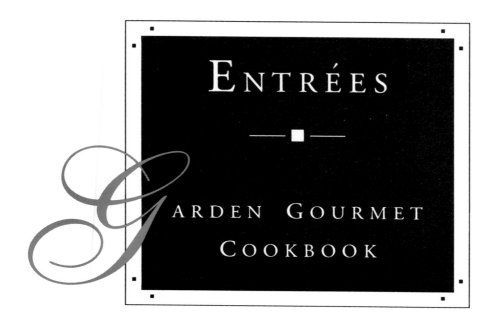

ENTRÉES

GARDEN GOURMET
COOKBOOK

VEAL SCALLOPS WITH AMONTILLADO

1 pound veal or turkey scallops,
    pounded thin
⅓ cup all-purpose flour
½ cup milk
2 tablespoons olive oil
2 tablespoons unsalted butter

Salt and freshly-ground pepper
½ cup medium-dry sherry, preferably
    Amontillado
1 4-ounce can sliced mushrooms, drained
1 tablespoon chopped fresh parsley

Dredge the veal in flour, dip in milk and then again in the flour; shake off any excess. In a large, heavy skillet, heat 1 tablespoon of the oil and 1 tablespoon of the butter. Add as many veal scallops as fit without crowding and sauté over moderately high heat for about 3 minutes on each side, until light brown. Transfer to a serving platter and season with salt and pepper to taste. Repeat with the remaining veal, oil, and butter. Add drained mushrooms and sherry to the skillet and boil over high heat, scraping up any browned bits from the bottom of the pan, until reduced by half, about 1 minute. Pour the sauce over the veal and garnish with the parsley. Serves 4.

Karen Bradshaw

VEAL PAPRIKA

2 pounds veal cutlets
2 tablespoons bacon drippings
1 large onion, chopped
    Salt and pepper to taste

2 tablespoons paprika
1 tablespoon flour
    Few drops cold water
½ cup sour cream

Cut meat into 1-inch cubes, trimming off fat. Sear in bacon drippings. When almost browned, add onion, and continue to cook until it is golden. Sprinkle with salt and pepper to taste; add paprika. Add hot water to barely cover. Place a lid on the pan and simmer for 1 hour. If necessary, add a little more water occasionally to prevent burning. Just before serving, thicken drippings by stirring in a paste made of the flour and a little cold water. Add sour cream. Serve in a rice ring. Serves 6 to 8.

Dorothy DeGolyer Arnold

FILET DE BOUEF

(Beef Wellington)

2½ pounds filet of beef
2 tablespoons cognac
   Salt
   White pepper, freshly cracked

5 strips bacon
   Duxelles of mushrooms
1 egg
1 teaspoon heavy cream

Pastry:
1¼ cups flour
  6 tablespoons sweet butter, very cold
  ¼ teaspoon salt

¼ teaspoon sugar
3 tablespoons ice water
2 tablespoons solid shortening

Duxelles of mushrooms:
  3 tablespoons sweet butter
  2 tablespoons shallots, finely chopped
  ¾ pound mushrooms, chopped fine

½ teaspoon salt
¼ teaspoon cracked white pepper

Mushrooms: Melt butter in a skillet and add the shallots. Cook on medium heat for 1 minute. Add mushrooms, salt, pepper and cook, mixing with a wooden spoon. Mushrooms will render their juices and when liquid is cooked down and dry and starts to sizzle, it is ready. Transfer to a bowl and cover with waxed paper.

Pastry: Place flour, butter, salt, shortening and sugar in a large bowl. Mix so that all butter pieces are coated with flour. Add the water. Start kneading the ingredients to gather dough into a ball. Do not worry if there are little pieces of butter here and there. Dough is manageable and usable immediately. (If overworked it would become elastic and shrink when used. Let "rest" in refrigerator for an hour before using.) Place on a floured board and roll uniformly. Be sure the board is well floured.

Beef: Preheat oven to 450 degrees. Rub filet with cognac. Lay bacon over top, securing with string. Place on rack or in roasting pan and roast 15 minutes (rare); 20 to 25 minutes (medium). Meat thermometer 115 degrees. Remove from oven and remove bacon. Cool to room temperature before proceeding. Spread top and sides of filet with duxelles. Preheat oven to 425 degrees. Roll out pastry into 18×12×¼-inch rectangle. Place filet top down in middle of pastry. Draw long sides up to overlap on bottom. Brush with mixture of egg and cream to seal. Trim ends of pastry and make an envelope. Brush with egg again to seal. Transfer to a baking sheet, seam-side down. Brush all over with egg. Cut decorative shapes from pastry trimmings and arrange on pastry. Brush shapes with egg wash. Let dry. Bake 30 minutes or until pastry is cooked. It is better to overcook pastry. Serve hot with Madeira sauce.

Martha Baker

LYNN'S LASAGNA

1½ pounds lean ground beef	1 teaspoon basil
Olive oil	½ cup green/red peppers, chopped
1 15-ounce can tomato sauce	¾ cup Parmesan cheese
1 to 1½ medium onions, chopped	1 teaspoon thyme
1 pound mozzarella cheese, grated	2 eggs, beaten
1 heaping teaspoon oregano	1 package lasagna noodles

Brown ground beef in olive oil. Add tomato sauce, onion, peppers, oregano, thyme, and basil. Simmer 20 minutes. Mix cheeses together with eggs, holding out a little of the mozzarella to sprinkle on top. Preheat oven to 350 degrees. Cook lasagna noodles according to package directions. In a 13×9×2-inch baking dish, layer the noodles, then the cheese, then the meat mixture 2 to 3 times. Sprinkle the extra mozzarella cheese on top. Bake at least 30 minutes. Remove from oven and let sit 5 to 10 minutes to set cheese.

Dedicated to Lynn Franzoni

BARBECUED BEEF BRISKET

1 teaspoon celery salt	2 ounces liquid smoke
1 teaspoon garlic salt	2 tablespoons Worcestershire sauce
1 teaspoon onion salt	2 cups barbecue sauce
1 teaspoon seasoning salt	5 to 8 pound brisket

Mix first 6 ingredients. Pour on meat, cover and refrigerate overnight in 9×13×2-inch pan or baking bag. When ready to bake, add 1 cup of barbecue sauce. Bake at 300 degrees for 4 hours. Add rest of barbecue sauce and cook 1 hour more at 325 degrees.

Glenna Clayton

DEVILED STEAK CUBES

1 tablespoon flour
1 teaspoon salt
Dash pepper
1 pound round steak,
    cut in 1-inch cubes
2 tablespoons fat

1 8-ounce can seasoned tomato sauce
1/4 cup water
1/2 teaspoon dry mustard
1 1/2 teaspoons Worcestershire sauce
1 medium onion, thinly sliced

Combine flour, salt and pepper. Dredge meat in flour mixture; brown slowly on all sides in hot fat. Add remaining ingredients. Cover; simmer 35 to 40 mintues or until meat is tender. Makes 4 servings.

Sadie Caropresi

PEPPER STEAK

1 1/2 pounds round steak,
    cut into strips or chunks
Oil to cover pan
1 medium onion, coarsely chopped
2 medium green peppers, chopped
1 cup beer
1 teaspoon garlic salt

1 teaspoon ginger
1 teaspoon pepper
1 teaspoon salt
1 tablespoon cornstarch
2 tablespoons sugar
2 tablespoons soy sauce
3 tomatoes

Heat oil in large skillet. Brown meat in oil about 5 minutes. Add onion, peppers. Stir in mixture of beer and seasonings. Heat to boiling, reduce heat, cover and simmer approximately 15 minutes. Blend cornstarch, sugar and soy sauce. Stir into meat mixture. Cook stirring constantly, until mixture thickens and boils. Boil and stir 1 minute. Cut each tomato into eighths. Place on meat mixture. Cook over low heat just until tomatoes are heated though, about 3 minutes. Serve over rice or wide noodles.

Gayla Ross

GREEN PEPPER STEAK

2 tablespoons oil
1 pound sirloin steak
1 teaspoon salt
  Dash pepper
2 tablespoons minced onion
1 clove garlic, minced

2 cups bouillon
2 green peppers, diced
4 small tomatoes, quartered
4 tablespoons cornstarch
4 tablespoons soy sauce
½ cup water

Cut steak into ⅛-inch thick slices. Heat oil in heavy skillet. Add meat, salt, pepper, onion and garlic. Cook over moderately hot heat, stirring constantly until meat is brown. Add bouillon and green peppers. Cover tightly and cook over low heat 10 minutes. Add tomatoes and cook one minute longer. Blend together cornstarch, soy sauce and water. Add to skillet and cook 3 to 4 minutes longer, stirring constantly, until mixture is hot and sauce is thickened. Serve over hot rice or Chinese noodles.

Lucy Martin

GUISO

(Mexican Stew)

1½ pounds boneless round steak
2 tablespoons shortening
2 ripe tomatoes
1 small green bell pepper, chopped
1 large onion, chopped

2 cloves garlic
1 teaspoon oregano
1 teaspoon powdered cumin
  Salt and pepper to taste
8 to 10 8-inch flour tortillas

Trim fat from steak. Cut into pieces about ½×2 inches. Skin tomatoes by dipping into boiling water to cover for 10 to 15 seconds. Slip off skin and chop. Melt shortening in Dutch oven. Add onion, stir until they begin to brown. Remove to a side dish with a slotted spoon. Add green pepper to pan and repeat process, removing to side dish. Repeat process with tomatoes. Finally, brown meat, adding a little more shortening if needed. Return vegetables to the pan and add enough hot water to cover, about 2 cups. Crush garlic in a mortar and add it and other seasonings. Simmer covered about 45 minutes. This may be done ahead of time and reheated as flavor improves after several hours. Heat a dry frying pan over medium heat and warm tortillas one at a time, turning once. Place some of meat mixture across center of each tortilla and fold sides over. Pour a little sauce over each. If Guiso seems too thin, thicken with a little flour and water when nearly done. Serves 4.

Pat Norvell

GONE ALL AFTERNOON STEW

1 pound stew meat or cubed round steak	1 can tomato soup
3 carrots, sliced	½ soup can water
2 onions, chopped	1 teaspoon salt
3 potatoes, quartered	½ teaspoon pepper
½ cup port wine or sweet pickle juice	2 ribs celery, chopped
	1 to 2 bay leaves

Put all ingredients in large casserole and cover tightly. Bake at 275 degrees for at least 5 hours.

Jimmie Smith

"GRANDMA'S" HOMEMADE SALAMI

¼ teaspoon red pepper	1 tablespoon mustard seed
1 tablespoon sugar	1 tablespoon whole peppercorns
2 pounds ground round beef	1 tablespoon Morton's Tender Quick curing salt
¼ teaspoon garlic powder (optional)	
½ teaspoon onion powder	1 cup water

Mix thoroughly all the ingredients. (Curing salt may be available at some hardware stores.) Divide into half and roll into foil. Cure rolls 2 days in refrigerator and bake at 275 degrees for 1½ hours on rack. Remove foil before baking.

Billie Tichenor

GOLDEN TREASURE MEATBALLS

1 pound lean ground beef	½ teaspoon garlic salt
½ cup milk	½ pound cheddar cheese, in chunks
1 slice bread, crumbled	Oil or margarine
1 teaspoon parsley, chopped	1 small can tomato sauce

Mix first 5 ingredients. Form meatballs *around* chunks of cheese. Press into round shape. Brown in oil or margarine in large skillet. Drain off oil. Turn heat to low and pour tomato sauce over meat balls. Watch carefully and turn as needed. Cook about 20 minutes, depending on size of meatballs. Makes 7 or 8 large meatballs. Serve 1 or 2 meatballs per serving over freshly cooked rice or noodles.

Jeanne Jarrell

COUNTRY MEAT LOAF

2 tablespoons salad oil
1 medium onion, chopped
1 celery stalk, finely chopped
3 white or whole wheat bread slices
2 pounds lean ground beef
1 or 2 (to your taste) medium carrots,
    finely shredded

1½ teaspoons salt
¼ teaspoon cracked black pepper
1 egg
1 8-ounce can tomato sauce
1 tablespoon light brown sugar
1 tablespoon cider vinegar
1 tablespoon prepared mustard

In 2-quart sauce pan, cook onion and celery in hot oil over medium heat for 10 minutes, stirring occasionally with a slotted spoon. Into large bowl, add bread slices which have been torn into small pieces. Add onion and celery mixture. Add ground beef, carrot, salt, pepper, egg and half the tomato sauce. Stir thoroughly to mix. Shape mixture into an 8×4-inch loaf or a 12×8-inch baking dish. Set aside. Combine brown sugar, vinegar, mustard and remaining tomato sauce in a cup and mix thoroughtly. Spoon sauce over meat loaf. Bake at 350 degrees for 1½ hours. Serve warm; or cover and refrigerate to serve cold.

Pauline Ellis

REUBEN LOAF

3¼ cups all purpose flour
1 tablespoon sugar
1 teaspoon salt
1 package yeast
1 cup hot water
1 tablespoon margarine, softened
¼ cup Thousand Island dressing

6 ounces corned beef, thinly sliced or
    one 7-ounce can
¼ pound sliced Swiss cheese
1 8-ounce can sauerkraut,
1 egg white, beaten
Caraway seed

Set aside 1 cup flour. In large bowl, mix remaining flour, sugar, salt, and yeast. Stir in hot water and margarine. Mix in only enough reserved flour to make soft dough. On floured surface, knead 4 minutes. On greased baking sheet, roll dough to 14×10 inches. Spread dressing down center third of dough length. Top with layers of beef, cheese, and sauerkraut. Cut 1-inch wide strips. Fold strips along sides of filling out to dough edges. Alternating sides, fold strips at an angle across filling. Cover dough; place baking sheet over large shallow pan half-filled with boiling water for 15 minutes. Brush with egg white. Sprinkle with caraway seed. Bake at 400 degrees for 25 minutes or until done. Cool slightly; serve warm.

Carol Cattoi Lanning

HUNGARIAN GOULASH

1 medium onion, chopped
1 tablespoon margarine
1 pound hamburger meat
1 15-ounce can English peas

1 15-ounce can diced carrots
1 10¾-inch can cream of mushroom soup
Canned biscuits

Sauté onion in margarine until soft. Mix in hamburger meat and brown as desired. Cook peas and carrots in their juice until soft. Drain meat mixture and vegetables. Mix with soup and place in baking dish. Bake 30 minutes at 325 degrees. Place biscuits on top and bake until biscuits are done.

Frieda Fiske

COTTAGE PIE

4 potatoes
1 pound ground round steak
½ onion, chopped

Salt and pepper
4 small or 2 large tomatoes
2 slices of cheese

Cook potatoes and mash. Set aside. Brown beef, onion and seasonings. Place a portion in bottom of small casserole dish. Peel and slice tomatoes, put on top of the meat. Repeat layers. Add the mashed potatoes to the final tomato layer. Cut the cheese slices into 3×½-inch ribbons and place on top of potatoes. Bake in a preheated 375 degree oven for 30 minutes. Serves 4. This recipe originated in England.

Anne Walker

BEEF AND BEAN ROUND-UP

1½ pounds ground beef
½ cup onion, chopped or
    1 tablespoon instant minced onion
2 or 3 tablespoons barbecue sauce

1 tablespoon brown sugar
1 16-ounce can baked style beans
1 10-ounce can refrigerated flaky biscuits
½ cup processed cheese, shredded

Heat oven to 375 degrees. In a skillet, brown ground beef and onion, then drain. Stir in barbecue sauce, brown sugar and beans. Heat until bubbly. Pour into a 2½-quart casserole. Separate dough into 10 biscuits, cut each biscuit in half crosswise. Place biscuits, cut side down over hot meat mixture in spoke fashion around edge of casserole. Sprinkle cheese over biscuits. Bake at 375 degrees for 22 to 27 minutes or until biscuits are golden brown. Serves 6.

Jeanne Bryant

MARY WILSON CASSEROLE

3 tablespoons oil
1 6- to 10-ounce package medium
    noodles
2 pounds hamburger meat or
    1 pound hamburger and
    1 pound ground turkey
2 onions, chopped

2 cloves garlic, chopped fine
1 green pepper, chopped
1 cup black olives, sliced
1 29-ounce can tomatoes
1 4-ounce jar mushrooms, drained
½ pound Velveeta, grated
    Salt and pepper to taste

In a large skillet, sauté onions, green pepper and garlic in oil. Drain oil, then brown meat. Mix all other ingredients except noodles and cheese. Cover and cook slowly while preparing noodles according to package. Drain noodles and add to skillet. Stir in cheese to melt. Place entire mixture in 9×13-inch casserole dish and cook in 325 degree oven 30 minutes. Freezes well. Serves a small army.

Joan Wright

BEEF AND SAUSAGE TAMALE PIE

1 pound ground beef
½ pound sausage
1 medium onion, chopped
1 teaspoon garlic salt
    Pepper to taste
1 green pepper, minced
1 15-ounce can tomatoes,
    partly drained

1 can whole kernel corn, partly drained
1 3-ounce can pitted black olives
1 teaspoon chili powder
1 cup corn meal mix
1½ cups sweet milk
3 eggs, well beaten
1 cup cheese, grated

Brown ground meat, sausage and onion and season with garlic salt and pepper. Drain well. Soak corn meal in sweet milk, then add all remaining ingredients except cheese. Mix well. Turn into greased 3-quart baking dish. Bake at 350 degrees for 40 to 50 minutes. Sprinkle with grated cheese 15 minutes before done and return to oven. Makes 6 to 8 portions.

Shirley Belcher

MEXICAN MANICOTTI

1 can refried beans	1½ cups water
1 pound lean ground beef	1 8-ounce carton sour cream
1 teaspoon cumin	½ cup green onion, finely chopped
1 teaspoon oregano	½ cup black olives, chopped
1 box manicotti shells	¾ cup mozzarella cheese, grated
1 8-ounce jar picante sauce	

Mix meat, refried beans, cumin, and oregano. Stuff into 8 uncooked shells. Put in microwave dish. Put picante and water on top. Cover with vented plastic wrap. Microwave on high 10 minutes. Take out, turn over and cook 10 minutes longer or until done. Mix sour cream, onions, olives, and spread on top. Top with cheese and microwave 2 to 3 minutes longer.

Pat Davies

BEEF AND BROCCOLI PIE

1 pound ground beef	1 beaten egg
¼ cup onion, chopped	10 ounces chopped broccoli, cooked
2 tablespoons flour	and drained
1 teaspoon garlic salt	2 packages refrigerator crescent rolls
1¼ cups milk	4 ounces Monterey Jack cheese
3 ounces cream cheese, softened	Extra milk

Brown beef and onions in large skillet, drain fat. Stir in flour, garlic salt, milk and cream cheese. Cook and stir until mixture is thick and smooth. Add small amount of mixture to beaten egg, blend together and return to skillet. Continue to cook over medium heat for a couple of minutes until thick. Stir in broccoli and turn off heat.

Unroll 1 package of rolls on floured surface. Place 4 sections together forming a 12×7-inch rectangle. Do the same with the other 4 sections and join both together. Seal all edges. Roll into a 12-inch square and fit into greased deep dish pie pan and trim. Spoon mixture into shell. Slice cheese and place on top to cover. Roll out second package of rolls as before to form top crust. Trim and seal all edges with a fork. Cut steam slits and brush with milk.

Bake at 350 degrees for 40 minutes. Let stand for 10 minutes before serving. If top browns too fast, cover with a foil strip for the last 10 minutes of cooking time. Makes 6 large or 8 small servings.

Susan Sadler

SAUSAGE~STUFFED TURBAN SQUASH

1 3-pound turban squash	1 egg, slightly beaten
Salt	½ cup sour cream
1 pound mild bulk sausage	¼ cup grated Parmesan cheese
1 cup celery, chopped	¼ teaspoon salt
¼ cup onion, chopped	Parsley sprigs (optional)
½ cup fresh mushrooms, sliced	Fresh mushroom slices (optional)

Remove small upper portion of squash, cutting down to seeds. Remove seeds to form a cavity; discard upper portion of squash and seeds. Sprinkle cavity with salt. Place squash, cut side down, in a 9-inch square baking pan. Fill pan with 1-inch water. Bake at 375 degrees for 1 hour or until tender. Remove squash from pan, reserving water.

Combine sausage, celery and onion in a heavy skillet; cook 5 minutes, stirring to crumble sausage. Stir in mushrooms and continue to cook until meat is browned. Drain well.

Combine egg, sour cream, cheese and salt; stir well. Add egg mixture to sausage mixture, and blend well. Spoon into cavity of squash. Place squash, stuffing side up, into same pan with reserved water. Bake 20 to 25 minutes. Before serving, garnish with parsley and mushrooms, if desired. Serves 6.

Tonya Calhoun

SAUCY SIRLOIN SUPREME

1½ pounds sirloin (or round) steak, cut into 1×¼-inch pieces	½ cup water
1 can golden mushroom soup	1 bay leaf
2 tablespoons sherry	1 10-ounce package frozen green beans

In skillet, sauté steak in a little oil until slightly brown. Add remaining ingredients except green beans. Cook 1 hour on very low heat, stirring occasionally. Add frozen beans and cook an additional 15 minutes. The beans will be crunchy. Serve over rice. Serves 5 to 6.

Irene Burleson

STUFFED PORK CHOPS

(Stuffed with Andouille, Apples, and Cornbread)

4 center-cut pork chops, 6 to 7 ounces each	1 unpeeled green apple, cored and diced
1 tablespoon olive oil	1 sage leaf, chopped
¼ cup small onion, diced	1 sprig rosemary, chopped
¼ cup stalk celery, diced	2 tablespoons crumbled cornbread
1 clove garlic	2 tablespoons sour cream
¼ cup red bell pepper, seeded and diced	Salt and freshly ground pepper to taste
1 serrano chile, seeded and minced	1 tablespoon vegetable oil or clarified butter
3 ounces andouille sausage, cut into ⅛-inch dice	¼ cup port wine
	½ cup chicken stock

Preheat the oven to 160 degrees. Place 1 pork chop flat on a work surface, and holding it down with one hand, slice it through the middle with the point of a knife to form a pocket. Cut deeply to the bone, open the chop, and flatten each half with a meat pounder to make it a little larger for stuffing. Repeat this procedure for the remaining pork chops.

Heat the olive oil in a large skillet over medium heat until lightly smoking. Sauté the onion, celery, garlic, bell pepper, and serrano for 2 to 3 minutes. Add the sausage to the pan and cook for 1 minute longer. Add the apples, herbs, and cornbread crumbs, and toss to heat through.

Remove the skillet from the heat, stir in the sour cream, and season with salt and pepper. When the stuffing has cooled, divide among the pork chops. Push the stuffing into the pockets and close securely. Do not overstuff, and make sure the meat is pressed together around the opening. Season the chops with salt and pepper.

Heat the vegetable oil or clarified butter in a large skillet over medium heat until lightly smoking. Add the chops and cook the first side for 3 to 4 minutes, until browned. Turn the chops over, cover the pan, and lower the heat. Cook for an additional 6 to 7 minutes. Remove the chops from the skillet and keep warm in the oven.

Deglaze the pan with the port and reduce by half while scraping the pan with a spatula to dissolve the solidified juices. Add the stock and reduce by half again. Season with salt and pour over the pork chops on a platter.

Chef Stephan Pyles

POT STICKERS

(Oriental Dumplings)

¼ head cabbage, chopped
4 green onions, chopped
1 pinkie size fresh ginger
   Cilantro (optional)
1 pound unseasoned ground pork

2 teaspoons soy sauce
½ teaspoon baking powder
1 package won ton or pot sticker wrappers
   Peanut oil
1 can chicken broth

Chop the cabbage up into small pieces. A food processer works well. Chop and add the onions and ginger. Add a few chopped leaves of cilantro, if desired. Combine all the greens with the meat, soy sauce and baking powder. Mix well. Take a won ton or pot sticker wrapper, wet the edges and add to it 1 heaping teaspoon of the seasoned meat and fold it over and press the edges together, using the back side of a spoon. Repeat making the dumplings until you run out of meat or wrappers. In electric skillet set the temperature to 350 degrees and add 1 tablespoon of peanut oil. Add dumplings to fill the bottom of the pan (about 12). Cover and cook for 5 minutes. Pour 1 tablespoon chicken broth over each dumpling (this will unstick them). Cook for another 5 minutes at 350 degrees in the covered skillet. Remove and serve with soy sauce or sweet and sour sauce. Repeat cooking until all the pot stickers are done. Makes 30 to 40 dumplings. Serves 6.

Bert Baker

CHICKEN AND SAUSAGE JAMBALAYA

3 pounds smoked sausage,
   cut into 3-inch pieces
8 chicken breasts
1 bunch green onions, chopped
2 medium yellow onions, chopped
2 bell peppers, cut in ¼-inch pieces
1 celery stalk, chopped

Chopped parsley
Cajun seasoning
Fresh garlic, chopped
Tabasco
Butter
3 boxes brown rice, minimum

Boil sausage and chicken in water to cover, seasoned with Cajun seasoning, for 20 to 30 minutes. Sauté the green and yellow onions, peppers, garlic, and celery in real butter. Cut boiled sausage and chicken into bite size pieces. Remove sauteed ingredients from skillet, leaving as much butter as possible. Brown sausage in skillet. Prepare rice (the more rice you use, the more servings) and stir in sauteed ingredients, sausage and chicken. Immediately prior to serving, stir in parsley. Cajun seasoning can be added during sauté stage and/or combining of ingredients with rice. Each guest can use Tabasco to own taste. Serves 20 to 24.

B. Leonard Critcher

BARBECUED SPARERIBS (CHINESE)

3 pounds spareribs
2 tablespoons cornstarch
⅔ cup brown sugar
⅔ cup soy sauce

¼ cup vinegar
¼ teaspoon ground ginger
2 cloves garlic, minced

Parboil the spareribs, simmering 45 minutes. Drain. Combine all other ingredients.Dip each piece of rib into mixture, coating thoroughly. Place on grill or under broiler for 5 minutes or until brown. Brush with sauce occasionally. Turn ribs and brush with sauce. Broil 3 minutes.

Carol Russell

HAM AND CHICKEN CASSEROLE

1½ cups thin spaghetti, broken
    into 1½-inch pieces
¼ cup margarine
6 green onions with tops, finely chopped
1 4-ounce can sliced mushrooms,
    drained
1½ cups ham, diced

1 cup cooked chicken, diced
½ teaspoon salt
⅛ teaspoon pepper
½ teaspoon celery salt
1 cup sour cream
1 cup creamed cottage cheese
1 cup sharp cheddar cheese, shredded

Cook spaghetti, drain. Sauté onions, mushrooms in margarine. Add ham, chicken, salts, and pepper and heat through. Combine sour cream and cottage cheese with spaghetti. Add ham and chicken mixture. Toss together lightly. Turn into 2 quart casserole. Top with cheese and bake at 350 degrees until brown and bubbly.

Dorothy Joe Ficken

PHYLLO ROLL WITH CRANBERRY SAUCE

⅓ cup celery, chopped
⅓ cup green pepper, chopped
¼ cup green onion, sliced
1½ teaspoons oil
1½ cup cooked ham, diced
4 ounces mushrooms, drained, sliced
½ cup cheddar or Monterey Jack
   cheese, shredded

1 tablespoon flour
¼ teaspoon pepper
⅓ cup unsalted butter or margarine,
   melted
1 tablespoon dry bread crumbs
8 sheets phyllo dough (18×14)
1 egg white, beaten
1 recipe cranberry sauce (below)

In large saucepan, cook celery, green pepper and onion in hot oil until tender. Remove from heat and drain well. Stir in ham, mushrooms, cheese, flour and pepper. Lightly brush some butter and sprinkle ½ teaspoon bread crumbs between each thawed phyllo sheet, stacking sheets. Brush top with egg white. Mound ham mixture on phyllo dough stack parallel to and about 3 inches from one short edge. Fold 3-inch edge of dough over ham mixture. Fold into about 1½ inches on the long sides, then roll up from the short side with the ham mixture. Make shallow cuts in diagonal crisscross fashion across the top. Place roll in 13×9×2-inch baking pan. Brush with more of the melted butter. Cover; chill up to 24 hours. To serve, uncover; bake in 400 degree oven 25 to 35 minutes, or until golden and heated through. Slice and serve with cranberry sauce. Great for Holiday brunch!

Cranberry Sauce:
½ cup cranapple juice
1 tablespoon cornstarch
   Dash cloves

8 ounces jellied cranberry sauce
1 tablespoon butter or margarine

In small saucepan, combine cranapple juice and cornstarch. Add cranberry sauce and dash cloves. Cook and stir until thickened and bubbly; cook and stir 2 minutes more. Stir in butter until melted. Makes about 1⅓ cups sauce.

Pamela Easter

SWEET 'N' SOUR PORK-LOIN 'N' VEGGIES

3 to 3½ pounds boneless pork loin
1 tablespoon olive oil
2 tablespoons onion, minced
½ cup sugar
2 tablespoons cornstarch
¾ cup red wine vinegar
½ cup catsup

¼ cup soy sauce
½ cup water
¼ teaspoon vegetable supreme
2 garlic cloves, crushed
2 tablespoons olive oil
Veggies (potatoes and onions)

Prepare outdoor grill for "indirect barbequing." Heat 1 tablespoon olive oil in sauce pan. Add onion. Sauté over medium heat until soft. Stir in remaining ingredients (except veggies). Bring to boil. Cook, stirring until thick and clear. Remove and set aside. Grill pork 6 inches from coals on medium low, covered, for 1½ hours or 170 degrees on meat thermometer, turning meat occasionally. Brush with sauce during last 30 minutes, using a disposable foil pan under rack and directly under roast. Meanwhile halve potatoes and cut onions into wedges. Place veggies in a single layer on double thickness, heavy duty foil, large enough to fold over veggies. Cover with crushed garlic, ½ teaspoon salt, ¼ teaspoon pepper and sprinkle with "vegetable supreme" and 2 tablespoons olive oil. Seal edges of foil together over vegetables. Place foil packet on rack next to meat. Cook 30 minutes or until veggies are tender, turning packet occasionally. Serve vegetables with pork; pass sauce separately.

Fran Darley

PEPPERED CHEF'S PRIME

1 2- to 4-pound boneless pork
  rib roast

1 to 2 tablespoons garlic pepper
1 to 2 teaspoons crushed rosemary

Preheat oven to 325 degrees. Coat roast with a seasoning mixture of garlic pepper and rosemary. Roast in a shallow pan for 45 minutes to 1½ hours, until meat thermometer registers 155 degrees. Let roast rest 5 to 10 minutes before carving.

Janet Trlica

TENDERLOIN PARMIGIAN

1 2½- to 3-pound boneless pork
   tenderloin*
1 egg
½ teaspoon seasoned salt
⅛ teaspoon pepper

½ cup bread crumbs (Italian)
2 tablespoons oil
15½ ounces spaghetti sauce with
   seasonings, preferably homemade
¼ cup Parmesan cheese
2 slices mozzarella cheese

Beat egg; add salt and pepper. Dip tenderloin into egg mixture, then crumbs. Brown on both sides in oil. Place in shallow pan. Pour sauce over meat. Sprinkle with Parmesan cheese. Bake covered in 350 degree oven 30 minutes. Remove cover. Top with mozzarella cheese. Cook 10 minutes or until cheese melts and meat reaches 170 degrees internal temperature. Serves 4 to 6.

*Chicken, veal or eggplant may be substituted for pork.

Pat Marshall

ORANGE PORK TENDERLOIN

2 pork tenderloins
1 tablespoon butter, softened
¼ teaspoon dried thyme, crushed
   Dash cayenne pepper

¾ cup orange juice
1 tablespoon flour
1½ teaspoons sugar
1 teaspoon aromatic bitters

Mix butter, thyme, and cayenne; spread evenly over tenderloin. Place tenderloin in shallow roasting pan and pour orange juice over meat. Roast at 375 degrees for 25 to 30 minutes (155 to 160 on meat thermometer). Baste occasionally. Remove tenderloin to serving platter; keep warm. Measure basting liquid into small saucepan, adding more orange juice if necessary to make ¾ cup. Quickly whisk in flour, sugar and bitters. Cook and stir until mixture boils and thickens. Cut tenderloin into 1-inch slices and serve with sauce.

Joan Jensen

ROAST LEG OF LAMB

(with Pesto, Radicchio and Shallots)

1 5- to 6-pound leg of lamb	2 medium heads radicchio
7 to 8 ounces pesto sauce	Fresh basil springs
8 ounces shallots, peeled	

Cut excess fat from lamb, leaving a thin layer. Set lamb in medium size roasting pan. Make several slits in lamb and spoon some pesto into each. Rub remaining pesto into lamb. Cover and let stand 2 hours at room temperature or refrigerate overnight. Preheat oven to 350 degrees. Roast lamb 30 minutes. Add shallots to pan, turning to coat in pan juices. Roast 45 minutes. Cut radicchio heads into 3 wedges, but do not core. Add radicchio, turning to coat in juices. Continue roasting until thermometer inserted into thickest part of meat registers 140 degrees for medium-rare, about 45 minutes longer. Remove from oven and let stand 15 minutes. Transfer lamb, shallots and radicchio to platter. Garnish with fresh basil sprigs and serve.

DyAnna Giltner

RACK OF LAMB FOR TWO

1 rack of lamb (1½ to 2 pounds)	3 tablespoons olive oil
(8 ribs)	3 tablespoons seasoned bread crumbs
Salt and pepper	1 cup sherry (optional)

Preheat oven to 450 degrees. Rub rack of lamb with salt and pepper and roast with ribs down in roasting pan for 25 minutes. Combine olive oil and seasoned bread crumbs to form a paste. Remove rack from oven, cover with paste and add wine to the pan if desired. Cook for another 5 to 10 minutes for medium rare to medium.

Seasoned bread crumbs: Combine approximately 3 tablespoons bread crumbs, 1 tablespoon finely grated Romano cheese and ½ cup fresh mint leaves in blender or processor. Blend until completely mixed. This may be made up in quantity and kept in freezer to use in other dishes.

Dick Jeffrey

GINI'S LAMB CHOPS

6 double thick lamb chops
1½ to 2 tablespoons good olive oil
1 tablespoon garlic powder

1 tablespoon parsley, fresh if possible
1 tablespoon thyme, fresh if possible
1 tablespoon rosemary, fresh if possible

Crust mixture:
½ cup fresh bread crumbs
4 ounces softened butter
1 teaspoon parsely, minced

1 teaspoon garlic powder
1 tablespoon Dijon mustard

Rub chops well with olive oil. Season heavily with mixture of the garlic powder, rosemary, thyme and parsley. Rub this in well. Refrigerate overnight.

Next day, bring back to room temperature. Mix crust ingredients. Preheat oven to 350 degrees. Put a pat of butter on each chop and roast for 15 to 20 minutes. Remove from oven and coat chops well with crust mixture. Broil until brown and crispy (about 5 minutes). This will produce pink lamb chops. If you like them more done, increase the roasting time about 5 minutes.

(Instead of the normal mint jelly to accompany the chops, mix *5 ounces of hot jalapeño pure jelly with 6 ounces of cran-fruit cranberry orange sauce*. This is an outstanding compliment for lamb.)

Gini Marston

LAMB CHOPS PAPRIKA

6 shoulder lamb chops
  (about 3 pounds)
1 cup sliced onion
1 clove garlic, crushed
2 teaspoons paprika
2 large green peppers
¼ cup tomato puree

1 10½-ounce can condensed beef
  broth, undiluted
½ cup red wine
2 teaspoons salt
1 8-ounce package noodles
  Dash cayenne
1½ cups sour cream

Wipe chops with damp paper towels. Trim excess fat. Heat fat in large skillet. Sauté lamb chops in hot fat until well browned on both sides. Remove chops and any pieces of fat. Add onion, garlic and paprika; sauté, stirring until onion is tender, about 5 minutes. Cut green peppers into ½-inch wide strips. Add to skillet with lamb chops, tomato puree, beef broth, wine and salt. Cook slowly, covered, 45 to 50 minutes, or until lamb is tender. During last half hour of cooking, cook noodles as package label directs; drain. Add cayenne and sour cream to lamb. Heat until just hot. Serve with noodles. Serves 6.

Carole Cohen

GRANDMOTHER'S INDIAN CURRY

2 pounds lamb shoulder
3 medium onions, finely chopped
  Salt and pepper
6 tablespoons butter or margarine
¼ cup flour

2 teaspoons curry powder (or to taste)
3 cups hot meat stock (or 3 bouillon
  cubes and 3 cups boiling water)
3 tablespoons lemon juice
4 cups hot cooked rice

Cut meat from bones and mix with onions. Season with salt and pepper, and sauté until brown in butter. Mix flour and curry powder and stir into meat. Add hot stock and lemon juice and simmer until meat is tender (about 45 minutes). Serves 4 to 6. Serve with hot cooked rice and condiments such as:

crushed pineapple
chutney
coconut

chopped peanuts
pickle relish
sieved hard-cooked eggs

Sarah Gardenhire

LAMB CURRY

4 cups stewing lamb, cubed
2 cups chicken broth
2 cups milk
½ teaspoon peppercorns
1 sprig thyme
1 sprig parsley
4 tablespoons butter
2 large onions, chopped

1 large green apple, chopped
4 tablespoons flour
3 tablespoons curry powder
½ teaspoon salt
⅛ teaspoon pepper
½ cup lime juice
½ cup seedless raisins
2 whole cloves

Cover meat with broth and milk, add peppercorns, thyme and parsley. Simmer until meat is tender. Drain off liquid and save. Sauté onion and apple in butter until yellow. Add flour mixed with curry powder, salt and pepper. Slowly pour on reserved liquid, bring to boil. Then add lime juice, raisins and cloves. Add meat mixture and simmer 30 minutes. Serve on very dry rice. Serves 8.

Betty Lou Winslow

SESAME CHICKEN

½ cup soy sauce
⅓ cup oil
2 tablespoons sesame seeds
1 teaspoon ginger
¼ cup water

1 tablespoon sugar (or substitute)
½ teaspoon garlic powder
⅛ teaspoon red pepper
2 tablespoons minced onion
6 to 8 boneless chicken breasts

Mix ingredients together in shallow pan. Marinate chicken breast in sauce about 12 hours. Grill or bake chicken.

Diana Sobey

BACKYARD GARDENER'S BARBECUE

2 broiler fryers
Seasoned salt
Garlic salt
Freshly ground pepper
Bottled barbecue sauce

1 lemon
1 cup water
¼ cup margarine
½ cup vegetable oil
½ cup onion, sliced
4 tablespoons vinegar
½ teaspoon freshly ground pepper
½ teaspoon garlic salt

To make basting sauce, combine ingredients in the second column in order listed. Bring to a rolling boil. Gently squeeze lemon and remove. Use to baste chickens. Leftover sauce will keep in refrigerator for several weeks, or add ½ cup bottled barbecue sauce and serve with chicken.

Wash chickens, pat dry, quarter and sprinkle generously with salts and pepper. Place on barbecue grill and cook at medium heat for approximately 2 hours. Baste frequently with basting sauce. Turn occasionally to insure uniform browning. Gently twist leg bone; if bone turns easily in socket, chicken is done. Add ½ cup bottled barbecue sauce to basting sauce. Baste chicken with this sauce during last 5 minutes of cooking. Place chickens on platter and pass extra sauce.

Irene and Gene Cerny

PICNIC HONEY CHICKEN

½ cup honey
¼ cup prepared mustard
3 tablespoons milk
2 to 3 pounds chicken pieces

3 tablespoons butter, melted
1 teaspoon curry powder
1 teaspoon salt

Mix all ingredients except chicken. Dip chicken pieces in the mixture and place in a roasting pan. Bake 1¼ hours at 350 degrees, basting occasionally with the remaining mixture. Serve hot or cold.

Dedicated to Boni Bennett

SANTA FE CHICKEN

6 chicken breasts, boned, skinless
2 teaspoons ground cumin (divided)
1 teaspoon garlic salt
1 tablespoon olive oil
1 16-ounce can black beans

1 15-ounce can white shoe peg corn
⅔ cup picante sauce
1 cup bell peppers, chopped
2 tablespoons cilantro, chopped

Sprinkle both sides of chicken with cumin and garlic salt. Brown in olive oil and cook until tender. Keep warm. Mix all ingredients except cilantro and heat until boiling. Spoon over chicken, decorate with cilantro.

Sunny Krutz

SHERRIED CHICKEN BREASTS

10 chicken breasts, browned in oil

Sauce:
1½ cups margarine, melted
1½ tablespoons Worcestershire sauce

1½ tablespoons red currant jelly
1½ cups golden sherry (not cooking)

Line pan with foil enough to pull up over chicken and seal. Place browned chicken on foil and pour sauce over it. Seal chicken in foil and bake at 350 degrees for 1 hour. Serve over wild and long grain rice mixture.

Annella Collins

CHICKEN BREAST IN SOUR CREAM

8 chicken breast halves, skinned
1 4-ounce can button mushrooms
1 can cream of mushroom soup
½ soup can sherry
1 cup sour cream
Paprika

Place chicken in baking dish. Combine other ingredients and pour over chicken. Sprinkle with paprika and bake at 350 degrees for 1½ hours. Serves 8.

Virginia Duncan

IMPERIAL CHICKEN

½ cup plus 2 tablespoons butter or
   margarine, melted
2 small cloves garlic, crushed
¾ cup dry breadcrumbs
½ cup Parmesan cheese, grated
1½ tablespoons parsley, minced
1 teaspoon salt
Pepper to taste
6 chicken breasts, boned and skinned
Juice of 1 lemon
Paprika

Combine butter and garlic; set aside. Pound the chicken breasts with a meat hammer until flat. Combine breadcrumbs, cheese, parsley, salt, and pepper; stir well. Dip each chicken breast in butter mixture, then in breadcrumb mixture. Roll tightly, starting at narrow end, and secure with a wooden pick. Arrange rolls in a shallow baking pan. Drizzle with remaining butter and lemon juice. Sprinkle with paprika. Bake at 350 degrees for 45 to 55 minutes. Serves 6.

Norma Slane

TEN MINUTE CHICKEN WITH BRIE

1 tablespoon olive oil
1 large clove garlic, peeled and
   put through a press
½ teaspoon basil or rosemary,
   crushed
4 chicken breast halves, boned and
   skinned
¼ teaspoon salt
Fresh ground pepper, to taste
⅓ pound Brie or Camembert cheese,
   rind removed, cut into 4 pieces

Preheat oven to 350 degrees. Stir together oil, garlic and basil. Brush onto chicken and sprinkle with salt and pepper. Place in foil-lined baking pan and bake 30 minutes. Remove from oven; turn oven to broil. Place a piece of Brie on each. Run under broiler just until cheese starts to melt.

Jeanne Barnes

CHICKEN SAUTÉ

2 tablespoons soy sauce
1/4 cup water
2 teaspoons cornstarch
1 teaspoon sugar
2 tablespoons oil
1 clove garlic, minced

1/2 teaspoon fresh gingeroot, grated
1 pound chicken breasts, cut in
    bite- size pieces
1 6-ounce package snow peas, thawed
1 8-ounce can sliced water chestnuts
1/2 small sweet red pepper, in slices

Combine first 4 ingredients. Set aside. Heat oil 1 to 2 minutes in large skillet. Add garlic and gingeroot. Sauté until tender. Add chicken and cook, stirring constantly, 3 minutes or until lightly browned. Drain water chestnuts. Add last 3 ingredients. Cook 1 minute, stirring constantly. Add soy sauce mixture. Cook 2 minutes or until thickened. Serves 4.

Leila C. McLendon

PICANTE CHICKEN SKILLET

1 pound chicken breasts, skinned
    and boned
    Salt (optional) and pepper
1 tablespoon olive or vegetable oil
1 clove garlic, minced
1 14 1/2- to 16-ounce can whole
    tomatoes
1/3 cup picante sauce

1 medium yellow or green pepper, cut
    in 3/4-inch chunks
1 medium onion, cut in 1/4-inch wedges
3/4 teaspoon ground cumin
1/2 teaspoon salt (optional)
1 tablespoon cornstarch
1 tablespoon water
1 to 2 tablespoons chopped cilantro
2 cups hot cooked rice

Cut chicken into 1 1/2×1/2×1/2-inch strips. Sprinkle with salt and pepper. Heat oil in 10-inch skillet. Add chicken and garlic; cook and stir until chicken is almost cooked through, about 5 minutes. Drain and coarsely chop tomatoes, reserving juice. Add tomatoes, reserved juice, picante sauce, pepper, onion, cumin and salt to skillet. Simmer 5 minutes, stirring occasionally. Dissolve cornstarch in water; stir into skillet. Simmer 1 minute or until sauce is thickened, stirring constantly. Serve over rice with cilantro and additional picante sauce. Makes 4 servings.

Krista Smith

CHICKEN WITH ARTICHOKE

6 boneless chicken breasts
2 tablespoons butter
½ cup flour
   Clove garlic, crushed
⅓ cup white wine

1 can artichoke hearts, drained
½ cup chicken broth
   Juice of one lemon
½ cup capers

Dredge chicken through flour. Brown in melted butter. Add all other ingredients and cook until tender, about 30 minutes. Serve over buttered noodles or rice. Serves 6.

Mrs. Ben R. Weber, Jr.

BOB HOPE'S FAVORITE CHICKEN HASH

2 chicken breasts, broiled
2 strips of bacon, crisp
½ small onion, chopped, sauteed
2 tablespoons butter

½ teaspoon lemon juice
   Salt and pepper to taste
2 tablespoons sour cream
1 teaspoon dry sherry wine

Cut chicken in fine strips. Crumble bacon and combine with the onion, butter, lemon juice and seasonings. Sauté until thoroughly heated in the butter. Shortly before serving add the sherry and sour cream. Do not allow to cook after adding. Just heat through.

Bob Hope

CHICKEN DaDa

8 chicken pieces
   Salt
3 tablespoons oil
1 clove garlic
⅓ cup parsley sprigs, chopped

   Pepper
1 teaspoon vinegar
4 ounces white wine
2 tablespoons catsup
   Water

Rub salt on chicken pieces. Cut garlic clove in half. Heat oil, add garlic, and brown chicken well. Add chopped parsley, pepper to taste, and vinegar. Cook for 2 minutes. Add wine and cook a few minutes longer. Add catsup and a few drops of water. Cover and simmer until chicken is done. Serve with potatoes or noodles.

Ila Post

TOM SELLECK'S FAVORITE CHICKEN
(with Wine and Vegetables)

1 tablespoon butter
1 medium onion, chopped
¼ teaspoon salt
⅛ teaspoon pepper
4 chicken breasts, boned and halved
½ cup all purpose flour

2 tablespoons butter
8 whole mushrooms, sliced
1 8-ounce can artichoke hearts, drained
1 cup orange juice
1 cup dry white wine
1 cup ginger ale
2 tablespoons lemon juice

In a skillet, brown onion in butter. Salt and pepper chicken. Roll chicken in flour to cover. Brown quickly in remaining butter. Place onion in bottom of Dutch oven. Layer chicken and mushrooms. Mix all liquid ingredients; pour over chicken. Cook covered for 1 hour at 325 degrees. Add artichoke hearts. Cook for 1½ hours more. Serve with brown rice. Serves 4.

Jeanne Bryant

EXCELLENT CHICKEN WITH WINE SAUCE

1½ tablespoons flour
½ teaspoon salt
⅛ teaspoon pepper
3 packages chicken breasts, skinned
4 tablespoons margarine
1 pound mushrooms with stems

3 medium onions, chopped
1 cup parsley, chopped
1 cup white wine
1 8-ounce can water chesnuts
2 cups cooked rice

Combine flour, salt and pepper. Coat chicken with mixture. Shake off and reserve excess flour. Melt 2 tablespoons margarine in large skillet over medium heat. Brown chicken; remove from skillet. Add remaining margarine, mushrooms, onion and 2 tablespoons chopped parsley. Saute' until onion is transparent. Remove from heat. Stir in reserved flour. Blend in wine. Bring to a boil, stirring frequently. Add chicken and water chestnuts. Cover, reduce heat and simmer 25 minutes or until chicken is tender. Serve over rice. Garnish with remaining parsley. Serves 4.

Janet Buttimer

CHAMPAGNE CHICKEN BREASTS

12 chicken breasts, skinned and boned (about 4.5 ounces each)
Garlic powder (optional)
Vegetable oil spray

3 tablespoons vegetable oil
Champagne
½ pound fresh mushrooms, sliced

Place chicken breasts between 2 sheets of wax paper and pound with flat hand until as thin as possible. Sprinkle lightly with garlic powder. Spray three 12-inch skillets with vegetable oil spray. Place 1 tablespoon oil in each pan and swirl. Sauté breasts 4 in each pan, 3 minutes on each side. Pour in enough champagne to cover, add one third of mushrooms to each pan. Simmer 10 to 12 minutes, adding champagne as needed, until breasts look done. Remove to Dutch oven with sauce and place in a 200 degree oven, just to keep warm. Add enough champagne to cover breasts to keep moist.

Donald McLaughlin

CHICKEN DIJON

4 chicken breast halves, skinned, boned
2 tablespoons olive oil
½ cup chicken broth
¼ cup dry white wine
2 cups fresh mushrooms, sliced

2 tablespoons parsley, chopped
2 tablespoons onion, minced
⅛ teaspoon pepper
2 tablespoons fresh parsley, chopped
1 tablespoon Dijon mustard

Flatten each piece of chicken between sheets of waxed paper, using mallet or rolling pin, to about ½-inch thickness. In a skillet, add chicken to hot oil over medium heat. Cook on each side until lightly browned. This will usually be enough cooking for the breasts. Remove from skillet and keep warm.

Combine chicken broth, wine, mushrooms, parsley, onion and pepper in the skillet. Cook over medium high heat 1 to 2 minutes until reduced to about half. Remove from heat, stir in parsley and mustard with wire whisk. Spoon sauce over chicken. Serve warm accompanied with rice. Serves 4.

Barbara Lake

CURRIED CHICKEN

½ cup margarine
½ cup onion, chopped
½ cup celery, chopped
½ cup bell pepper, chopped
1 medium apple, chopped
2 teaspoons curry powder

1 teaspoon powdered ginger
2 tablespoons flour
¼ cup water
4 cups chicken broth
4 cups chicken, cooked, diced
3 tablespoons grated coconut
Salt and pepper to taste

Melt margarine; sauté vegetables and apple until clear and tender. Combine curry powder, ginger, flour and water in a small bowl. Mix to a smooth paste. Stir into skillet mixture. Add chicken broth and bring to gentle boil. Reduce heat and add chicken and coconut. Heat thoroughly. Serve on hot, fluffy rice. Serve with peanuts, coconut, stuffed or chopped dates, chutney, etc.

Leila C. McLendon

HEAVENLY CHICKEN WITH DUMPLINGS

1 chicken, cut into serving pieces
2 cups water
1 teaspoon salt
¼ teaspoon pepper

1 onion, sliced
1 stalk celery, chopped
2 tablespoons parsley

Put all ingredients in large stew pot and cover. Cook until chicken is tender, about 45 minutes. Meanwhile mix dumplings.

Dumplings:
1½ cups flour
3 teaspoons baking powder
½ teaspoon salt

2 tablespoons shortening
⅔ cup milk

Sift together flour, baking powder and salt. Cut in shortening, add milk and mix quickly, just until mixture holds together. Drop by spoonfuls into chicken and broth. Cook until done, about 10 minutes. Serve hot.

Noreen Collins

PRESIDENT'S CHOICE CHICKEN PASTA FOR A POSSE

8 *to 10 chicken breasts, boneless,*
  skinless, sliced thin
2 *cups butter*
2 *packages herb and garlic pasta*
  sauce mix (dry packages)

2 *to 3 dozen mushrooms, sliced thin*
2 *red bell peppers, sliced thin*
1 *cup almonds, sliced*
1 *to 2 cups white wine*

Cook chicken with 1 cup butter and 1 package of sauce mix. Add mushrooms, peppers, almonds, the remaining cup of butter, sauce mix, and wine. Cook until peppers and mushrooms are tender. Toss with your favorite pasta.

Jack Gorman

CREAMED CHICKEN CASSEROLE

1 *8 ounce package stuffing mix*
3 *cups cooked chicken, cubed*
½ *cup margarine*
½ *cup flour*

Pepper
4 *cups water*
4 *chicken flavored bouillon cubes*
1½ *cups egg substitute or 6 eggs*

Sauce:
1 *can lite cream of mushroom soup*
¼ *cup skim milk*

1 *cup lite or non-fat sour cream*
¼ *cup chopped pimiento*

Prepare stuffing and put in a 13×9-inch pan. Put chicken on top. In a large saucepan, melt margarine. Blend in flour and seasonings. Gradually add 4 cups of bouillon and stir until thickened. Stir a little of the hot mixture into the eggs or egg substitute and then add it to the rest of the hot mixture. Pour the mixture over the chicken and stuffing. Bake 45 minutes at 325 degrees. Cut into squares to serve. Mix sauce ingredients, heat and stir. Serve over casserole squares. Serves 12 to 16.

Marie McNiel

CHICKEN SPECTACULAR

3 cups chicken, cooked, chopped
1 box original long grain white and
   wild rice, cooked according to
   package directions
1 can cream of celery soup, undiluted
1 4-ounce can or jar pimiento

1 medium to large onion, chopped
1 16-ounce can French-style green
   beans, drained
1 cup mayonnaise
1 8 ounce can sliced water chestnuts, drained
1 cup buttered breadcrumbs

Mix all ingredients except breadcrumbs. Spread evenly in buttered 9×13-inch baking dish. Top with buttered breadcrumbs. Bake at 350 degrees, 25 to 30 minutes. If cold from refrigerator, allow another 15 minutes. Serves 12 to 15.

Louise Hargrave

CHICKEN CASSEROLE

1 cup (or more) chicken breasts,
   cooked and cut up
1 medium onion, finely chopped
½ teaspoon salt
½ cup mayonnaise

1 cup celery, finely chopped
1 can cream of chicken soup
1 teaspoon lemon juice
1 cup cooked rice
½ cup almonds, toasted and chopped
   Buttered crumbs

Mix all ingredients. Cover with buttered crumbs. Bake at 375 degrees for 30 minutes. Serves 4.

Catherine Jones

CHICKEN STRATA

2 eggs, slightly beaten
1½ cups milk
12 to 14 slices day-old white bread
2 cups chicken, cooked and diced
½ cup onion, chopped
½ cup green pepper, chopped
½ cup celery, chopped
½ cup mayonnaise
¾ teaspoon salt (or less)
Dash of pepper
1 can mushroom soup
½ cup sharp cheese, shredded

Beat eggs and milk together. Cut bread into ½-inch cubes. Put one half of bread in bottom of 8×8×2-inch greased pan. Place chicken, vegetables, mayonnaise and seasoning over bread. Add second layer of bread. Pour egg mixture over all. Put in refrigerator overnight. Pour undiluted soup over top when you get ready to bake. Bake at 325 degrees for 45 minutes. Sprinkle cheese on top for last 15 minutes. The dish should puff. Cut in squares to serve. Serves 8.

Jeanne Jarrell

CHICKEN CASSEROLE

2 cans long asparagus
2 cups cooked chicken, sliced or cut up
1 can mushroom soup
1 can cream of chicken soup
1 teaspoon lemon juice
1 cup mayonnaise
¼ teaspoon curry powder
½ cup grated cheese
1 tablespoon margarine, melted
Bread crumbs

Put asparagus on bottom of dish. Place chicken over asparagus. Mix soups, mayonnaise, lemon juice and curry; pour over chicken. Sprinkle cheese over all. Mix bread crumbs and margarine and spread over top. Bake at 350 degrees for 25 to 30 minutes. Freezes well.

Jo Almgren

BAKED CHICKEN WITH MUSHROOMS

1 pound chicken breast pieces (or
   halves), boned and skinned
2½ tablespoons canola oil
 ½ cup Parmesan or Romano
   cheese, grated
 ½ pint sour cream (light)
1 can mushroom soup
   Buttered breadcrumbs (optional)

 ½ cup mushrooms, sliced
1 teaspoon white pepper, freshly ground
 ½ teaspoon garlic salt
1 teaspoon paprika
 ½ cup parsley flakes
   Paper towels
   Foil

Preheat oven to 350 degrees. Brown chicken pieces in oil on both sides in an oven proof frying pan. Turn off burner. Remove chicken pieces and pat dry with paper towels to remove excess oil. Also, wipe out frying pan to remove excess oil.

Return chicken pieces to baking dish. Spread mushroom soup, then sour cream over chicken. Sprinkle mushroom pieces and seasonings: white pepper, ¼ cup parsley flakes, garlic salt and paprika on top. Cover with foil. Bake 30 minutes in preheated 350 degree oven. Remove foil. Turn over chicken and spoon sour cream and soup mixture over top. Sprinkle cheese and another ¼ cup parsley flakes on top and a little more paprika for color. Optional: Sprinkle with buttered crumbs. Just before serving, run baking dish under the broiler 5 minutes or until lightly brown on top. Serves 4. Serve with rice and a green vegetable.

Cookbook Committee

CREAMY BAKED CHICKEN BREASTS

8 chicken breast halves
   skinned and boned
8 4-inch slices Swiss cheese
1 can cream of chicken soup,
   undiluted
¼ cup dry white wine

1 teaspoon Italian herb seasoning
1 teaspoon garlic powder
1 teaspoon poultry seasoning
1 teaspoon lemon pepper seasoning
1 cup herb-seasoned stuffing mix, crushed
¼ cup butter or margarine, melted

Arrange chicken in a lightly greased 13×9×2-inch baking dish. Top with cheese slices. Combine soup, wine and spices; stir well. Spoon evenly over chicken. Sprinkle with stuffing mix. Drizzle butter over crumbs. Bake at 350 degrees for 45 to 55 minutes. Serves 8.

Donald McLaughlin

CHICKEN WITH TOMATOES AND EGGPLANT

4 to 6 chicken breasts
Flour for dredging
Salt and pepper
¼ cup olive or vegetable oil
1 onion, chopped
3 large tomatoes, chopped

¼ cup white wine (optional)
¼ pound mushrooms, sliced
1 medium eggplant, chopped
4 slices mozzarella cheese
Large handful of fresh herbs
    (thyme, basil, oregano, rosemary)

Dredge chicken in flour, salt and pepper. Sauté chicken and onion to a medium brown. Transfer to an oven proof casserole, add tomatoes, wine, mushrooms, and eggplant. Spread fresh herbs over ingredients and bake 25 minutes at 350 degrees. Remove from oven. Discard the herbs, cover with mozzarella and return to oven for 5 minutes. Garnish with additional fresh herbs and serve immediately.

Rosa Schachle

ITALIAN CHICKEN

4 large chicken breasts, skinned
    boned, cut in half lengthwise
Salt, pepper, garlic powder to taste
2 eggs, beaten
½ cup seasoned Italian breadcrumbs
½ cup Parmesan cheese
4 tablespoons butter
4 tablespoons light olive oil

7 medium mushrooms, thickly sliced
1 green pepper, julienned lengthwise
½ red pepper, julienned lengthwise, optional
1 medium onion, sliced thin
2 15½-ounce bottles marinara sauce
8 slices mozzarella cheese
Italian seasoning

Season breasts with salt, pepper and garlic powder. Dip breast portions in beaten eggs, then roll in mixture of breadcrumbs and Parmesan. Put butter and the olive oil in a large skillet and fry the breasts until brown (not quite done). Remove to a 9×13-inch Pyrex baking dish, evenly spaced.

Warm the marinara sauce in the same (unwashed) skillet in which chicken was fried. Place a slice of mozzarella on each chicken breast. Scatter the onion, mushrooms and peppers on top. Then pour over the warmed marinara, and sprinkle Italian seasoning over all. Bake covered for 45 to 50 minutes at 325 degrees. Serve with ample "soppin' sauce." Can be made the day before and refrigerated or it can be frozen.

Gini and John Marston

BAKED CHICKEN LASAGNA

1 pound chicken breast, ground
2 tablespoons onion, finely chopped
1 clove garlic, chopped fine
2 teaspoons parsley, chopped fine
1 teaspoon dried oregano leaves

½ teaspoon dried basil leaves
¾ teaspoon salt
   Dash pepper
2 tablespoons Parmesan, grated
1 egg (or 2 whites, or egg substitute)

Combine all ingredients in a medium bowl. Shape mixture into approximately 30 balls. Spray pan with vegetable oil spray and lightly brown chicken balls. Remove and set aside.

Add to pan:

¼ cup onion, finely chopped
1 clove garlic, finely chopped

2 teaspoons parsley, finely chopped
1 teaspoon dried basil leaves

Sauté until tender, about 5 minutes. (Add a few drops of water if needed to prevent sticking.)

Add:

1 can (1 pound 12 ounces) whole
   tomatoes, undrained, cut up
2 cans (6 ounces) tomato paste
2 teaspoons dried oregano leaves
1 teaspoon dried basil leaves

2 teaspoons salt (can be omitted)
1 teaspoon garlic powder
¼ teaspoon pepper
⅛ teaspoon cayenne

Stir and add chicken to mixture along with ½ cup water. Bring to boil. Reduce heat and simmer uncovered 1½ hours, stirring occasionally. Preheat oven to 350 degrees. Spray 13×9×2-inch baking pan with vegetable oil spray (can be divided into smaller pans).

½ pound lasagna noodles
8 to 12 ounces low fat/skim mozzarella

16 ounces low fat/skim ricotta
1 cup Parmesan, freshly grated

Cook noodles as label directs. In prepared baking dish layer half the ingredients in order: noodles, mozzarella, ricotta, tomato sauce/chicken, Parmesan. Repeat layers. Bake 30 to 35 minutes or until cheese is melted and lasagna is heated through.

Note: This is a low fat adaptation of a high fat beef lasagna recipe. Use fresh tomatoes if available, and fresh parsley. Chicken can be frozen and used for spaghetti sauce or other pasta combinations.

DyAnna Giltner

POLYNESIAN CHICKEN

2 broiler fryers, or 4 to 6 chicken
   breasts, split
1 teaspoon salt
¼ teaspoon pepper
¼ cup butter, melted
1 8-ounce bottle sweet/sour sauce

1 pound can peach slices, drained
1½ cups dark sweet cherries, drained
   (1 large can)
1 medium onion, sliced
½ cup chili sauce

Place chicken in pan. Salt and pepper. Drizzle with melted butter and broil until brown. Combine other ingredients and pour over chicken. Bake for 1 hour at 325 degrees. Makes 6 to 8 servings.

Ebby Halliday

SPANISH CHICKEN AND RICE

3 tablespoons olive oil
1 fryer or cut up chicken parts
1 to 3 cloves garlic, depending upon taste
1 medium onion, chopped

1 green pepper, chopped
1 package of yellow rice
8 to 10 pimiento-stuffed olives, sliced
1 14- to 16-ounce can crushed tomatoes,
   drained, reserving juice

In large skillet, add olive oil and sauté chicken parts on medium heat for 8 to 10 minutes. Add green pepper and onion during last few minutes, stirring often. Press garlic cloves onto mixture. Measure juice from the tomatoes and add the crushed tomatoes, and enough water to cook rice (usually 2½ cups; check package). Add rice and green olives. Cover and cook on low heat for 20 to 25 minutes. Serves 4.

Wendy Seldon

CHICKEN OLÉ

2 plump fryers
  Water to cover
1 tablespoon salt
1 teaspoon celery salt
¼ cup butter
4 to 5 green onions with tops, chopped
1 medium onion, chopped
2 cans cream of chicken soup
1 15½-ounce can tomatoes with
  green chilies and liquid, chopped

1 cup broth (from stewed chicken)
2 teaspoons instant chicken boullion
2 teaspoons chili powder
1 tablespoon cumin
1 tablespoon garlic, minced
  Salt and Accent to taste
12 tortillas, diced
1 cup sour cream
  Sharp cheddar cheese, grated

Stew fryers in water with salt and celery salt. Debone and cut into bite-sized pieces. In a large pan, melt butter and sauté onion and green onions. Add soup, tomatoes, broth, boullion, spices and seasonings, and tortillas. Simmer until tortillas absorb some of the liquid. Add chicken pieces and sour cream. Pour into 13½× 8¾×1¾-inch Pyrex dish. Top with cheddar cheese. Bake at 350 degrees until bubbly (20 to 30 minutes). Serves 8 to 10.

Martha Baker

GREEN CHICKEN ENCHILADAS

4 cups cooked chicken, cut in
  1-inch pieces
8 ounces cream cheese, softened
1 small onion, finely chopped
  Salt and pepper
  Fresh cilantro, chopped

1 pound tomatoes
1 4-ounce can mild green salsa
1 cup whipping cream
15 to 18 corn tortillas
2 tablespoons oil
8 ounces Monterey Jack cheese, grated

Preheat oven to 350 degrees. In a large bowl, mix chicken, cream cheese, onion and cilantro. Season to taste with salt and pepper and set aside. In a large saucepan, cook tomatoes in water over low heat until tender, about 10 minutes. Cool, drain, then liquefy in blender for about one minute. Transfer to medium bowl. Add salsa and cream. Whisk until well blended. Set aside. In a medium skillet, soften tortillas in hot oil. Drain well. Place one tablespoon tomato sauce on a tortilla with 1 tablespoon chicken mixture. Roll and place in a 9×13-inch baking dish, seam side down. Repeat with remaining tortillas. Pour remaining sauce over enchiladas and top with grated cheese. Bake for 20 minutes, or until hot. Serves 6 to 8.

Helen Tieber

CHICKEN ENCHILADAS

2 large chicken breasts	1 teaspoon ground cumin
1 cup chopped onion	½ teaspoon salt
1 clove garlic, minced	½ teaspoon dried oregano, crushed
2 tablespoons butter	½ teaspoon dried basil, crushed
1 16-ounce can tomatoes, cut up	12 frozen flour tortillas, thawed
1 8-ounce can tomato sauce	2½ cups (10 ounces) Monterey Jack cheese
¼ cup chopped green chilies	¾ cup sour cream
1 teaspoon sugar	

Bake chicken in 350 degree oven for one hour. Carefully remove skin and bones. Sprinkle chicken with a little salt. Cut into 12 strips. Set aside. In saucepan, cook onion and garlic in butter or margarine until tender. Add tomatoes, tomato sauce, chilies, sugar, cumin, salt, oregano and basil. Bring to boiling, reduce heat and simmer, covered, for 20 minutes. Remove from heat. Dip each tortilla in tomato mixture to soften. Place one piece of chicken and about 2 tablespoons shredded cheese on each tortilla; roll up, and place, seam side down, in a 13½×8¾×1¾-inch baking dish. Blend sour cream into remaining sauce mixture; pour over tortillas. Sprinkle with remaining cheese. Cover and bake in 350 degree oven for about 40 minutes, or until heated through. Makes 6 servings.

Mary Alice Shepherd

GREEN CHILI ENCHILADAS

1 can cream of chicken soup	½ pound cheddar cheese, grated
1 soup can of milk	1 dozen corn tortillas
¼ cup (or more) onion, chopped	4 to 5 cooked chicken breasts,
1 4-ounce can green chilies, chopped	diced or chopped
(less if mild flavor preferred)	

Mix soup, milk, onion and chilies to make sauce. Dip tortillas, one at a time into sauce and cover bottom of 9×9-inch baking dish. Cover with a layer of chicken. Spread sauce over chicken and sprinkle cheese over sauce. Continue layers until tortillas are gone. Pour remaining sauce over dish and sprinkle generously with cheese. Bake at 350 degrees until hot and cheese melts (about 30 minutes).

Mary Ann Gardenhire

CHICKEN LIVERS PAPRIKASH

1 pound chicken livers
3 tablespoons margarine
1 medium onion, diced
½ teaspoon salt
½ teaspoon black pepper
1 tablespoon sweet paprika

1 cup water
1 clove garlic, sliced in half
½ teaspoon thyme
1 tablespoon flour
¼ cup sour cream

Clean liver, removing all fat and connective tissue. Heat margarine in 10-inch skillet and sauté onion until soft and bright yellow, not brown. Add livers and brown on all sides. Sprinkle with salt, pepper and paprika and sauté for a minute or two or until paprika loses raw smell. Add 1 cup water or just enough to half cover livers. Add garlic and thyme and simmer, covered, 15 to 20 minutes or until livers are done. Blend flour into sour cream. Stir into skillet and simmer 3 or 4 minutes. Adjust seasoning to taste and serve. Serves 4.

Adell Campbell

BAKED CORNISH HEN

8 Cornish hens
Salt and pepper
8 whole onions

¾ cup butter or margarine
¼ cup kitchen bouquet
1 8-ounce jar orange marmalade

Clean and dry hens. Season inside and out with salt and pepper. Refrigerate overnight. When ready to bake, insert a whole onion in cavity of each hen and place in open roasting pan, leaving space between them.

In small saucepan put butter, kitchen bouquet, and orange marmalade. Heat together until butter has melted and mixture is blended. Spoon over the hens and bake at 350 degrees until hens are tender, about 1½ hours, basting often. If sauce cooks down before hens are done, add a little hot water to the pan to assure having some of the sauce left to accompany the hens. If hens appear to be getting dry during the baking, place a piece of foil loosely over the pan to retard the browning.

Note: For entertaining, onions should be removed from hens before serving, but for family enjoyment, leave them there.

Chloye Whitson

HERB~BUTTER~BASTED TURKEY BREAST

½ cup butter or margarine, melted	½ teaspoon salt
¼ cup lemon juice	½ teaspoon thyme
2 tablespoons soy sauce	½ teaspoon celery salt
1 teaspoon dried sage, crushed	¼ teaspoon pepper
1 teaspoon dried whole marjoram	1 turkey breast, 5 to 7 pounds

Combine first 9 ingredients in a saucepan; bring to boil. Remove from heat. Place turkey breast in an oiled 13×9×2-inch pan; baste with butter mixture. Cover with foil. Insert meat thermometer into thickest portion of breast. Bake at 325 degrees for 3 hours or until thermometer reaches 190 degrees. Baste often. Cool slightly before slicing. Serves 10 to 12.

Cook instant rice in the broth from the turkey breast. The two are great served together.

Glenna Clayton

TURKEY FLORENTINE

8 ounces egg noodles	2 cans cream of mushroom soup
8 slices bacon, cooked crisp and crumbled	2 eggs, beaten
	1 cup sour cream
1 cup chopped onion	1½ teaspoons salt
1 10-ounce package frozen chopped, spinach, cooked and drained	4 cups cooked turkey, cubed
	1 cup bread crumbs
½ cup celery, thinly sliced, sauteed	3 tablespoons butter, melted
¼ cup pimiento, chopped	Slivered almonds

Cook noodles. Sauté onions. Combine noodles, onions and bacon pieces, spinach, celery and pimiento. Combine soup, eggs, sour cream and salt. Stir half of soup mixture into noodle mixture. Pour into 13×9×2-inch dish. Arrange turkey on top, and pour remaining soup mixture over turkey. Top with crumbs and melted butter. Sprinkle with slivered almonds. Bake at 350 degrees for 35 to 40 minutes.

Dorothy Lovett

WHITE ROCK DUCK

2 4- or 5-pound ducks
Garlic salt
Onion salt
1/4 cup butter or margarine
1 medium onion, chopped
1 cup red plum preserves
2 cups Dr. Pepper

2 tablespoons lemon juice
1/3 cup chili sauce
1/4 cup soy sauce
2 teaspoons prepared mustard
3 drops Tabasco sauce
4 thin-skinned oranges, halved

Have ducks cut in quarters. Sprinkle with garlic salt and onion salt. Place skin-side up in large shallow baking or broiler pan. Roast at 325 degrees for 1 1/2 hours. Meanwhile, melt butter in saucepan. Add onion and cook until tender. Add remaining ingredients, except oranges. Simmer for 15 minutes.

Pour off fat of roasted ducks and arrange orange halves in the pan with ducks. Pour about half of the plum sauce over both oranges and ducks. Roast for 45 minutes more or until tender, basting with extra sauce every 10 to 15 minutes. Arrange on platter. Serve with rice (wild, brown or white) and extra sauce. Makes 8 servings.

Note: This sauce is also delicious with roast pork or fryer halves. For pork, proceed as directed, but increase roasting time as necessary. For chicken, roast for 45 minutes. Then proceed as directed, except there will be no fat to pour off.

Barbara L. Adamson

CAJUN CRAWFISH AND ANGEL HAIR

1 pound crawfish tails	4 tablespoons butter
1 bunch green onions	½ pound angel hair or vermicelli
½ teaspoon Zatarin seafood seasoning	½ cup half-and-half cream
½ teaspoon garlic	

Sauté first 4 ingredients in butter until green onions and crawfish are done. Just before serving, add cream; let simmer. Serve over angel hair.

Helen Wood

OYSTER PUDDING

6 slices white bread	2 8-ounce cans oysters, drained reserving liquid
Butter or margarine, softened	Milk, enough to make 2½ cups
8 slices sharp Old English cheese	measured with oyster liquid
2 eggs, beaten	
1 teaspoon salt	¼ teaspoon pepper

Spread one side of bread slices with butter. Cut into cubes. Place half the cubes in bottom of 11¾×7½×1¾-inch baking dish. Top with cheese slices. Arrange oysters over cheese slices. Top with remaining bread cubes. Blend oyster-milk mixture with eggs, salt and pepper. Pour over ingredients in baking dish. Bake at 325 degrees until knife inserted just off center comes out clean, about 1 to 1¼ hours. Serves 4 to 6.

Donald McLaughlin

DEVILED-CRAB CASSEROLE

1 pound crab meat, preferably lump, picked over to remove shell	1 egg
	1 cup mayonnaise
1 cup saltine crackers, crushed	2 tablespoons prepared mustard
1 large stalk celery, finely diced	1 tablespoon Worcestershire sauce
1 egg, hard-boiled and finely diced	Lemon wedges for garnish

Preheat oven to 375 degrees. Mix all ingredients together, making sure the saltines are blended in well. If the mixture is still dry, add a little more mayonnaise. Pack into a decorative baking dish. Bake for 30 to 35 minutes, until top is golden brown. Serve with lemon wedges on the side. Serves 4 to 6.

Peggy Dawson

CRABMEAT CASSEROLE

1 14-ounce can artichoke hearts	½ teaspoon salt
1 pound crabmeat	1 teaspoon Worcestershire sauce
½ pound fresh mushrooms,	¼ cup medium-dry sherry
sliced and sauteed	Paprika, to taste
4 tablespoons butter	Ground red pepper, to taste
2½ tablespoons flour	Black pepper, to taste
1 cup heavy cream	¼ cup Parmesan cheese, grated

Drain and quarter artichokes and place in bottom of baking dish; sprinkle with the crabmeat and top with sauteed mushrooms. Melt butter in a saucepan; stir in flour to make a smooth paste. Cook until bubbly; stir in cream and remaining ingredients except cheese. Cook until thickened; adjust seasoning. Pour sauce over artichoke-crab layers; sprinkle cheese on top. Bake 20 minutes at 375 degrees. Serves 8.

Jarrel and Tonya Calhoun

MADALYNNE'S HOT CRAB SOUFFLÉ

20 slices bread, crusts removed	2½ cups milk
2 cups crabmeat	1 10½-ounce can mushroom soup
1 onion, chopped	1 teaspoon dry mustard
1 green pepper, chopped	Dash garlic and onion salt
1 cup celery, chopped	1½ cups grated cheddar cheese
½ cup mayonnaise	Paprika
4 eggs	

Dice 10 slices bread into a 3-quart Pyrex dish that has been sprayed with oil. Mix mayonnaise, onion, pepper, celery and crab. Spread mixture evenly over the bread. Place the remaining slices of bread evenly over the crab mixture. Mix eggs and milk with dashes of the salts and dry mustard. Pour over the bread. Cover and refrigerate overnight. Bake at 350 degrees for 15 minutes. Take from oven and pour the soup over. Top with cheese and paprika. Bake 1 hour at 325 degrees. Serves 8. This is a great make ahead dish for brunch.

Madalynne Callahan

RICH CRAB CAKES

1 pound blue crab
1 tablespoon flour
1 egg
¼ cup whipping cream

Salt
Black pepper
Cayenne to taste
4 tablespoons butter

Dredge flour over crab and stir gently to coat. Beat egg, cream and seasonings together, pour over crab and mix gently. Melt butter in thick skillet, then drop large spoonfuls of crab in hot butter and brown. Makes 8 cakes.

Landon Scarlett

CRAB AVOCADO CAKES

1 pound blue crabmeat, flaked
1 avocado, peeled and chopped
¼ cup onions finely chopped
1 egg, beaten
2 tablespoons margarine

2 tablespoons fresh lemon juice
1 tablespoon spicy mustard
½ teaspoon dried dill weed
¼ cup olive oil
¾ cup dry bread crumbs

Place crabmeat in a large mixing bowl. Remove any remaining shell and cartilage. Add remaining ingredients except bread crumbs and stir until blended. Add ¼ cup bread crumbs, reserving remaining ½ cup. Form the crab mixture into 6 cakes. Place remaining bread crumbs into flat pan. Dredge crab cakes in crumbs. Heat half the oil and cook 3 crab cakes until golden brown, turning once. Drain and keep warm. Cook remaining crab cakes in oil and serve with avocado slices and lemon wedges, if desired. Serves 3.

Pat Holder

CREVETTES "MARGARITA"

(Shrimp with Tequila)

¾ pound (about 20) raw shrimp
¼ cup lime juice
   Salt and freshly ground pepper
1 small ripe, unblemished avocado
2 tablespoons butter

1 tablespoon shallots, finely chopped
¼ cup tequila
¾ cup whipping cream
1 tablespoon cilantro, finely chopped, optional

Shell and devein shrimp and "butterfly" them; that is, split them partly down the back and flatten lightly. Place shrimp in a bowl and add the lime juice, salt and pepper. Let stand briefly until ready to cook. Peel avocado and cut into ½-inch slices.

Heat the butter in a skillet and when it is quite hot, but not smoking, add the shrimp, stirring rapidly and cook about 2 minutes. Sprinkle with the shallots and cook stirring about 10 seconds. Add the tequila and cream and cook over high heat about 1 minute. Add salt and pepper to taste. Add the avocado and cook just until the slices are piping hot, no longer. Using a slotted spoon, transfer the shrimp and avocado pieces to hot serving dishes. Bring the sauce to a full rolling boil for about 30 seconds and add the chopped cilantro. Spoon the sauce over the shrimp and avocado and serve with rice.

Billye Garonzik

PICKLED SHRIMP

2 pounds raw shrimp, peeled and
   deveined (41 to 50 count)
2 medium white or purple onions,
   sliced into rings
1 cup vegetable oil

1½ cups white vinegar
½ cup sugar
1½ teaspoons salt
1½ teaspoons celery seed
4 tablespoons capers with juice

Place shrimp in boiling salted water, reduce heat and simmer for 3 to 5 minutes. Shrimp are done when they are pink and tender. Drain and rinse with cold water, then chill. Make alternate layers of shrimp and onion rings in a sealable container. Mix remaining ingredients and pour over shrimp and onions. Seal and place in refrigerator for 6 hours or more, shaking or inverting occasionally. Drain and serve. Makes 6 servings.

Carole Cohen

BARBECUED SHRIMP

1½ pounds fresh shrimp in shells,
   headless (large size is best)
8 tablespoons unsalted butter
2 teaspoons garlic, minced
1 teaspoon Worcestershire sauce
½ cup chicken stock (granules
   may be used)
¼ cup beer at room temperature

Seasonings:
1 teaspoon cayenne pepper
1 teaspoon black pepper
½ teaspoon salt
½ teaspoon crushed red pepper
½ teaspoon dried thyme
½ teaspoon dried rosemary leaves, crushed
⅛ teaspoon dried oregano leaves

Combine seasonings in small bowl. Combine butter, garlic, Worcestershire and seasonings in a large heavy skillet over high heat. When butter is melted, add the shrimp. Cook for 2 minutes, shaking the pan in a back-and-forth motion; do not stir. Add stock and turn shrimp; cook and shake for 2 minutes. Add the beer and cook and shake for 1 minute longer. Remove from heat. Serve immediately. To serve, put on plate with a rice mound in center, with shrimp arranged around and plenty of sauce. Serve with plenty of napkins, French bread, and finger bowls. Make rice mound with custard dish. Fill with packed rice and invert on plate. Serves 4.

Barbara Lake

SHRIMP CREOLE

1 bunch celery, chopped
1 green pepper, chopped
2 onions, chopped
1 clove garlic, minced
7 tablespoons shortening

1 16-ounce can tomatoes
1 tablespoon Worcestershire sauce
1 tablespoon Tabasco sauce
2 pounds cooked, deveined shrimp
1 8-ounce can tomato sauce

Cook celery, pepper, onion and garlic in shortening until tender. Add all ingredients except shrimp, and simmer for 45 minutes. Add shrimp and simmer for an additional 15 mintues. Serve over rice.

Barbara Bigham

SHRIMP AND MUSHROOMS ELEGANTE

3 tablespoons butter or margarine
2 7-ounce packages frozen shelled
  shrimp, partially thawed
½ pound fresh mushrooms, sliced
¼ cup butter or margarine
¼ cup all-purpose flour

¼ teaspoon dry mustard
  Dash cayenne
2 cups light cream
3 tablespoons cooking sherry
¼ cup shredded Parmesan cheese
  Parsley rice, cooked

Melt 3 tablespoons butter in skillet. Add shrimp and mushrooms. Cook over medium heat, stirring frequently, about 5 minutes, or until mushrooms are tender and shrimp turn pink and are done. Remove from skillet and set aside. Add ¼ cup butter to skillet. When melted, blend in flour and seasonings. Stir in cream all at once. Cook, stirring constantly until mixture thickens and boils. Add shrimp and mushrooms to sauce. Reserve a few shrimp for garnish. Heat through, 2 or 3 minutes. Stir in cooking sherry and Parmesan cheese. Salt to taste. Keep warm in chafing dish over hot water. Trim with bouquet of parsley or watercress and reserved shrimp. Serve over hot fluffy parsley rice. Pass extra Parmesan cheese. Makes 6 servings.

Noreen Collins

SHRIMP VICTORIA

1 pound raw shrimp
2 tablespoons shallots, minced
¼ (or more) cup butter or margarine
½ pound mushrooms, sliced
1 tablespoon all-purpose flour

½ teaspoon salt
¼ teaspoon pepper (freshly ground)
3 tablespoons sherry
1½ cups sour cream

Shell and clean shrimp. Sauté shrimp and minced shallots in butter until shrimp are pink. Add mushrooms and cook 5 minutes, adding another tablespoon butter if needed. Sprinkle with flour, salt, pepper. Add sherry and sour cream. Cook gently until hot. Serve with wild rice or on toast. Serves 6.

Pauline Steele

WILD RICE, SHRIMP AND ARTICHOKE SKILLET

1¾ cups water
1 6¼-ounce package fast-cooking
    long grain and wild rice
½ teaspoon black/ red pepper blend
1 pound medium shrimp, cleaned,
    deveined, tails removed

1 14-ounce can artichoke hearts,
    drained and cut into bite size pieces
2 to 4 teaspoons chopped cilantro
    (or parsley)
    Lime or lemon wedges

Combine water, rice, rice seasoning packet, and black/red pepper in pan. Bring to vigorous boil. Stir in shrimp. Cover tightly and simmer until all water is absorbed, about 5 minutes. Stir in artichokes; heat through. Cover; remove from heat. Let stand 5 minutes or until liquid is absorbed. Sprinkle with cilantro and serve with lime. Makes 4 to 6 servings.

Tonya W. Calhoun

RIGATONI WITH SHRIMP, FETA AND TOMATO SAUCE

½ cup onion, finely chopped
1 garlic clove, minced
3 tablespoons olive oil
½ cup dry white wine
3 14- to 16-ounce cans plum
    tomatoes, with juice
2 tablespoons fresh parsley leaves,
    finely chopped

½ teaspooon dried basil, crumbled
½ teaspoon dried oregano, crumbled
¾ teaspoon salt
    Dried red pepper flakes, to taste
1¼ pounds medium shrimp, shelled,
    deveined, and rinsed
1 pound rigatoni or other tubular pasta
8 ounces feta cheese, crumbled

In a large kettle, heat oil over moderate heat. Sauté the onion and garlic, stirring occasionally until softened. Add the wine. Boil the mixture for 1 minute. Stir in the tomatoes and juice, 1 tablespoon parsley, the basil, oregano, salt, and red pepper flakes. Boil the mixture, stirring occasionally for 5 minutes or until it is thickened. Add the shrimp and cook over moderate heat, stirring, for 4 to 5 minutes, or until the shrimp are just firm.

In a large kettle of boiling water, cook the rigatoni until just al dente. Drain well; stir it into the shrimp mixture. Stir in 6 ounces of feta cheese and salt and pepper to taste. Transfer mixture to a lightly oiled, 4 quart, shallow glass baking dish. Sprinkle the top with the remaining parsley and remaining feta. Bake uncovered at 450 degrees for 20 minutes or until bubbling, and the top is crusty.

Toby Rives

CRAB AND SHRIMP CASSEROLE

1 can crabmeat, drained	1 can shrimp, drained
1 can water chestnuts, drained, sliced thin	1 4-ounce can mushrooms, drained
1 medium onion, chopped	1 medium green pepper, chopped
1 cup celery, chopped	2 boiled eggs, chopped
1/2 cup almonds, slivered	2 cups mayonnaise
	Buttered breadcrumbs

Combine all ingredients, place in buttered casserole. Top with buttered breadcrumbs. Bake at 350 degrees 40 to 50 minutes. Serves 6 to 8 for dinner or 8 to 10 for lunch.

Ruth Pruitt

SEAFOOD CASSEROLE

1 pound medium shrimp, unpeeled	1 cup half-and-half
1 cup dry white wine	1/2 cup Swiss cheese, shredded
1 tablespoon butter or margarine	2 teaspoons lemon juice
1 tablespoon fresh parsley, chopped	1/8 teaspoon pepper
1 teaspoon salt	1/2 pound crab-flavored seafood product
1 medium onion, thinly sliced or coarsely chopped	1 4-ounce can sliced mushrooms, drained
1 pound fresh bay scallops	1 cup soft breadcrumbs
3 tablespoons butter or margarine	1/4 cup Parmesan cheese
3 tablespoons all-purpose flour	Paprika

Peel and devein shrimp: set aside. Combine wine, butter, parsley, salt and onion in a Dutch oven; bring to a boil. Add shrimp and scallops and cook 3 to 5 minutes, drain, reserving 2/3 cup liquid. Put 3 tablespoons butter in Dutch oven over low heat. Add flour, stirring until smooth. Cook 1 minute, stirring constantly. Gradually add half-and-half; cook over medium heat, stirring constantly until mixture is thickened and bubbly. Stir in Swiss cheese. Gradually stir in reserved liquid, lemon juice and pepper; add shrimp mixture, crab-flavored seafood and mushrooms. Spoon into a lightly greased 11×7×1 1/2-inch baking dish. Cover and refrigerate up to 8 hours (do not use Pyrex). Remove baking dish from refrigerator, and let stand for 10 or 15 minutes. Cover and bake at 350 degrees for 40 minutes. Combine breadcrumbs and Parmesan cheese, and sprinkle over casserole. Bake an additional 5 minutes. Sprinkle with paprika. Let stand 10 minutes before serving. Garnish with 3 peeled cooked shrimp and fresh parsley sprigs, if desired. Serves 8.

Faye Gould

SEAFOOD CASSEROLE

½ cup raw shrimp, chopped
½ cup raw lobster meat, chopped
½ cup raw snapper, chopped
½ cup raw oysters, chopped
½ cup fresh mushrooms, chopped
¼ cup onion, chopped
1 cup flour
6 medium potatoes, cooked and mashed

½ teaspoon red pepper sauce
Salt to taste
1 cup sherry
½ cup butter or margarine
1 quart milk
¼ cup grated Parmesan cheese
1 egg, beaten

Place shrimp, lobster, snapper, oysters, mushrooms, onions, salt, pepper sauce and sherry in a deep kettle. Bring to a boil. Cook for 10 minutes. Remove ingredients from stock; keep hot. Melt butter in saucepan, blend in flour. Add milk gradually. Cook over low heat until sauce thickens, stirring constantly. Add fish mixture and 2 tablespoons cheese to white sauce. Turn mixture into 6 individual casseroles. Add egg to potatoes; blend. Force potatoes through pastry tube around each casserole. Sprinkle each with 1 tablespoon cheese. Place casseroles on baking sheet. Place under broiler until lightly browned. Serves 6.

Dedicated to Charles P. Bowman

SEAFOOD STEW

2 tablespoons olive oil
1 onion, thinly sliced
2 cloves garlic, minced
1 28-ounce can tomatoes, drained and chopped
1 cup clam juice
½ cup dry white wine

12 ounces firm white fish, cut into 1-inch pieces
12 mussels, scrubbed
12 large shrimp, peeled and deveined
12 littleneck clams, scrubbed
¼ cup fresh parsley, chopped

In a large heavy saucepan, heat oil over medium heat. Add onion and garlic and cook until wilted, about 10 minutes. Add chopped tomatoes and cook 5 minutes. Add white wine and clam juice and cook 5 minutes more. Add fish and shellfish to simmering broth. Simmer covered 3 to 5 minutes until clams and mussels open, fish turns opaque and shrimp turn pink. Sprinkle with parsley. Makes 4 servings.

Herdercine Nash

SOUTHERN BAKED CATFISH

⅓ cup stoneground yellow cornmeal
¼ teaspoon freshly ground black pepper
2 tablespoons evaporated skim milk

2 tablespoons Dijon mustard
4 5- to 6-ounce catfish fillets
2 teaspoons olive oil

Heat oven to 425 degrees. Coat a nonstick baking sheet with oil. Mix cornmeal and pepper in a shallow pan. Mix milk and mustard in a shallow bowl. Dip catfish in milk mixture then cornmeal, and bake 10 minutes turning once or until fish flakes easily. Place under broiler 1 to 2 minutes to brown. Serve with cocktail sauce. Serves 4. This is a good low-fat substitute for fried catfish.

Shirley Moseley

OVEN CATFISH PARMESAN McLAUGHLIN

⅔ cup grated Parmesan cheese
¼ cup all-purpose flour
½ teaspoon salt
¼ teaspoon pepper
1 teaspoon paprika

1 egg, beaten
¼ cup milk
6 small catfish fillets (about 2 pounds)
¼ cup butter or margarine, melted
⅓ cup pecans, chopped

Combine cheese, flour, salt, pepper and paprika; stir well. Combine egg and milk; stir well. Dip fillets in egg mixture, dredge in flour mixture. Arrange fillets in a lightly greased 13×9×2-inch baking dish; drizzle with butter. Sprinkle pecans evenly over tops of fillets; bake at 350 degrees for 35 to 40 minutes or until fish flakes easily when tested with a fork. Makes 4 to 6 servings.

Donald McLaughlin

FRIED SNAPPER

¼ cup evaporated skim milk
3 cloves garlic, mashed
1 teaspoon oregano
1 teaspoon lemon juice

2 4- to 5-ounce snapper fillets
¼ cup whole-wheat breadcrumbs
1½ tablespoons grated Parmesan cheese

Combine milk, garlic, oregano, and lemon juice and marinate fish in mixture 10 to 20 minutes per side. Combine crumbs and cheese and press fish fillets in mixture until well coated on each side. Place fish in non-stick baking dish and pour remaining milk mixture over top. Bake at 450 degrees 12 to 15 minutes or until fish flakes easily. Serves 2.

Shirley Moseley

RED SNAPPER FLORIDIAN

2 pounds red snapper fillets,
    fresh or frozen, thawed
3 tablespoons oil or melted fat
2 tablespoons orange juice

2 tablespoons grated orange peel
1 teaspoon salt
Dash nutmeg
Dash pepper

Cut snapper fillets into serving pieces. Place, skin side down, in single layer in greased 12×8×2-inch baking dish. Combine remaining ingredients and pour over fish. Bake in 350 degree oven 25 to 30 minutes or until fish flakes easily when tested with a fork. Makes 6 servings.

Doris Westermeier

SALMON PATTIES

1 16-ounce can pink salmon, drained
1 small onion, chopped
2 tablespoons oatmeal
1 egg
¼ teaspoon salt

½ teaspoon garlic powder
¼ teaspoon thyme
1 tablespoon prepared mustard
⅓ to ½ cup flour
Peanut oil

Remove bones and skin from salmon, separate and crumble fine. Add all other ingredients, except flour and oil. Mix well. Spoon out into flour; roll and slightly pat into patties. Place in large skillet with hot oil (about ¼-inch deep). Fry to golden brown.

M. Oleta Walls

EGGS FROMAGE

6 eggs, well beaten
8 teaspoons cream
1 3-ounce can deviled ham

½ cup grated American cheese
Salt and pepper to taste

Add cream, ham, cheese and seasonings to eggs. Mix well. Cook over boiling water, while stirring, until soft scrambled. Serve on thin triangles of buttered toast.

Cecilia DeGolyer McGhee

OEUFS AU VIN

1 tablespoon butter or margarine
4 eggs
⅛ teaspoon pepper

1 cup dry white wine
½ teaspoon salt
1 tablespoon Parmesan cheese, grated

Melt butter in skillet. Add wine and heat until barely bubbling. One by one, break eggs into saucer and slide into hot wine. Sprinkle with salt, pepper, cheese. Cook 3 to 5 minutes, until eggs are done as desired. Drain eggs, serve on hot buttered toast or rice. Serves 4.

Adell Campbell

BAKED EGGS

Eggs
Celery, green onion, squash,
Mushrooms (or other
    vegetables of your choice)

Olive oil
Cheese

Pour 1 teaspoon olive oil in ovenproof dish. Add chopped vegetables. Crack 1 or 2 eggs on top of vegetables. Grate cheddar or parmesan cheese on top of eggs. Bake at 450 degrees until done. Check often so you don't overbake.

Julie Hogg

OVERNIGHT BRUNCH CASSEROLE

2 to 3 English muffins, crumbled
1 pound bulk sausage, browned
    and drained
2 cups cheddar cheese, shredded
1 4-ounce can green chilies
6 eggs, beaten

1½ cups milk
½ teaspoon dry mustard
    Salt and pepper to taste
    Corn flakes, rice chex, or any
    Unsweetened cereal, crumbled
¼ cup margarine, melted

Spread crumbled English muffins in 9×13-inch baking pan. Top with sausage, one half the cheese, chilies, and the remainder of the cheese. Mix eggs, milk and seasonings together and pour over sausage-cheese mixture. Combine cereal and melted margarine and spread on top. Cover and refrigerate overnight. Bake at 350 degrees for 50 minutes.

Sue Smith

GREEN CHILI QUICHE

1 9-inch pie shell, unbaked
3 eggs
1 4-ounce can chopped green
    chilies, drained
½ cup Swiss cheese, grated

½ cup sharp cheddar cheese, grated
1½ cups milk
½ teaspoon salt
    Several grinds pepper
3 drops Tabasco sauce

Cook shell 8 to 10 minutes at 400 degrees. You may fill shell with dried beans to prevent puffing. Remove beans and lower oven temperature to 375 degrees. Beat eggs until foamy and add remaining ingredients. Place in shell and bake 30 minutes. Serves 9.

Pat Norvell

BLUE CHEESE QUICHE

1 8-inch pie shell, unbaked
3 ounces blue cheese, grated
2 3-ounce packages cream cheese

3 tablespoons milk
1 tablespoon chives, finely chopped
2 eggs

Bake pastry shell at 450 degrees 8 to 10 minutes until it begins to brown. Cool. Reduce heat to 325 degrees. Add milk and chives to cheeses which should be at room temperature. Beat until light and fluffy. Add eggs one at a time, beating well after each. Pour into pastry shell. Bake 30 minutes. Cool 15 minutes before serving. Can be frozen. Thaw uncovered at room temperature.

Ruth Branham

BAKED FRENCH TOAST

1 loaf French or Italian bread
6 eggs
½ cup milk or cream

1 teaspoon vanilla
1 teaspoon cinnamon
1 teaspoon nutmeg

Heat oven to 350 degrees. Cut bread into 1 to 2 inch slices. Whip eggs, add milk, vanilla, cinnamon, and nutmeg. Let bread soak in egg mixture for 10 to 15 minutes. Spray pie plate with vegetable oil spray and place bread on plate. Bake for about 25 minutes. Serve with butter, powdered sugar or syrup.

Julie Hogg

My Favorite Entrées

VEGETABLES

—◾—

GARDEN GOURMET
COOKBOOK

GREEN BEAN WRAP-UPS

2 16-ounce cans Blue Lake whole
   green beans
1 package bacon slices, cut in half

½ cup margarine or butter
⅓ cup brown sugar
1 teaspoon garlic salt

Bundle together 15 green beans. Wrap with bacon (like a tie). Place in a greased casserole. Melt sugar and garlic salt in margarine or butter. Pour over green beans. Bake at 350 degrees uncovered for 30 minutes. Serves 20. (Do *not* double the garlic salt if you double the recipe.)

Dedicated to Keri Dawson

GREEN BEANS WITH GRAPEFRUIT

4 tablespoons butter or margarine
¼ teaspoon Tabasco sauce
1 teaspoon instant minced onion

6 tablespoons (½ of a 6-ounce can frozen)
   grapefruit juice, thawed, undiluted
2 10-ounce packages frozen whole green beans

In saucepan over low heat, melt butter with Tabasco and onion. Stir in undiluted grapefruit juice concentrate; heat. Meanwhile, cook green beans according to package directions. Serve grapefruit sauce over green beans. Garnish with grapefruit sections, if desired. Serves 4 to 6.

Virginia Salter

ORIENTAL GREEN PEAS

1 tablespoon unsalted butter
2 teaspoons honey
¼ cup chicken stock
1 teaspoon soy sauce
1 10-ounce package frozen peas

1 8 ounce-can sliced water chestnuts
2 large scallions, trimmed and sliced,
   including most of the green
Salt to taste
Few drops red pepper oil

In a medium, microwave safe bowl, combine the butter, honey, stock and soy sauce, and cook on high (100% power) for 3 minutes. Stir in the peas, and drained water chestnuts and cook uncovered for 4 minutes, or until the peas are just tender and hot, stirring once during this time. Add the scallions, salt and pepper oil and cook 1 minute longer. Serve at once. Makes 4 servings.

Virginia Salter

ASPARAGUS WITH SOUR CREAM

6 tablespoons onion, finely chopped
2 tablespoons butter
2 cups sour cream
⅔ cup mayonnaise
2 tablespoons fresh lemon juice

½ teaspoon salt
¼ teaspoon white pepper
4 pounds fresh cooked asparagus, or
    two 15-ounce cans long spears

Sauté onion in butter. Stir in sour cream, mayonnaise and lemon juice. Heat until hot, but do not boil. Season with salt and pepper and pour over asparagus.

Cookbook Committee

SCALLOPED ASPARAGUS

⅓ cup butter
¼ cup flour
1 teaspoon salt
   Pepper to taste
2 cans green asparagus spears

1 small jar pimiento
4 hard boiled eggs
½ cup grated cheddar cheese
⅓ cup bread crumbs
   Milk

Melt 4 tablespoons of butter, add flour, salt and pepper to make a smooth paste. Drain asparagus; add enough milk to liquid to make 2 cups of liquid. Cook until thickened. Add pimiento. Cover bottom of a 9×9-inch casserole dish with half of the asparagus, sliced eggs and cheese. Repeat with remaining ingredients. Top with bread crumbs. Melt remaining butter and pour over top. Bake at 425 degrees for 20 minutes.

Congressman Sam Johnson

CELERY AU GRATIN

1 large bunch celery
1 10-ounce package frozen peas
1 10¾-ounce can cream of celery soup

2 tablespoons pimiento
½ teaspoon basil
½ cup cheese, grated

Cut celery in 1-inch pieces, boil 15 minutes and drain. Mix all ingredients except cheese in buttered casserole. Top with cheese and bake at 350 degrees for 20 minutes. Serves 8.

Lill Clayton

COINTREAU CARROT COINS

4 cups carrots, sliced into coins
2 tablespoons Cointreau (or any
    orange-flavored liqueur)
1/3 cup fresh lemon juice

3 tablespoons brandy
1/4 cup honey
1 tablespoon parsley, finely chopped

Simmer carrots in boiling salted water until tender crisp; drain. Arrange in a single layer in a buttered baking dish. Blend together Cointreau, lemon juice, brandy and honey; pour over carrots and bake in 350 degree oven for 10 minutes. Baste several times. Sprinkle with parsley and serve. Serves 8 to 10.

Nancy Spicer

SUNSHINE CARROTS

10 medium carrots
2 tablespoons sugar
2 teaspoons cornstarch
2 tablespoons butter

1/2 teaspoon salt
1/2 teaspoon ground ginger
1/2 cup orange juice

Peel and cut carrots (bias) in 1-inch chunks. Cook covered in boiling salted water until just tender (about 20 minutes). Drain and keep warm. Meanwhile, combine next 4 items in small sauce pan. Add orange juice a little at a time. Cook, stirring constantly until mixture thickens and bubbles. Boil 1 minute. Stir in butter. Pour over hot carrots, tossing gently to coat evenly. Serves 8 to 10.

Vi Kimbrell

CARROT SOUFFLÉ

1 16-ounce can carrots (or
    fresh cooked)
1/2 cup margarine
2/3 cup sugar

3 eggs (or 6 egg whites)
1 teaspoon baking powder
3 tablespoons flour
1/2 teaspoon vanilla

Drain carrots. Melt margarine, add carrots and put in blender. Add remaining ingredients and blend. Pour in greased casserole. Bake at 350 degrees for 45 minutes. Serves 6.

Linda Holder

ZUCCHINI SQUASH CASSEROLE

2 tablespoons rice
1 pound zucchini squash, sliced
1 large onion, sliced
1 large green pepper, sliced
1 stalk celery, chopped

1 large tomato, sliced
Salt and pepper
1 tablespoon dried basil leaves
1 tablespoon brown sugar
2 tablespoons butter

Butter casserole dish. Place ingredients in casserole in order listed. Cover with foil. Bake at 350 degrees for 2 hours. Stir after the first hour. Serves 6 to 8.

Grace Enlow

CREAMED ONIONS

3 Bermuda onions, sliced
　　in 1/4-inch rings
3 tablespoons butter
3/4 pound Swiss cheese, grated

1 can cream of chicken soup
1/2 cup milk
2 slices white bread, cubed
10 slices party rye, buttered

Glaze sliced onions in butter until golden. Put in 2 1/2 quart buttered casserole. Combine cheese, soup and milk. Stir until smooth. Add bread cubes to onions and pour sauce over all. Place buttered party rye on top and bake in 350 degree oven for 40 to 45 minutes. Serves 10.

Elaine Russ

EGGPLANT / SQUASH CASSEROLE

1 medium eggplant, peeled
　　and cubed
1 pound yellow squash (3 to 4), cubed
3 ounces cream cheese

2 tablespoons Worcestershire sauce
1 small can green chilies
2 eggs, beaten
Corn chips, crushed

Use equal amounts of eggplant and squash. Boil together in salted water until tender. Drain and put into mixer. While still hot, whip in cream cheese, Worcestershire sauce and chilies. Add eggs. Put into buttered glass casserole dish (quiche dish or large pie plate). Top with corn chips and bake at 350 degrees for 30 minutes.

Renee Morris

BROCCOLI MADELEINE

1 pound frozen cut broccoli
4 tablespoons butter
2 tablespoons flour
2 tablespoons onion, chopped
1/2 cup milk
1/4 to 1/2 cup vegetable liquid
1/2 teaspoon black pepper

1/4 teaspoon celery salt
3/4 teaspoon garlic powder
1/2 teaspoon salt
6 ounce roll of jalapeño cheese
1 teaspoon Worcestershire sauce
Red pepper to taste
Buttered bread crumbs

Cook broccoli according to package directions. Drain and reserve liquid. Melt butter in saucepan over low heat. Add flour, stirring until blended and smooth, but not brown. Add onion and cook until soft, but not brown. Add liquid and milk slowly, stirring constantly to avoid lumps. Cook until smooth and thick; continue stirring. Add seasonings and cheese that has been cut into small pieces. Stir until melted; combine with cooked broccoli. Put into a buttered casserole and top with buttered bread crumbs. Run under broiler and serve immediately; or refrigerate overnight and warm in moderate oven just before serving. (May also be frozen.) Serves 6 to 8.

Jo Ann Hancock

THE BEST DISH EVER

1 cup celery
1 cup onion, chopped
1/2 cup butter
20 ounces chopped broccoli, frozen
1/2 cup water
1 can cream of chicken soup

1/2 cup milk
16 ounces cheese whiz
4 cups cooked rice
Salt
Pepper
Garlic powder

Sauté celery and onion in butter until limp. Add water and broccoli. Cook until broccoli is thawed. Add soup, milk, cheese whiz and seasoning. Mix. Add cooked rice and pour in casserole sprayed with vegetable oil. Bake at 325 degrees for 30 to 45 minutes.

Nancy Jernigan

STIR-FRIED CABBAGE

1 tablespoon vegetable oil
1 onion, sliced
4 cups shredded cabbage

1 cup celery, sliced
½ cup chicken broth
2 tablespoons soy sauce

Heat oil. Add remaining ingredients. Cook over high heat. Stir constantly until tender.

Lucy Martin

EGGPLANT PIE

½ recipe for 2-crust pastry
2 cups eggplant, unpeeled, cubed
¼ cup butter
1 cup fresh mushrooms, coarsely chopped
1 clove garlic, minced

½ cup scallions, chopped
2 tablespoons parsley, coarsely chopped
¼ cup tomato paste
1 teaspoon mixed salad herbs
½ teaspoon seasoned salt

Prepare pastry, roll out and line 9-inch pie pan. Flute edges. Sauté eggplant in butter, covered, for 10 minutes over low heat. Add all fresh ingredients and cook until mushrooms begin to wilt, stirring constantly. Add salt, herbs, tomato paste. Stir once to mix and turn into pie shell. Bake for about 45 to 50 minutes at 400 degrees until filling is bubbly and crust is browned. Check from time to time to make sure pie does not get too brown. Cool slightly before serving. Make double quantity of filling for a pie shell if it is to be used as main dish. Can be served hot or chilled, or cut in slices as hors d'oeuvres.

Adell Campbell

MIDDLE EASTERN MAJEDORAH

1½ cups lentils
4 cups water
1 tablespoon salt
2 cups onions, cut up

¼ cup olive oil
1 teaspoon salt
¾ cup brown rice
1½ tablespoons butter

Soak lentils 8 to 9 hours, then drain. Simmer in 4 cups water with 1 tablespoon salt, covered, for 2 hours. Cook onions in olive oil with salt, covered, until yellow, about 20 minutes. Parch brown rice in butter for 2 minutes (until opaque). Add rice and lentils to onions in big pot with up to 2 cups water slowly added. Cook until soft (not mushy) stirring frequently to avoid sticking, over low heat. Top with salad (must include celery or cucumbers). Serve with beer and French bread.

Landon Scarlett

HERBED TOMATO HALVES

4 large tomatoes.
2 tablespoons green onion, chopped
¼ cup butter or margarine
1 teaspoon salt

½ teaspoon pepper
¼ teaspoon leaf marjoram, crumbled
¼ teaspoon leaf basil, crumbled
1½ cups fresh bread crumbs

Core tomatoes; cut in half crosswise. Place cutside up in shallow baking pan, just large enough to hold tomatoes. Sauté onion in butter in a large skillet until soft. Add salt, pepper, marjoram, basil and bread crumbs. Stir until crumbs are thoroughly moisted. Divide mixture evenly over tomato halves. Bake at 350 degrees for 20 minutes.

Mimi Jernigan

SPINACH-ARTICHOKE CASSEROLE

½ cup onion, chopped
½ cup butter or margarine, melted
2 10-ounce packages frozen spinach,
    thawed, well-drained
½ cup sour cream
¼ cup Parmesan cheese, grated

¾ teaspoon salt
    Dash of ground red pepper
¾ teaspoon ground white pepper
2 14-ounce cans artichoke hearts,
    drained and halved
2 tablespoons Parmesan cheese, grated

Cook onion in butter in a large skillet over medium high heat, stirring constantly, until tender. Stir in spinach and next 5 ingredients. Place artichokes in a lightly greased 8 inch square baking dish (not Pyrex if put in refrigerator). Spoon spinach mixture over artichokes and sprinkle with 2 tablespoons Parmesan cheese. Bake at 350 degrees for 25 to 30 minutes. Serves 8.

Note: Casserole may be assembled in advance, reserving 2 tablespoons cheese, cover and refrigerate up to 8 hours. To serve, remove from refrigerator and let stand 30 minutes. Uncover, sprinkle with cheese and bake as directed.

Faye Gould

LAYERED SPINACH SUPREME

1 cup biscuit mix
¼ cup milk
2 eggs
¼ cup onion, finely chopped
1 10-ounce package frozen chopped
  spinach, thawed and drained

½ cup Parmesan cheese, grated
2 eggs
1 12-ounce carton creamed cottage cheese
4 ounces Monterey Jack cheese
½ teaspoon salt
2 cloves garlic, crushed

Heat oven to 375 degrees. Grease a 12×7½×2-inch baking dish. Mix vigorously together, biscuit mix, milk, 2 eggs, and onion. Spread into dish. Cut Jack cheese into 1½-inch cubes. Mix cheeses, spinach, 2 more eggs and seasonings. Spoon evenly over first layer. Bake until set, about 30 minutes. Let stand 5 minutes. Serves 6 to 8.

Peggy Hasse

CORN CASSEROLE

8 tablespoons margarine
8 ounces cream cheese
2 15-ounce cans white shoe peg corn

Salt and pepper to taste
1 4½-ounce can green chilies, chopped
1 tablespoon sugar

Melt margarine and cream cheese; add (drained) corn and chilies, sugar, salt and pepper. Bake uncovered for 30 minutes at 350 degrees.

Nancy Beene

BAKED CORN CASSEROLE

1 16½-ounce can cream style corn
1 12-ounce can whole kernel corn
½ cup grated onion
½ cup green pepper, chopped
¼ cup margarine, melted
2 tablespoons sugar

1 tablespoon pimiento
⅔ cup milk
1 egg, well beaten
1 cup cracker crumbs
1 cup American cheese, grated
Salt and pepper to taste

Combine all ingredients; mix well. Pour into buttered 2-quart casserole. Top with buttered, slightly browned, coarse cracker crumbs. Bake at 350 degrees for 1 hour. Serves 8.

Maxine Brown

CORN PUDDING

4 large eggs
6 tablespoons butter, melted
2 tablespoons flour
½ teaspoon onion powder
½ teaspoon salt

¼ teaspoon red pepper
¼ teaspoon garlic powder
1 10-ounce package frozen whole corn
1 16½-ounce can cream style yellow corn
1 cup heavy cream

Preheat oven to 325 degrees. Grease deep 1½-quart casserole or soufflé dish. Beat eggs in large bowl. Beat in butter, flour and all dry ingredients until blended. Stir in remaining ingredients. Pour in casserole and bake 1 to 1½ hours until knife inserted in center comes out clean. Let stand 5 minutes before serving.

Marseda McHolland

HOT CHEESE HOMINY

¾ cup chopped onion
2 tablespoons butter
2 14½-ounce cans hominy
2 4-ounce cans green chilies

8 ounces sour cream
1 teaspoon chili powder
Salt and pepper to taste
½ pound cheddar cheese, grated

Sauté onion in butter. Mix onion and all other ingredients, except cheese, in a greased casserole. Sprinkle cheese on top. Bake at 400 degrees for 20 to 30 minutes. Serve hot. May be prepared ahead. Serves 4 to 5.

Marci Wells

MUSHROOMS LUISA

1 pound mushrooms, sliced
1 to 2 shallots, chopped
4 tablespoons butter or margarine

Sherry
1 to 2 teaspoons Worcestershire sauce
Salt and pepper

Melt butter and add shallots. Sauté, then add mushrooms. Once cooked down (all butter absorbed), add some Worcestershire sauce and then sherry to taste. Cook a little longer. Season to taste. Serve with steak.

Luisa Bridges

VEGETABLE CASSEROLE

2 tablespoons butter
2 cups onions, chopped
8 medium potatoes, peeled,
  cooked and sliced
4 hard-boiled eggs, sliced

½ cup fresh parsley, minced
4 fresh tomatoes, peeled and sliced
1½ teaspoons salt
⅛ teaspoon pepper

Sauce:

2 tablespoons butter, melted
3 tablespoons flour
2 cups sour cream
1 cup cheddar cheese, grated

1 teaspoon salt
¼ teaspoon pepper
⅛ teaspoon paprika
1 cup fresh bread crumbs
½ cup cheddar cheese

Sauté onions in butter. Put half the potatoes on bottom of buttered casserole. Add eggs, onion, parsley and tomatoes. Sprinkle with salt and pepper. Top with remaining potatoes.

Mix sauce ingredients (except crumbs and cheese). Cook sauce until thick and pour over casserole. Sprinkle with bread crumbs, top with cheese and dot with butter. Bake at 350 degrees for 45 minutes.

Charlotte Stoltz

POTATO BAKE

2 pounds frozen hash brown
  potatoes, thawed
⅓ cup margarine, melted
¼ cup onions, chopped

1 can cream of chicken soup
1 cup sour cream
8 ounces sharp cheese, grated

Mix all ingredients and put in 13×9-inch baking dish. Bake for 1 hour in 350 degree oven, uncovered. Serves 10 to 12.

Neva Muller

POTATOES WITH ROSEMARY

3 pounds new potatoes, approximately
2 tablespoons extra virgin olive oil
4 tablespoons margarine

1 teaspoon fresh rosemary leaves
Salt and pepper

Clean and chop into bite-sized chunks, equal parts of new red potatoes and white potatoes; *do not peel.* Cover with water and boil until not quite done. Drain well. Put olive oil and margarine in bottom of 3-quart casserole dish. Add cooked, hot potatoes, rosemary, salt and pepper. Stir gently to coat potatoes. Place in hot oven (400 to 450 degrees) for about 30 minutes, turning often so all potatoes brown nicely. Check often so they do not burn.

Kathleen Grandjean

POTATOES AND HERBS

1 teaspoon thyme
1 teaspoon marjoram
1 teaspoon chervil
¼ cup flour
6 uniform white potatoes

5 tablespoons butter
Salt and pepper
2 bay leaves
2 cloves garlic

Mix herbs and flour on sheet of wax paper. Peel potatoes and roll in mixture. Put in buttered casserole and dot with butter, season with salt and pepper. Add whole bay leaves and garlic buds stuck with a toothpick (easy to recover). Cover and bake in 450 degree oven 45 to 60 minutes or until potatoes are tender. Serves 6.

Mrs. Blair Mercer

GOURMET POTATOES

6 medium potatoes
2 cups cheddar cheese, grated
1½ cups sour cream
¼ cup butter

1 cup green onions, chopped
1 teaspoon salt
¼ teaspoon pepper
2 tablespoons butter

Cook potatoes in skins, cool, peel and grate. Heat the cheese, sour cream and ¼ cup butter to make smooth sauce. Add onions, salt and pepper to sauce. Fold sauce into potatoes. Place in a greased casserole. Dot with 2 tablespoons butter. Bake 30 minutes at 350 degrees.

Charlotte Stoltz

SWEET POTATO COCONUT CASSEROLE

3 cups mashed sweet potatoes
1 cup sugar
½ teaspoon salt
2 eggs

4 tablespoons margarine, melted
1 teaspoon vanilla
½ teaspoon cinnamon
½ teaspoon nutmeg

Topping:
1 cup coconut
⅓ flour
¾ teaspoon baking powder

1 cup brown sugar
1 cup chopped nuts
4 tablespoons margarine, melted

Mix all ingredients and pour into greased 2-quart baking dish. Mix topping ingredients and pour on top of sweet potato mixture. Bake at 300 degrees for about 35 minutes. (You may use half the topping and refrigerate the other half for next time.)

Pauline Steele

DUCHESS SWEET POTATOES

1 large can sweet potatoes
¾ cup sugar
½ cup margarine, melted

3 eggs
1 teaspoon vanilla
½ cup milk or cream

Topping:
1 cup corn flakes, crushed
½ cup brown sugar

½ cup nuts, chopped

Mash potatoes. Add other ingredients and mix well with mixer. Place in a 9-inch square or 11×7×2-inch baking dish. Mix topping ingredients well and spread over potatoes. Bake at 350 degrees for 30 to 45 minutes.

Pearl Scott

YAM-APPLE CASSEROLE

2 Delicious apples, peeled and sliced
⅓ cup pecans, chopped
½ cup brown sugar, packed
½ teaspoon cinnamon

2 17-ounce cans yams, drained
¼ cup margarine
2 cups miniature marshmallows

Toss apples and nuts with sugar and cinnamon. Alternate apple mixture and yams in 1½-quart casserole, then dot the top with margarine. Cover and bake at 350 degrees for 35 to 40 minutes. Sprinkle with marshmallows and continue baking until brown. Serves 8 to 10.

Dorothy Jones

SWEET POTATO SOUFFLÉ

3 sweet potatoes, boiled and peeled
½ cup cream
⅓ cup sugar
½ teaspoon salt
2 tablespoons butter, melted

2 eggs, lightly beaten
1 teaspoon nutmeg
¾ cup chopped pecans
1½ cups marshmallows

Beat potatoes until light and smooth. Fold in cream, sugar, salt, butter, eggs and nutmeg. Top with pecans and marshmallows. Bake at 350 degrees for 30 minutes (325 degrees for glass baking dish).

Martha Weisend

SWEET POTATO PONE

4 cups sweet potatoes, peeled
   and shredded
1 orange rind, grated
1½ cups sugar
½ teaspoon salt
¾ cup butter or margarine, softened

1 cup milk
2 eggs, slightly beaten
1 teaspoon cinnamon
¼ teaspoon nutmeg
1 teaspoon vanilla

Combine sweet potatoes and orange rind in a large mixing bowl. Mix well. Add sugar, salt, butter, milk, eggs, cinnamon, nutmeg and vanilla. Blend thoroughly. Spoon mixture into a greased 8-inch square baking dish. Bake at 325 degrees for 1 hour and 30 minutes. Serve hot or cold. Yields 10 to 12 servings.

Mae Dobbs

CHILI~CHEESE CASSEROLE

2 4-ounce cans whole green chilies,
   drained and seeded
2 cups chopped tomatoes
2 cups cheddar cheese, shredded

1 cup biscuit mix
1 cup milk
3 eggs
½ teaspoon salt

Heat oven to 375 degrees. Grease an 8×8×2-inch baking dish. Arrange chilies in single layer in dish. Sprinkle with tomatoes and cheese. Beat remaining ingredients with hand beater until smooth; pour over top. Bake until knife inserted in center comes out clean, 30 to 35 minutes. Serves 6 to 8.

Donald McLaughlin

CHILI RELLENO CASSEROLE

1 cup milk
3 to 4 eggs
¼ cup flour
4 4-ounce cans green chopped chilies

1 pound Monterey Jack cheese, grated
Butter
1 8-ounce can tomato sauce

Mix milk, eggs and flour together. Layer chilies and cheese in baking dish; repeating each layer. Pour mixed ingredients over top, dot with butter. Bake at 350 degrees for 45 minutes, covered. Uncover, pour tomato sauce over top. Cook 15 minutes longer.

Annella Collins

EASY CHEESE SOUFFLE

12 slices white bread, toasted
1½ pounds medium or
   sharp cheddar cheese
3 cups milk

4 eggs
Salt and pepper to taste
1½ teaspoons dry mustard
1½ teaspoons fines herbes

Butter a 9×13-inch glass casserole. Cube the toasted bread slices. Grate cheese and toss with toast cubes. Mix the remaining ingredients in a bowl and pour over cheese and toast in casserole. Bake at 325 degrees for 1 hour.

Sue Smith

WELSH RAREBIT

1 pound Wisconsin cheese, cut up
1/2 cup beer
1 egg, slightly beaten

1 teaspoon prepared mustard
1 teaspoon Worcestershire sauce
Few dashes Tabasco

Melt cheese over boiling water. Add beer. Add seasonings to egg and combine well with cheese. Let cook for a few minutes until it thickens. Pour over toasted crackers, or crisp toast. Serves 6.

Katherine Pitman (Roberta Camp's cousin)

GRITS WITH GREEN CHILIES

1 cup dry grits, cooked according
    to package directions
1/2 cup margarine
1/4 clove garlic, or garlic salt

2 eggs lightly beaten
1/2 pound sharp cheddar cheese, grated
1 small can chopped green chilies (not hot)

Add remaining ingredients to grits. Add salt to taste. Pour into greased 11×7-inch baking dish, and bake 1 hour at 350 degrees, or until set.

Maxine Brown

CHEESE GRITS

4 cups water
1 cup quick grits
3 eggs, well beaten
6 tablespoons butter or margarine
    (less than a 1/2-pound tub)

1/2 pound processed cheese, cubed
1/2 pound sharp cheddar cheese, grated
    (medium or mild, if preferred)
3 to 4 drops Tabasco sauce
2 teaspoons seasoned salt

Preheat oven to 325 degrees. Cook grits 3 minutes. Add butter and cheese and continue heating until melted. Add salt and Tabasco to beaten eggs and fold into grits/cheese mixture. Bake in a 9×12-inch buttered dish for 45 minutes.

Dedicated to Lillian LaFountaine

GARLIC CHEESE GRITS SOUFFLÉ

1 cup grits
4 cups water
1 teaspoon salt
1 roll garlic cheese

½ cup butter
2 eggs, separated
¼ cup milk
Salt and fresh ground pepper to taste

Cook grits in water with salt added. After grits are cooked, add roll of garlic cheese. Break in pieces and add butter, 2 egg yolks well beaten, milk, salt and pepper. In a separate bowl, beat egg whites until stiff peaks form. Add to grits and pour in 1½-quart well-greased casserole and bake for 40 minutes to 1 hour at 325 to 350 degrees.

Lynda Sanders

EMERALD RICE

4 eggs, separated
4 cups rice, cooked
1 cup snipped raw (or thawed) spinach
½ cup green pepper, minced
⅓ cup Parmesan cheese
¼ cup onion, minced

1 teaspoon paprika
1 teaspoon salt
1 teaspoon dry chives
2 teaspoons dry parsley
¼ teaspoon MSG
1 cup heavy cream, whipped

Beat egg whites and set aside. Beat egg yolks and add remaining ingredients, folding in whipping cream and egg whites last. Pour into lightly buttered casserole or ring mold. Set casserole in a pan of water and bake at 350 degrees for 45 minutes.

Renee Morris

CONFETTI RICE

1 cup sliced mushrooms
½ cup onion, chopped
⅓ cup margarine or butter
3 cups hot cooked rice
1 10-ounce package frozen peas, cooked and drained

1 teaspoon salt
½ teaspoon pepper
¼ teaspoon crushed rosemary (more if desired)
¼ cup slivered almonds, toasted

Cook mushrooms and onion in butter until slightly brown. Add rice, peas and all seasonings. Makes 6 to 8 servings.

Ebby Halliday

GARDEN VARIETY RICE

1½ cups cooked white or brown rice
½ cup olive oil
2 medium onions, chopped
1 large fresh carrot, cut up for blender
1 cup fresh broccoli heads
2 stalks fresh celery with leaves,
    cut up for blender

2 tablespoons parsley, chopped
1 teaspoon oregano or Greek seasoning
1 teaspoon salt
1 teaspoon horseradish
¼ cup walnuts, finely chopped
    Coarse ground pepper, to taste

In a large sauce pan, sauté onions in olive oil until onions are golden brown. Reduce heat to simmer. Add cooked rice; stir and cover. Put all fresh vegetables into blender container with enough cold water to cover them. Run blender for a few seconds at the recommended speed for finely chopping fresh vegetables. Drain. Add drained vegetables to rice along with all other ingredients. Stir well; cover and simmer for 10 minutes. Serve hot with shrimp, crab claws, gumbo, or by itself. Makes 4 to 6 servings.

Jarrel W. Calhoun

CREOLE RICE FILÉ

1½ cups rice, cooked according
    to package instructions
5 young green onions, chopped,
    tops and all
½ bell pepper, chopped
½ cup parsley, chopped
⅓ cup oil

½ pound processed cheese, cubed
1 cup chicken broth (can be made
    from bouillon cube and water)
    Salt and pepper
2 teaspoons gumbo filé (available in spice section)
2 eggs, beaten

Stir into rice above ingredients, except eggs. Then add beaten eggs. Pour mixture in a greased casserole dish. Bake at 350 degrees for 45 minutes. This is very good with ham or chicken. It is similar to "Green Rice."

Peggy Dawson

SPICY RICE

1 cup (4 ounces) mild Mexican
    pasteurized process cheese spread
1½ cups original minute rice
1 cup water

¼ cup green onion, sliced
1 cup tomato, chopped
2 teaspoons chopped cilantro (optional)

Microwave cheese spread as directed on package. Mix with rice, water and onions in 1½-quart dish. Cover. Microwave on high 3 minutes. Mix in tomato and cilantro. Cover. Microwave on high 4 minutes. Let stand 5 minutes before serving. Stir before serving. Serves 4 to 6.

Tina Lewis

BUDDY'S SPANISH RICE

1 tablespoon cooking oil
1½ cups seasoning, (chopped onions,
    green pepper, celery, cut clove garlic)
1 pound ground meat

1 cup washed rice
2¼ cups tomato juice (or less)
1½ tablespoons Worcestershire sauce
Salt and pepper to taste

Melt cooking oil in large Dutch oven. Pour in seasonings and cook about 10 to 15 minutes, then put in meat and cook 15 minutes more. Mash down meat and seasonings in bottom with large spoon. Spread rice evenly over top, then pour tomato juice slowly over all. Cook exactly 1 hour with lid on (*do not* take lid off during the hour). Put heat down as low as possible. This makes a complete meal when accompanied with a green salad and garlic toast.

Sadie Caropresi

PECAN RICE

1 cup raw brown rice
3 cups chicken broth
¼ cup butter
1 cup celery, chopped
1 cup onion, minced

⅛ cup parsley, chopped
1 4-ounce jar pimiento, drained, chopped
1 cup pecans, sliced
½ teaspoon poultry seasoning
Salt and pepper

Cook the rice in the broth over very low heat until tender. Combine butter, onion, celery, and parsley in a skillet. Sauté on low until tender. Combine rice and sauteed vegetables. Add remaining ingredients. Put into a baking dish and bake for 30 minutes at 325 degrees. May be used as a stuffing for fowl. Serves 6.

Dorothy Lovett

WILD RICE

½ cup (4 ounces) wild rice, uncooked
1 onion, chopped
2 cloves garlic, chopped
2 stalks celery, chopped
½ cup white wine

1 can water chestnuts, chopped or
  sliced thin, drained
2 cups hot water plus 1 package butter
  buds dissolved in it
Pepper, sage, ½ teaspoon salt (all optional)

Combine all ingredients. Place in a casserole and bake covered at 325 degrees for 2 hours. Decorate top with sliced mushrooms, if desired.

Natalie Ornish

WILD RICE WITH MUSHROOMS AND ALMONDS

1 cup wild rice
¼ cup butter
½ cup almonds, slivered
1 cup white wine

Chopped green onions and garlic
1 8-ounce can mushrooms, drained
3 cups chicken broth

Wash and drain rice. Melt butter in skillet. Add rice, almonds, onions, garlic and mushrooms. Cook and stir until almonds are golden brown (about 20 minutes). Pour rice mixture into ungreased 1½-quart casserole. Heat chicken broth to boiling and add to casserole. Add wine. Cover tightly. Cook in a preheated 325 degree oven for 1½ hours or until all liquid is absorbed and rice is tender and fluffy. Serves 6 to 8.

Nancy B. Hamon

WILD RICE CURRY

¾ cup wild rice
6 slices bacon, diced
½ cup onion, chopped
½ cup raw carrot, grated
2 egg yolks

1 cup light cream
1½ teaspoons curry powder
½ teaspoon salt
4 tablespoons butter

Cook the rice until done. Drain and wash in cold water. Fry the bacon, add onions and carrots, sauté until onions are soft. Strain out and mix with the rice. Place in buttered casserole. Beat the egg yolks, add the cream and seasonings, and pour over the mixture. Dot with butter and bake at 300 degrees in a pan of water, until set. Serves 6 to 8.

Linda Civiletto

WILD RICE DATES

4 tablespoons butter
1 onion, chopped
4 celery stalks, diced
1 cup wild rice

3 cups chicken stock
1 teaspoon salt
½ cup walnuts, toasted
½ cup dates, chopped

Heat butter; add onion and celery and sauté for 10 minutes. Add rice and stir for 3 minutes more. Add stock and salt; bring to boil. Reduce heat, cover and simmer 1 hour. Add nuts and dates and let stand for 5 minutes. Serves 6.

Pat Yanigan Eigen

CHESTNUT STUFFING

12 cups of soft broken biscuits
1 cup celery, chopped
1 cup onions, chopped
1 cup chestnuts, chopped
2 eggs, beaten

½ cup milk
2 teaspoons salt
2 tablespoons parsley, chopped
2 teaspoons poultry seasoning
Broth from stewing giblets

Combine all ingredients. Use just enough broth to moisten. Mix thoroughly.

Mae Dobbs

MANICOTTI

Sauce:

1 medium onion, chopped
4 cloves garlic, minced
4 tablespoons oil
1 teaspoon salt
1 tablespoon sugar

½ teaspoon black pepper
4 6-ounce cans tomato paste
4 cans water
2 tablespoons parsley flakes
1 teaspoon basil

Sauté onions and garlic in oil. Add remaining ingredients and simmer 30 minutes, covered.

Filling:

1 16-ounce carton ricotta cheese
   (or small curd cottage cheese)
¼ pound mozzarella cheese, grated
1 teaspoon parsley flakes
3 tablespoons Romano cheese, grated

2 teaspoons sugar
1 egg, lightly beaten
½ teaspoon salt
¼ teaspoon pepper
   Uncooked manicotti shells

Mix all of the above ingredients and fill uncooked manicotti shells, using knife. Pour a little sauce in bottom of 9×12-inch dish and arrange filled shells in a single layer side by side. Add sauce to cover. Cover dish with foil to seal tightly. Cook at 400 degrees for 40 minutes, then uncover and cook 5 minutes more.

Jo Boyd

PRIMA PASTA

1 head cauliflower
1 bunch broccoli
3 zucchini squash
   Handful snow peas (optional)
3 firm tomatoes

1 package large shell macaroni
½ cup butter
2 to 3 whole garlic cloves, mashed
1 cup half-and-half (optional)
1 to 2 wedges Romano cheese, grated

Slice or floweret vegetables. Cook macaroni. In large skillet, melt butter, add garlic and vegetables. Sauté, cover and cook 2 to 3 minutes. Mix pasta and vegetables. If desired, add half-and-half, then add 1 to 2 wedges of grated Romano. Serve warm or cold, with French bread and wine.

Beverly Holmes

STUFFED SHELLS~CHEESE

Pasta Sauce:

6 tablespoons oil	16 ounces tomato sauce
1 clove garlic, minced	1 to 1¼ teaspoons salt
1 medium onion, minced	Dash pepper
2 16-ounce cans tomatoes	1 teaspoon sugar
2 tablespoons chopped parsley	1 teaspoon crumbled basil, or to taste

Filling:

1 pound ricotta cheese	1 tablespoon parsley, chopped
¼ pound mozzarella cheese, grated	½ teaspoon sugar (optional)
3 tablespoons Romano cheese, grated	Salt and pepper to taste
1 egg	20 pasta shells

Pasta sauce: Heat oil in heavy sauce pan. Add garlic, onion and parsley. Sauté several minutes, stirring a few times until garlic is golden. Add tomatoes, tomato sauce, salt, pepper, sugar and basil. Simmer uncovered, stirring occasionally until thickened, about 20 minutes. Taste to adjust seasoning if necessary. Makes 6 cups. Recipe can be doubled for freezing, but do not double oil.

Filling: Combine all ingredients, blending and mixing well together. Stuff uncooked shells. Arrange shells in one layer, side by side, stuffed side up. Add hot pasta sauce to completely cover shells. Cover pan with aluminum foil, crimping edges to seal tightly. Place in preheated 400 degree oven and bake for 50 minutes. Remove foil, sprinkle with additional grated Romano cheese. Bake uncovered 5 minutes longer. Let stand 5 minutes before serving. Fills 20 pasta shells.

Pat Marshall

GNOCCHI VERDI

10 ounces frozen or fresh spinach	½ cup flour
1 large egg, lightly beaten	Extra flour to sprinkle on plate
1 pound ricotta cheese	Boiling salted water
½ teaspoon nutmeg	Melted butter
1 teaspoon salt	½ cup Parmesan cheese, grated

Sprinkle the extra flour onto dinner-sized plate. Barely cook spinach; drain, squeeze and mince. Mix with egg and ricotta in bowl. Add seasonings and ½ cup flour. Roll 2½ teaspoons (approximately) of the mixture in palm of hand. Roll in flour that is on plate. (Balls can sit in refrigerator, wrapped in plastic, for several hours.) Bring a large pot of salted water to full boil. Drop gnocchi one by one into boiling water. Do not crowd. When done they rise to the water's surface. Remove with slotted spoon. Put on warm platter. Spread gnocchi with melted butter and Parmesan cheese. Be sure to continue adding flour to dinner plate as it is used up.

Jarrel W. Calhoun

ITALIAN PASTA FAGIOLI

1 16-ounce can crushed tomatoes	4 tablespoons olive oil
Italian seasoning	1 12-ounce package elbow macaroni
Salt and pepper to taste	1 can cannellini beans
4 garlic cloves, finely chopped	

In medium pot, place crushed tomatoes, Italian seasoning, salt and pepper. Cook slowly. In separate small skillet slowly brown garlic in olive oil. Add to tomatoes. Cook 1 hour. Boil water, cook macaroni, drain well. Add beans to tomatoes. Cook 5 minutes, then add macaroni. Serves 4 to 6. Serve with salad and garlic bread.

Grace Tambourine

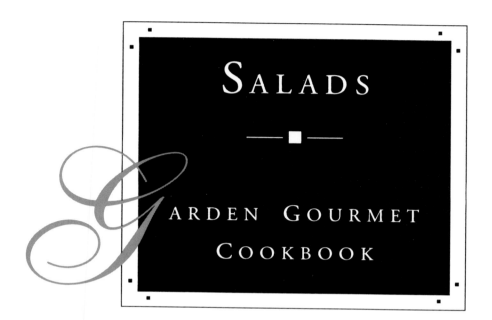

SALADS

■

GARDEN GOURMET COOKBOOK

The Arboretum has a small, well-planned, walled herb garden adjacent to the Camp House. Herbs are not a new thing . . . we can trace their history back 50,000 years.

Herbs have been a topic of conversation and interest since the beginning of time. In the Book of Genesis, plants served as symbols of life. Herbs have had a significant value in the physical, mental and spiritual development of mankind.

Herbs have been used for medicinal purposes, nutritional value, food seasoning or coloring and dyeing of other substances. Historically, the most important uses of herbs were medicinal.

Our present day interests in herbs tends to be centered in culinary and aromatic usage. Colonial forefathers brought herbs with them to these shores and conversely took many back to the Old World.

In using fresh herbs for culinary purposes one tablespoon of fresh equals one teaspoon of dried. The finer they are minced the more flavor they will release. Sugar can be flavored with lemon balm leaves or rose geranium leaves. Vinegar and oil can be flavored with fresh leaves, whole seeds. Salt can be blended with dry herbs for a seasoning blend.

In addition to the leaves and seeds of herbs, their flowers, as well as several well-known non-herb flowers can also be used for culinary enjoyment. Edible flowers started to bloom in our culinary world around 1988. There are many growers now who deal exclusively in this edible product. Boxes of petals are available in supermarkets and farmers' markets. There are year-around flowers available (violas, pansies and Johnny-jump-ups). However, we must give credit to the ancient Greeks and Romans who valued flowers as food long before they were appreciated for their beauty. Roses were pickled, boiled and potted and nasturtium, an herb of the New World, was added as a spice for its peppery taste.

Edible flowers can be added raw to salads, dried and infused in oil or used as a garnish on meat dishes, pasta and desserts. Popular ones are: sweet violets, marigolds, clove pink, poppy, seated geraniums, pansy, rose, daisy and nasturtium.

In deciding what makes a flower edible: make sure the flower is not poisonous; make sure it has not been sprayed with an insecticide: never use flowers from a florist in cooking or as a garnish, and avoid wild flowers as they may be tainted with exhaust fumes.

The wonderful new herbs now being offered can enhance, excite and delight . . . go boldly forth and become heady with the myriad possibilities that await you and your family.

ASPARAGUS MOLD

1   8-ounce package cream cheese,
    softened
1   10¾-ounce can cream of
    asparagus soup, undiluted
1   small package lime flavored gelatin
½   cup mayonnaise
1   8-ounce can cut asparagus
¾   cup chopped celery
½   cup sliced almonds

Mash cream cheese in a saucepan and gradually add soup. Place over low heat, stirring until smooth. Add gelatin to soup mixture; stir until gelatin is dissolved. Remove from heat, and stir in mayonnaise. Drain asparagus, reserving ¼ cup liquid. Stir liquid into gelatin mixture and chill until partially set. Fold asparagus, celery and almonds into gelatin mixture. Pour into an oiled 4 cup mold and chill until firm. Yields 8 to 10 servings.

Stella Klein

ASPARAGUS VINAIGRETTE

1   teaspoon salt
½   teaspoon pepper
½   teaspoon garlic, finely minced
¼   teaspoon sugar
½   teaspoon dry mustard
⅛   teaspoon cayenne pepper
24 fresh asparagus spears, trimmed

Dash Worcestershire sauce
Dash of Tabasco
3   tablespoons tarragon vinegar
10 tablespoons salad oil
2   tablespoons whipping cream
2   teaspoons parsley, chopped

To prepare the sauce, combine ingredients in a jar. Shake well and chill. To serve: Steam asparagus until tender but still crisp. Drain and arrange on individual plates. Drizzle cold sauce over tips. Serves 4. Sauce can also be used on cold vegetables, avocados, etc.

Susan Wells

BROCCOLI SALAD

3 bunches broccoli flowerets
   and tender tops
½ cup raisins
½ red onion, chopped
3 slices bacon, crumbled (optional)

1 cup salted sunflower seeds, toasted
1 cup mayonnaise
2 tablespoons sugar
2 teaspoons rice vinegar
1 cup white grapes, halved (optional)
1 cup red grapes, halved (optional)

Break up broccoli into bite-size pieces. Mix all ingredients and pour over broccoli to marinate. Let set for 24 hours, then serve chilled. Serves 8.

Patricia Hamilton, Annette Banks, Cal Small and Florene Doswell

CARROT AMBROSIA

4 cups shredded carrots
¼ cup lemon juice
1 3½-ounce can flaked coconut
1½ cups miniature marshmallows
3 tablespoons honey

1 cup chopped fresh navel orange
   segments
¼ cup mayonnaise
½ cup sour cream

Combine first 5 ingredients, tossing gently. Combine other 3 ingredients. Add and toss.

Beverly Cameron

CURRIED CARROT SALAD

2 pounds carrots, peeled and grated
¼ to ½ cup capers, rinsed
¼ cup onion, grated
   Juice of 1 lemon
2 to 3 teaspoons curry powder

½ teaspoon ground cumin
¼ teaspoon ground allspice
   Pinch cayenne
¼ cup canola oil

Mix carrots, capers and onion. Mix remaining ingredients (except oil) and toss with carrot mix; allow to chill and rest at least 10 minutes. Add oil and toss again. Chill.

Jill Cooke

GREEN BEAN SALAD

½ cup sugar
¾ cup white vinegar
½ cup cooking oil
1 can French cut green beans or
   green beans with pimiento, drained

1 can small English peas, drained
1 can white shoe peg corn, drained
1 cup onion, chopped
1 cup celery, chopped
1 cup green pepper, chopped

Combine sugar, vinegar and oil in saucepan and heat to boiling point. Combine remaining ingredients and pour syrup over all. Refrigerate for at least 2 hours before serving. Will keep well in refrigerator.

Jeannette Johnson

SPRING PEA SALAD

1 10-ounce package frozen peas
1 cup diced celery
1 cup cauliflower, chopped
¼ cup green onion (scallions), diced
1 cup cashews or sunflower seeds

¼ cup crisp cooked bacon, crumbled
½ cup sour cream
1 cup prepared ranch dressing
½ tablespoon Dijon mustard
1 clove garlic, minced

Rinse peas in hot water, then drain. Combine with celery, cauliflower, onion, nuts and bacon. Mix other ingredients for dressing, and pour over salad.

Kay Damms

TOMATO ASPIC SALAD

3¾ cups tomato juice
2 3-ounce packages lemon gelatin
¼ cup vinegar
1 teaspoon chopped onion

1 cup green pepper, chopped
1 cup celery, chopped
4 ounces cream cheese
Chopped pecans

Heat tomato juice to boiling. Add gelatin and mix to dissolve. Cool. Add vinegar, onion, green pepper and celery. Grease 12 individual salad molds with oil. Make 12 cheese balls from cream cheese and roll each in pecans. Place one ball in each mold. Fill with aspic. Chill. Unmold and serve on lettuce leaf. You may also put this in an oblong dish and cut into squares. Serves 12.

Lill Clayton

VEGGIE SALAD

2 cups broccoli, cut up
2 cups cauliflower, cut up
½ cup raisins

5 green onions, sliced
8 slices bacon, cooked, chopped
½ cup pecans

Toss together with dressing.

Dressing:
1 cup mayonnaise
2 tablespoons milk

2 tablespoons sugar

Annella Collins

FABULOUS COLE SLAW

1 large head cabbage (4 to 5 pounds)
4 onions, sliced thin
⅞ cup sugar
1 cup white vinegar
2 tablespoons dry mustard

¾ cup salad oil
1 teaspoon celery seed
1 tablespoon salt
2 teaspoons sugar

Slice cabbage thin. Place cabbage and onions in large bowl alternating layers. Place part of the ⅞ cup sugar over each layer. Set aside. In a saucepan, mix remaining ingredients, for dressing. Heat to boiling point and pour over cabbage and onions while hot. Cover tightly and chill in refrigerator for 8 hours. This will keep approximately 1½ weeks. Serves a crowd.

Vi Kimbrell

RED CABBAGE SLAW

½ head red cabbage
1 apple

1 cup green seedless grapes
Poppy seed dressing

Shred the cabbage. Core, peel and slice the apple. Toss all ingredients together with poppy seed dressing and serve.

Ruth Kopplin

TWENTY-FOUR HOUR CABBAGE SLAW

1 medium head cabbage, shredded
1 small onion, chopped
1 green bell pepper, chopped
6 stuffed olives, sliced (optional)
½ cup sugar

½ cup white vinegar
1 teaspoon salt
1 teaspoon celery seed
1 teaspoon prepared mustard
⅛ teaspoon black pepper
½ cup salad oil.

Combine cabbage, onion, green pepper, olives and sugar and set aside. Combine remaining ingredients in a saucepan and boil for 3 minutes. Pour hot dressing over cabbage mixture. Cover and chill for 24 hours. Keeps very well in refrigerator. Serves 12 to 16.

Marjorie Weber

HOT POTATO SALAD

4 to 5 medium potatoes, unpeeled
¼ pound bacon
½ medium onion, chopped
⅛ cup white vinegar

¼ cup water
Pinch salt and pepper
½ cup parsley, chopped

Steam potatoes until just tender. Peel and cut into ½-inch slices. Keep warm. Fry bacon until crisp, drain and crumble. Sauté onion to light color. Stir in vinegar, water, salt and pepper. Cook until heated and pour over potatoes, gently tossing to coat slices evenly. Sprinkle with bacon and parsley. Serve hot. Serves 4.

Betty Holyfield

ANNA'S POTATO SALAD

Must be prepared the day before serving.

8 medium potatoes, boiled
1½ cups mayonnaise
1 cup sour cream
1½ teaspoons horseradish

1 teaspoon celery seed
½ teaspoon salt
1 cup fresh parsley, chopped (do not omit or decrease)
2 medium onions, finely chopped

Peel potatoes and cut into ⅛-inch slices. Combine mayonnaise, sour cream, horseradish, celery seed; set aside. In another bowl, mix parsely and onion.

In large serving bowl, layer potatoes, salt slightly; cover with layer of mayonnaise-sour cream mixture, then layer of parsley-onion. Repeat. Cover and refrigerate overnight. Serves 8 to 10.

Anna Bradberry

CINDY'S POTATO SALAD

7 or 8 medium size new potatoes
1 bunch green onions, sliced
1 small purple onion, chopped

3 stalks celery, chopped
1 4-ounce jar pimiento
2 boiled eggs (optional)

Sauce:

1 cup mayonnaise
1 teaspoon prepared mustard
1 tablespoon vinegar
2 teaspoons sugar

2 teaspoons lemon juice
2 teaspoons celery seed
Salt and pepper to taste

Quarter and boil potatoes until tender. Meanwhile prepare and combine next 5 ingredients. Cut cooled potatoes into bite-size pieces and stir into chopped vegetables. Combine sauce ingredients in order given. Add salt and pepper to taste. Pour over salad being sure to coat evenly. Chill 3 to 5 hours or overnight.

Cindy Wiles

WATER CHESTNUT SALAD

1 head lettuce (romaine or iceberg)	1 small jar mayonnaise
3/4 cup chopped chives (or scallions)	Grated Parmesan cheese
3/4 cup sliced water chestnuts, drained	8 ounces shredded Swiss cheese

Cut up lettuce in large salad bowl. Toss in chives and water chestnuts. Scoop mayonnaise onto salad and smooth, completely covering lettuce. Shake grated cheese lightly over mayonnaise and then sprinkle shredded Swiss cheese over that. Cover with plastic wrap and place in refrigerator for several hours. Best if made the night before serving.

Grace Tambourine

WATER CHESTNUT SALAD

1/2 cup mayonnaise	1/8 cup chives
1/4 cup half-and-half	1/8 cup parsley
1 tablespoon tarragon vinegar	1/2 clove garlic
2 teaspoons anchovy paste	1 can water chestnuts

Mix half-and-half and tarragon vinegar together. Mix this with other ingredients except water chestnuts. Pour mixture over the water chestnuts. Serve on lettuce leaves.

Greta Rees

RICE AND BLACK BEAN SALAD

1 cup uncooked rice	1/3 cup peanut oil
1 16-ounce can black beans, drained and rinsed	1/4 cup fresh lime juice
1 medium red bell pepper, minced	Salt and freshly ground pepper
1 medium green bell pepper, minced	Lettuce leaves
4 green onions, minced	2 avocados, peeled and sliced
1/4 cup fresh cilantro, minced	1 papaya, peeled, seeded and sliced

Cook rice according to package directions and cool to room temperature. Combine with next 5 ingredients in a large bowl. Whisk together oil and lime juice in small bowl. Pour over rice mixture and toss to coat. Season with salt and pepper. (Can be prepared 1 day ahead. Cover and refrigerate.) Line large bowl with lettuce. Mound salad in bowl. Garnish with avocado and papaya and serve.

B. Copeland

C.A.R. Salad

(Chicken ~ Avocado ~ Rice)

1 box long grain and wild rice, cooked	Salt and "lots of" cracked pepper
4 lemon pepper chicken breast patties, (ready to serve), chopped	½ cup honey mustard dressing mix Orange juice
1 medium onion, chopped	1 large avocado

Prepare honey mustard dressing, using orange juice instead of water. Mix all ingredients except avocado. Chill. Just before serving, slice avocado lengthwise and place decoratively on top of salad. Serves 4.

Carol Little

Pasta Salad

1 pound imported pasta, preferably PENNE	½ to 1 cup dried Roma tomatoes
1 can ripe olives	¼ pound sliced pepperoni, cut into pieces
2 small bell peppers (or use pieces of different color peppers)	½ 10-ounce box frozen peas
½ pound mozzarella cheese, cut in ½-inch chunks	¼ cup fresh basil, finely chopped Extra virgin olive oil
2 small jars marinated artichokes, drained, chopped	Red wine vinegar Salt and pepper

Cook the penne *al dente*. (The literal translation is "to the teeth," but to an Italian cook it means "still a bit crunchy"). Drain the pasta well and place in a large casserole dish, coating with enough olive oil to keep the pasta from sticking together. Cool about 20 minutes. Chop all the ingredients into bite-sized pieces, but not too small, because the beauty of this dish depends on the recognizable, but varied shapes of the ingredients. Add all ingredients to the cooled pasta, including the peas, which should still be frozen. Dress with about ¼ cup olive oil, the chopped basil, and enough red wine vinegar to add some bite to it. Salt and pepper to taste. Chill for several hours for the tastes to mingle, but let sit out at room temperature about 20 minutes before serving.

Kathleen Grandjean

VERMICELLI SALAD

1 pound vermicelli	1 cup salad dressing
6 teaspoons seasoning salt	1 large bell pepper
6 tablespoons vegetable oil	1 small jar pimiento
4 tablespoons lemon juice	1 small can chopped black olives
1 cup celery	4 to 6 green onions

Cook vermicelli as directed. Rinse in cold water until cool. Drain. Mix season salt, oil and lemon juice with noodles. Cover and set overnight. Next day, chop celery, pepper and green onions. Add along with the salad dressing, chopped pimiento and chopped olives to salad.

Faye Brooks, Marjorie Cerf

COMPANY PASTA SALAD

1 12-ounce package garden spiral pasta	1 2½-ounce can sliced black olives, drained
1 cup broccoli flowerets	¼ cup sliced green olives
1 pound shrimp, cooked, shelled and deveined	1 can hearts of palm, sliced
1 cup cauliflower flowerets	1 8-ounce bottle low calorie Italian dressing
1 pint cherry tomatoes, halved	Salt and pepper to taste
1 small purple onion, halved and sliced	Garlic salt (optional)

Cook pasta according to package directions. Add broccoli to boiling pasta for last 30 seconds. Drain. Rinse under cold running water. Add shrimp and next 6 ingredients. Toss with ½ bottle of salad dressing. Add salt and pepper (may use garlic salt). Chill for at least 2 hours. Pasta will absorb liquid. Pour remaining salad dressing over salad before serving.

Cindy Wiles

OVERNIGHT PASTA SALAD

1 cup (4 ounces) small shell macaroni
2 cups lettuce, shredded
2 hard cooked eggs, sliced
1 cup ham, cut in julienne strips
1 cup frozen peas, thawed
½ cup Swiss cheese, grated

½ cup mayonnaise
¼ cup sour cream
1 tablespoon green onion, chopped
1 teaspoon prepared mustard
Dash hot pepper sauce
Chopped parsley

Cook macaroni in boiling water. Drain, rinse and drain again. Cool. Place lettuce in bottom of 2-quart casserole or glass bowl. Sprinkle with salt and pepper. Top with macaroni. Layer sliced eggs on top of macaroni. Then top with layers of ham strips, peas and grated cheese. Combine mayonnaise, sour cream, green onion, mustard and hot pepper sauce. Spread over top of salad, sealing to edge of dish. Cover and refrigerate 24 hours or overnight. Sprinkle with parsley, paprika or Parmesan cheese. Toss before serving. Serves 4.

Sue Smith

TURKEY AND PASTA SALAD

4 ounces spiral pasta, uncooked
2 cups cooked turkey (may be smoked)
1 6½-ounce jar marinated
   artichoke hearts
2 large tomatoes, chopped
1 cup fresh mushrooms, sliced
½ cup black olives, sliced
2 tablespoons fresh parsley, chopped

¼ cup vegetable oil
¼ cup red wine vinegar
1 clove garlic, minced
¼ teaspoon salt
¼ teaspoon dried whole basil
⅛ teaspoon pepper
Lettuce leaves

Cook pasta according to package directions, omitting salt. Drain and set aside. Drain artichoke hearts, reserving ¼ cup marinade. Chop artichokes. Combine pasta, turkey, artichokes, tomatoes, mushrooms, olives and parsley. Mix well and set aside. Combine reserved marinade, oil, vinegar, garlic, salt, basil and pepper in a jar. Cover tightly; shake vigorously. Pour over pasta mixture; toss gently. Cover and chill well. Arrange salad over lettuce leaves to serve. Serves 6.

Maurice Buchanan

PINK ADOBE AVOCADO HALVES

(with Chicken in Chili Sauce)

3 cups cooked chicken, cubed
6 large romaine lettuce leaves
3 ripe avocados, halved, peeled, pitted
1 medium tomato, peeled, cut in wedges

3 hard cooked eggs, cut into wedges
12 black olives, pitted
2 tablespoons fresh chives, minced

Dressing:
1 cup mayonnaise
1 cup chili sauce
1 teaspoon capers
1 teaspoon chili powder

1 teaspoon chopped, pickled jalapeño
  Pepper
¼ teaspoon salt
1 teaspoon fresh cilantro, minced

Mix together the dressing ingredients. Add some dressing to the cubed chicken; use just enough to moisten chicken. On chilled plates, place a lettuce leaf and one avocado half per plate. Divide the chicken among the avocados. Garnish plates with tomato, eggs, olives, and sprinkle with chives. Serve remaining dressing on the side. Good served with hot, buttered flour tortillas. Serves 6.

Sherry Crow

CHICKEN SNOW PEA SALAD

5 tablespoons vegetable oil
  (divided use)
½ cup pine nuts
3 garlic cloves, minced (divided use)
½ pound fresh snow peas, ends trimmed
2 red bell peppers, cut in 1-inch pieces

2 cups cut up cooked chicken
2 tablespoons balsamic vinegar
1 tablespoon lemon juice
1 teaspoon Asian sesame oil
¼ teaspoon salt
6 or 7 cups salad greens, assorted

In 3-quart saucepan, heat 1 tablespoon oil and cook pine nuts and 1 clove garlic until golden. Drain on paper towels. Fill pot ¾ full and cook pods and peppers until firm (3 to 4 minutes). Drain well. Rinse under cold water, drain. Add to pot along with 4 tablespoons oil and 2 minced garlic cloves, chicken, vinegar, lemon juice, sesame oil, salt and pine nuts. Toss well. Refrigerate several hours before serving. Serves 4.

Mary Franz

CHICKEN AND RICE SALAD

1 cup cooked chicken, diced
1 cup cooked wild rice
⅓ cup mandarin oranges
1 cup white grapes

1 green scallion, chopped
1 rib of celery, chopped
Slivered almonds

Dressing:

¼ cup mayonnaise
1 tablespoon Durkee dressing
2 tablespoons creamy French dressing

½ teaspoon salt
Dash of pepper
1 tablespoon milk

Mix salad ingredients, except almonds. Mix dressing ingredients. Add to salad, toss and chill. Serve on lettuce leaf. Garnish with orange slices and almonds.

Nina Ross and Mary Jackson

CHICKEN SALAD MOLD

1 4- to 5-pound stewing chicken, cut up
1 teaspoon salt
2 cups water
1 envelope unflavored gelatin
½ cup cold water
1 cup celery, finely chopped

1 cup tiny peas
1 cup blanched almonds, salted, chopped
5 hard cooked eggs, chopped
1½ tablespoons lemon juice
1 teaspoon salt
1 cup mayonnaise

Rub chicken pieces with salt. Place in Dutch oven or large saucepan. Add the 2 cups water and simmer, covered, about 2 hours or until tender. Add water as needed during cooking so that there is always 2 cups of liquid. Remove chicken. Keep broth hot. Cool chicken pieces. Remove meat from bones. Discard skin. Finely chop meat. Soften gelatin in ½ cup water. Add to 2 cups of the hot broth; stir until dissolved. Add remaining ingredients, except mayonnaise. Cool. Fold in mayonnaise. Pour into a 12×8×2-inch pan. Chill until firm. Cut into squares and serve with additional mayonnaise, if desired. Yield 20 portions.

Stella Klein

CHICKEN TACO SALAD

1 cup plain low fat yogurt
⅓ cup mild or hot salsa or taco sauce
1 tablespoon butter
⅓ cup onion, sliced
2 cups cooked chicken, chopped
1 cup canned whole kernel corn, drained
½ cup water

1 package taco seasoning mix
4 cups salad greens, torn
1 cup tomatoes, chopped
⅔ cup green pepper, chopped
¾ cup cheddar cheese, shredded
¾ cup corn chips, broken

Combine yogurt and salsa. Cover and refrigerate 1 to 2 hours to blend flavors. In saucepan, melt butter. Stir in onion, chicken, corn, water and yogurt mixture. Reduce heat to low; simmer 20 minutes. Toss tomatoes and green pepper and combine with torn salad greens. To serve, place tossed greens on 4 serving plates; top each with hot chicken mixture. Sprinkle with cheese and corn chips. Serve immediately. (Approximately 370 calories per serving.)

Annella Collins

SHRIMP SCAMPI SALAD

8 cups assorted salad greens torn
   in small pieces
*1 7-ounce jar roasted red peppers
   drained, coarsely chopped
2 6-ounce jars marinated artichoke
   hearts, drained (reserve marinade)
1 pound medium shrimp, shelled
   and deveined

2 small cloves garlic, crushed
2 tablespoons lemon juice
3 teaspoons honey mustard
2 cups garlic and cheese flavored
   Croutons, freshly made with
   Parmesan cheese and French
   Bread
Pepper and salt

In large bowl or platter, arrange salad greens. Sprinkle with peppers and artichokes. Set aside. In large skillet, heat 6 tablespoons reserved artichoke marinade over medium high heat. Add shrimp and saute until pink and just cooked, about 4½ minutes. Using a slotted spoon, place shrimp on salad greens. To drippings in pan, add garlic, lemon juice and mustard. Bring to boil, stirring. If necessary, boil to reduce liquid to ½ cup. Stir in ½ teaspoon pepper and ¼ teaspoon salt. Pour liquid over salad greens. Toss to coat. Sprinkle with croutons. Serve immediately. Serves 4 to 6.

* Sun-dried tomatoes may be substituted for roasted red peppers.

Peggy Dawson

SHRIMP REMOULADE

1 pint small curd cottage cheese	8 teaspoons fresh parsley, chopped fine
1½ cups mayonnaise	1 teaspoon paprika
½ teaspoon salt	¾ teaspoon cayenne pepper
1 teaspoon sugar	1 teaspoon mustard
3 teaspoons lemon juice	2½ quarts water
3 teaspoons onion, finely grated	2 bay leaves
1 clove garlic, large pod crushed or grated very fine	Salt
	Juice and rind of 1 lemon
8 teaspoons celery, cut very fine	1½ pounds frozen shrimp, shelled

Drain cottage cheese in colander. Stir well several times to remove some of the cream. Drain while preparing other ingredients. Combine mayonnaise and next 10 ingredients; place in a large bowl, add cottage cheese and mix well.

Boil water with bay leaves, salt and lemon for 5 minutes. Add frozen shrimp, bring to a boil again. Cook shrimp only 2 minutes. Drain immediately. While shrimp are still hot, cut and add to prepared mixture. If shrimp are very small, do not cut. Mix well and store in covered jar or bowl. Refrigerate. *Must marinate overnight!* May be used as a dip with crackers or to stuff tomatoes or avocados.

Joyce Doyle Murphey

TUNA MOUSSE

1 envelope unflavored gelatin	1 tablespoon green onion, minced
2 tablespoons lemon juice	1 teaspoon prepared mustard
½ cup chicken broth	1 teaspoon dried dill weed
½ cup mayonnaise	¼ teaspoon white pepper
¼ cup milk (or half-and-half)	1 7-ounce can tuna, drained
2 tablespoons parsley, chopped	½ cup cucumbers, shredded

Soften gelatin in lemon juice in a large bowl. Heat broth and add milk, parsley, onion, mustard, dill and pepper; add gelatin mix. Beat until frothy. Fold in tuna and cucumber. Turn into a 2 cup mold. Chill until firm.

Carol Russell

SALMON MOUSSE

1 tablespoon unflavored gelatin
½ cup water
1 16-ounce can salmon
1 tablespoon capers, chopped
½ cup whipping cream
½ cup celery, diced

¼ cup green pepper, minced
1 tablespoon onion, grated
1 tablespoon lemon juice
½ cup mayonnaise
1 teaspoon salt
¼ teaspoon pepper

Soften gelatin in water and dissolve over hot water; mix again and cool. Mash salmon, including liquid. Add capers and blend well. Whip cream and add to salmon mixture. Then add celery, green pepper, onion, lemon juice, mayonnaise, salt and pepper and blend well. Stir in the gelatin and pour into an oiled fish mold (or any mold). Chill until set. Unmold and garnish with watercress, cucumber, lemon slices and sliced pimiento. Serve with sauce.

Sour cream dill sauce:
1 cup sour cream
1 tablespoon lemon juice
1 teaspoon grated onion

1 tablespoon chopped fresh dill, or
    2 healthy teaspoons of dill weed
Salt and pepper

Blend well.

Carole Cohen

SALMON MOLD

1 10¾-ounce can tomato soup
6 ounces cream cheese
1½ envelopes unflavored gelatin
1 cup celery, chopped
1 cup pecans, toasted and chopped

1 dash onion salt
½ cup salad dressing
    Sliced olives to taste
1 9½-ounce can red sockeye
    Salmon, skin and bone removed

Combine soup and cheese in blender or mixer. Place over heat and bring to boiling point. Add gelatin which has been softened in 2 tablespoons of cold water. Add remaining ingredients. Tuna may be substituted for salmon.

Lula Stewart

CRANBERRY RELISH

2 12-ounce packages fresh cranberries
3 apples, pared, cored, diced
2 pears, pared, cored, diced
2 cups golden raisins
2 cups sugar

1 cup fresh orange juice
2 tablespoons grated orange peel
2 teaspoons cinnamon
1/4 teaspoon nutmeg
1/2 cup orange liqueur

Combine all ingredients except liqueur in saucepan and heat to boiling. Reduce heat and simmer uncovered about 5 minutes or until cranberries pop. Stir in liqueur. Refrigerate covered, 4 hours or overnight. Serve slightly chilled. Serves 10 to 12 generously.

Stella Klein

AVOCADO GRAPEFRUIT SALAD

3 large grapefruits, peeled and
    sectioned (about 2 cups)

2 large ripe avocados, peeled, sliced
1 large sweet onion, sliced

Dressing:
1/4 cup vinegar
1/4 cup undiluted frozen orange juice
    Juice of 1 lemon
1/2 teaspoon salt

2 teaspoons orange peel, grated
1/4 cup sugar
1/2 teaspoon dry mustard
1 cup salad oil

Mix dressing ingredients and pour over salad. Cover and refrigerate overnight. To serve, lightly turn salad and arrange on leaf of Boston lettuce. Keeps for several days and additional fruit may be added to the marinade. This makes a wonderful luncheon dish, served with hot bread. Serves 8.

Manilla Franks

BERRY SALAD

1 envelope honey mustard salad
  dressing mix
¼ cup apple cider vinegar
2 tablespoons orange juice
½ cup salad oil
8 cups assorted greens (spinach,
  romaine lettuce, leaf lettuce)

2 cups assorted berries, (raspberries,
  blueberries, sliced strawberries)
1 8-ounce package frozen sugar
  snap peas, thawed
½ cup toasted pecans or slivered
  Almonds

Prepare dressing as directed on package, using vinegar and oil and substituting orange juice for the water. Toss with the remaining ingredients in large bowl. Makes 4 to 6 servings. (I have added cooked chicken breast strips, for a beautiful luncheon salad.)

Barbara Swearingen

JERRY'S FROZEN FRUIT SALAD

16 marshmallows
2 tablespoons strawberry juice
1 cup (frozen) crushed strawberries,
  thawed

½ cup crushed pineapple, drained
1 3-ounce package cream cheese
½ cup mayonnaise
1 cup whipping cream

Melt marshmallows in strawberry juice in double boiler. Cool. Add strawberries and pineapple after cooling. Soften cream cheese; add mayonnaise and whipped whipping cream. Fold together. Then fold into cooled fruit and juice mixture. Freeze in muffin tins with paper liners. May be doubled, but add only a *little* more mayonnaise when doubling. Makes about 24 when doubled.

Marilyn Thomas

PINEAPPLE CUCUMBER SALAD

(It's a Dilly)

1 No. 2-can pineapple chunks
1 large cucumber, sliced thin
4 tablespoons sour cream

Salt and pepper to taste
Dill weed to taste

Mix pineapple and cucumber, add sour cream. Sprinkle with salt, pepper and dill weed. Toss, then chill 1 hour.

Frances Collins

TWENTY-FOUR HOUR SALAD

2 cups white cherries, pitted, halved
2 cups diced pineapple
2 cups orange sections

½ pound miniature marshmallows
½ to ¾ pound green seedless
   grapes
½ to ¾ cup pecan pieces

Sauce:
  2 eggs
  2 tablespoons sugar
  ¼ cup light cream

Juice of one lemon
1 cup heavy cream, whipped
Maraschino cherries
Fresh mint leaves

Combine well-drained fruits, marshmallows and nuts. Beat eggs until light, gradually add sugar, light cream and lemon juice. Mix and cook in double boiler until smooth and thick, stirring *constantly*. Allow to cool. Fold in whipped cream, pour mixture over fruit and mix lightly. Chill 24 hours but do not freeze. Garnish with big red maraschino cherries and fresh mint, if possible.

Gladys Norman

BLUEBERRY SALAD

1 6-ounce package black raspberry
   gelatin
2 cups hot liquid (water plus juice from
   blueberries and pineapple to
   make 2 cups)

½ cup cold water
1 can blueberries, drained,
   reserve liquid
1 cup crushed pineapple, drained,
   reserve liquid

Bring water and juices to boil. Dissolve gelatin and add drained fruit and cold water. Chill until firm and cover with topping.

Topping:
  1 8-ounce package cream cheese,
    softened
  1 cup sour cream

¼ cup sugar
½ teaspoon vanilla
½ cup chopped pecans

Cream the first 4 ingredients and spread on the top of salad. Sprinkle with pecans. Serves 8.

Doris LaPorte

ORANGE-PINEAPPLE BAVARIAN

1 11-ounce can mandarin oranges
1 8¾-ounce can crushed pineapple
1 3-ounce package orange or orange/
   pineapple gelatin

2 tablespoons sugar
1 cup boiling water
1 teaspoon grated orange rind
1 envelope whipped topping mix

Drain fruits, measuring ¾ cup of the combined syrups. Dissolve gelatin and sugar in boiling water. Add orange rind and measured syrup. Chill until slightly thickened. Prepare whipped topping mix as directed on package (or use 1 carton whipped topping). Blend 1½ cups into the gelatin mixture. Chill until thickened. Fold in fruits. Chill until firm. Makes 5 cups or 8 servings.

Maxine Brown

MANGO SALAD

3 3-ounce packages lemon gelatin
3 cups boiling water
8 ounces cream cheese

1 large can mangos, drain (reserve juice)
1 cup mango juice

Dressing:
1 16-ounce carton sour cream
   Honey (to taste)

Brown sugar, to sprinkle on top

Dissolve gelatin in boiling water in large bowl. Blend mangos, juice and cream cheese in blender and add to gelatin mixture. Gel in refrigerator. Mix sour cream and honey for dressing. Sprinkle brown sugar over all. Serves 8. This salad goes well with *everything:* beef, pork, fish, game, Mexican, Italian, etc. It's quick and can be made a day or two ahead.

Susie Yeckel

RIBBON SALAD

5 3-ounce packages gelatin dessert
    used in the following order:
        black cherry, blackberry or grape
        lime
        lemon
        orange
        strawberry

1⅔ cups sour cream

Use 6×8-inch or 8×10-inch glass dish to make layers thin and even. Be sure refrigerator shelves are level.

Add 1 cup hot water to 1 package gelatin. Divide this liquid in half; slowly add ½ to ⅓ cup sour cream. Pour in dish and chill 30 minutes or until set. Add 3 tablespoons cold water to remaining half of gelatin mixture. Pour on top of "sett" layer and chill another 30 minutes. Continue with remaining packages of gelatin, adding another layer every half hour until 10 layers are formed.

Note: Don't be discouraged by instructions. It is truly worth the effort.

Sondra Juetten

CEASAR SALAD

1 head romaine lettuce, torn into
    bite sized pieces
2 cloves garlic
⅜ cup olive oil
½ tablespoon Worcestershire sauce
½ teaspoon Tabasco
½ teaspoon salt
½ teaspoon pepper
    until brown

¼ lemon, juiced and strained
½ teaspoon dry mustard
1 egg, beaten
4 slices bacon, fried crisp and crumbled
1 ounce anchovy fillets, chopped into
    very small bits (optional)
½ cup Parmesan cheese
¾ cup croutons, baked at 200 degrees

Place olive oil and pressed garlic in wooden bowl 1 hour prior to making salad. (Alternatively, use olive oil that has had garlic soaking in it for a week or two and forget the pressed garlic.) Add Worcestershire sauce, Tabasco, salt, pepper, lemon and dry mustard, and mix. Just before serving add lettuce and egg and toss well. Then add bacon, anchovies, Parmesan and croutons, and toss again. Serves 4.

Greg Baker

GREEK SALAD

½ head romaine lettuce
½ head iceberg lettuce
1 cucumber, peeled and sliced
1 bell pepper, sliced
½ red onion, thinly sliced
2 celery stalks, chopped
1 large tomato, diced

½ cup black olives, sliced
8 ounces feta cheese, crumbled
⅓ cup lemon juice
⅓ cup oil
½ teaspoon dried oregano, crumbled
½ teaspoon dried dill weed
½ teaspoon pepper

Tear romaine and iceberg lettuce into pieces. Combine with cucumber, pepper, onion, celery, tomato and olives in a large salad bowl. Sprinkle with feta cheese. Whisk lemon juice, oil, herbs and pepper in a small bowl to blend. Pour over salad and toss well. Serves 8.

Nancy Bogardus

SUFFERN INN SALAD

6 tablespoons mayonnaise
  Juice of 1 lemon
1 small onion, finely minced, or
  2 tablespoons minced chives
8 slices crisp bacon, crumbled

2 cups frozen peas, unthawed
1 cup Swiss or cheddar cheese strips
  Salt and pepper to taste
2 cups lettuce, torn in bite size pieces

Twenty-four hours before serving, combine mayonnaise, lemon juice, onion, frozen peas, and cheese strips in a bowl. Stir well. Add salt and pepper to taste; cover and refrigerate. Before serving, add lettuce and bacon, toss well and taste again. Serves 6.

Greta Rees

CALCUTTA SALAD

½ pound fresh spinach, torn
1 head romaine lettuce

1 bunch scallions, chopped
1 cup broken cashews

Dressing:
¾ cup vegetable oil
¼ cup vinegar
¼ cup plain or pineapple yogurt
1 tablespoon Dijon mustard

1 tablespoon chopped chutney
1 teaspoon salt
½ teaspoon curry powder
1 tart apple, grated, unpeeled

Combine spinach, romaine and scallions. Combine dressing ingredients and mix well (may use a blender). Toss with salad greens. Add nuts and toss again lightly. Serves 8. The unusual flavor of this slightly different green salad compliments grilled fish or meat. Try it with shrimp saffron.

Susan Wells

SPINACH SALAD

8 ounces colored swirl macaroni
1 10-ounce package fresh spinach
8 ounces mozzarella cheese, shredded
8 ounces cooked ham, cut small

1 4-ounce can green chilies
½ cup sliced black olives
¼ cup chopped pimiento

Cook and cool macaroni. Wash and tear spinach. Mix all ingredients and toss with Parmesan Pepper dressing.

Nell Denman

LIZ'S SPINACH SALAD

1 1-pound bag spinach
3 tablespoons soy sauce
3 tablespoons salad oil
1½ teaspoons sugar

3 tablespoons vinegar
1 small clove garlic, minced
3 tablespoons sesame seeds
1 11-ounce can mandarin oranges, drained

Wash and chill spinach. Combine other ingredients, except mandarin oranges. Just before serving, pour dressing over spinach; add mandarin oranges. Toss lightly. Serves 4 to 6.

Liz Minyard

A DIFFERENT SPINACH SALAD

1 10-ounce bag spinach, washed
1 8-ounce can water chestnuts,
    sliced
1 14-ounce can bean sprouts, drained

8 ounces fresh mushrooms, sliced
4 hard-cooked eggs, sliced
¼ pound bacon, fried crisp, crumbled

Dressing:
1 cup salad oil
¼ cup vinegar
½ cup catsup

¾ cup sugar
1 tablespoon Worcestershire sauce
¾ to 1 cup chopped onion

In a blender or jar, combine ingredients. Refrigerate overnight. Shake or stir well before serving over salad. In a large bowl, toss salad ingredients. Add dressing. Serves 8 to 10.

Variation: Fresh bean sprouts may be substituted for canned sprouts.

Jeanne Bryant

INDIAN SPINACH SALAD

8 cups fresh spinach
1½ cups apples, pared, chopped
½ cup raisins

½ cup salted peanuts
3 tablespoons green onion, chopped

Dressing:
¼ cup white wine vinegar
¼ cup salad oil
3 tablespoons chutney

2 tablespoons sugar
½ teaspoon salt
1½ teaspoons curry powder

Combine dressing ingredients in jar. Cover, shake and chill. Clean spinach and tear into bite-size pieces. Place in bowl; top with apples, raisins, peanuts, and onion. Pour dressing over all and toss.

Beatrice M. Haggerty

My Favorite Salads

BREADS

—◼—

GARDEN GOURMET
COOKBOOK

POPPY SEED MUFFINS

2½ cups sugar
3 eggs
1 cup vegetable shortening
1½ cups milk
1½ teaspoons vanilla

1½ teaspoons almond extract
3 cups flour
1½ teaspoons baking powder
⅓ cup poppy seeds

Cream sugar and eggs. Blend in shortening, milk, vanilla and almond flavors. Add flour and other dry ingredients. For a large loaf pan, bake at 325 degrees for 50 minutes. For small muffin tins, bake at 325 degrees for 10 to 12 minutes.

Glaze:

¾ cup sugar
½ teaspoon almond extract
2 tablespoons margarine

½ teaspoon vanilla
1¼ to 1⅓ cups orange juice

Mix all ingredients. Heat to a boil and pour over loaves or muffins.

Mary Scoggins and Kala Casebolt

BRAN MUFFINS

1 15-ounce box raisin bran cereal
5 cups flour
3 cups sugar
2 teaspoons salt
5 teaspoons baking soda

1 quart buttermilk
1 cup oil
8 egg whites (or 4 whole eggs)
2 cups chopped nuts (optional)

Mix dry ingredients well. Mix oil, eggs, and buttermilk with beater. Add to dry ingredients; mix thoroughly. Fill muffin cups ¾ full. Bake at 400 degrees for 20 to 25 minutes. Dough can be refrigerated up to 6 weeks if you want to bake a few at a time. Also freezes well after baking. Makes 6 dozen.

A. Schmieman and B. Copeland

BLENDER BRAN MUFFINS

1 cup flour
1/2 teaspoon salt
2 1/2 teaspoons baking powder
3 tablespoons shortening

1/4 cup sugar
1 egg
1 cup bran
3/4 cup milk

Sift flour, salt and baking powder into a bowl. Put shortening, sugar, egg, bran and milk into container; cover and process until blended. Pour into flour mixture, mixing only until flour is moistened. Fill greased muffin pans 2/3 full. Bake at 400 degrees for 30 minutes. Makes 12 muffins. May add 2 ripe bananas to blender contents to make Banana Bran Muffins

Sadie Caropresi

NEW YORK LUNCHEONETTE CORN MUFFINS

1 cup all-purpose flour
1 cup yellow cornmeal
1 tablespoon baking powder
1 teaspoon salt

1/3 cup solid vegetable shortening
1/3 cup sugar
2 large eggs
1 cup milk

Heat oven to 425 degrees. Grease twelve 2 to 2 1/2-inch muffin pan cups. Mix flour, cornmeal, baking powder and salt in medium-sized bowl. Using electric mixer, cream shortening and sugar in large bowl until fluffy. Beat in eggs to blend well, then milk. Stir flour mixture into milk mixture only until just blended. Spoon batter into prepared muffin pan cups, filling each 2/3 full. Bake 18 to 20 minutes until lightly browned and sharp knife inserted in muffin comes out clean. Makes 12 muffins. (Makes 8 to 10 jumbo muffins. Bake a bit longer.)

Deborah Grant

BLUEBERRY MUFFINS

1/4 cup butter
1/2 cup sugar
1 egg
1/2 cup milk

1 1/2 cups flour
2 teaspoons baking powder
1/4 teaspoon salt
3/4 cup blueberries

Heat oven to 350 degrees. Cream butter and sugar. Add egg and milk. Stir in flour, baking powder and salt until moistened. Batter will be lumpy. Stir in blueberrries. Divide batter among 12 well-greased muffin cups. Bake 20 to 25 minutes.

Sue Matlock

BLUEBERRY MUFFINS

1½ cups plus 4 tablespoons whole wheat
    pastry flour
6 teaspoons low sodium baking powder
4 tablespoons date powder
2 cups plus 4 tablespoons uncooked
    old-fashion rolled oats

4 teaspoons pumpkin pie spice mix
4 egg whites, beaten slightly
1 cup fresh orange juice
1 cup skim milk
½ cup apple juice concentrate
1 cup blueberries (fresh or frozen)

Combine first five dry ingredients in large mixing bowl, stirring to blend. In another bowl combine egg, juice, milk and apple juice concentrate. Pour liquid ingredients into dry ingredients, stirring with wooden spoon until all liquid is absorbed. Fold in blueberries. Fill *foil-lined* muffin pans ¾-full with batter (do *not* use paper liners). Bake in preheated 400 degree oven for 25 minutes. Muffins should be well-browned. Remove from oven, placing muffin pans on cooling rack. Allow to cool 10 minutes before removing muffins from foil liners. Makes 24 muffins.

Tonya Calhoun

ZUCCHINI NUT MUFFINS

3 eggs, lightly beaten
1 cup oil
1 tablespoon vanilla
2 cups zucchini, shredded, unpeeled
1 tablespoon cinnamon
½ teaspoon ground cloves

1 teaspoon salt
¼ teaspoon baking powder
2 cups sugar
2 cups flour
1½ teaspoons soda
1 cup nuts, chopped

Mix eggs, oil, vanilla and zucchini. Stir in remaining ingredients, but do not beat. When ready to use, fill cups ⅔ full and bake 20 minutes at 400 degrees. Yields 3 dozen muffins or 2 large loaves (bake loaves 1 hour at 350 degrees). Batter may be refrigerated up to two weeks and used as needed.

June Thomes

COFFEE RING

1 package dry yeast	¾ cup milk
¼ cup warm water	4¼ cups flour
1 cup margarine	2 small eggs
3 tablespoons sugar	½ teaspoon vanilla
1 teaspoon salt	

Filling:

1 cup pecans, chopped	1 cup Granny Smith apples, chopped
1 cup white raisins	1 cup canned apricots, drained well
⅔ cup brown sugar	and chopped
1 teaspoon cinnamon	

Dissolve yeast in warm water (115 to 120 degrees) and set aside. Cream margarine, sugar and salt in large bowl. Add milk, 1 cup flour, yeast mixture, eggs and vanilla and beat well. Add another cup of flour and beat again. Gradually incorporate remaining flour, using hands, if necessary. Place in greased bowl, turning once to grease surface; cover and let rise in warm place for 2 hours. Punch down and divide into 2 parts. Let rest for 10 minutes.

Combine filling ingredients. On a floured surface, roll one part of dough to a 9×15-inch rectangle. Sprinkle with half of filling. Fold in half lengthwise, pinching edges under to seal. Form a circle and join edges together. With scissors, make 1-inch slits on outside edge about an inch apart. Turn the sections sideways a bit to expose a little of the filling. Repeat the process for the second ring. Bake at 350 degrees for 20 to 25 minutes. Remove from pan immediately and place on serving platter. Glaze.

Glaze: Sift 2 cups confectioners' sugar. Add 1 tablespoon fresh-squeezed lemon juice and enough hot water to allow the glaze to flow from a spoon. Drizzle glaze over the warm coffee ring and decorate with a few pecan halves.

Kathleen Grandjean

MORNING GLORY MUFFINS

2 cups flour
1 cup sugar
2 teaspoons baking soda
2 teaspoons cinnamon
½ teaspoon salt
2 cups carrots, peeled and finely shredded
½ cup raisins

½ cup walnuts, chopped
½ cup shredded coconut
1 large tart green apple, cored, peeled, and chopped
⅔ cup oil
3 eggs

Preheat oven to 350 degrees. Grease 18 muffin cups or line with paper liners. Mix together flour, sugar, baking soda, cinnamon and salt, blending well. Add carrots, raisins, nuts, coconut and apple to dry ingredients. In separate bowl combine eggs, oil. Add to flour mixture, mixing just until all ingredients are moistened. Do not over mix. Batter will be stiff. Fill muffin cups and bake 20 to 25 minutes or until brown and toothpick inserted in center comes out clean. Makes 18 muffins.

Laura Arnone

FAVORITE PUMPKIN MUFFINS

2 cups flour
1½ cups whole-wheat flour
1 teaspoon salt
1 teaspoon cinnamon
1 teaspoon allspice
1 teaspoon nutmeg
1 cup raisins or nuts

1½ cups sugar
¾ cup vegetable oil
4 eggs, slightly beaten
1 teaspoon vanilla
⅔ cup water
1 16-ounce can pumpkin

Measure dry ingredients into mixer bowl; mix. Make a well in center and add remaining ingredients except raisins or nuts. Blend until moistened. Add raisins or nuts. Fill muffin cups or tins sprayed with vegetable oil. Bake at 350 degrees for about 20 minutes or until toothpick inserted in middle comes out clean. Cooking time will vary with size of muffin tins used. Makes 36 regular muffins.

Marsella Fults

SOUR CREAM COFFEE CAKE

Batter:

½ cup margarine
1 cup sugar
2 eggs
¼ teaspoon salt
1 cup sour cream

1 teaspoon vanilla
2 cups sifted flour
1 teaspoon soda
1 teaspoon baking powder

Topping:

½ cup brown sugar
1 cup flour

1 cup nuts
½ teaspoon cinnamon
4 tablespoons butter or margarine

Preheat oven to 350 degrees. Cream margarine and sugar. Add eggs one at a time. Add salt and vanilla. Sift dry ingredients and add alternately with sour cream, beating on slow speed just until smooth. Begin and end with addition of dry ingredients. Spread half of batter in greased 9×13-inch baking pan. Sprinkle with half of topping. Add remaining batter and cover with remainder of topping. Bake for 35 to 40 minutes.

Susan Rumble

APPLE PIE MUFFINS (VEGETARIAN)

2 tablespoons tofu
3 large ripe bananas (1½ cups) mashed
  Egg substitute for 1 egg
3 tablespoons sunflower oil
⅓ cup honey
1 cup whole-wheat pastry flour
1 scant cup oat flour
1 tablespoon soy flour

2 teaspoons baking powder
½ teaspoon baking soda
2 teaspoons ground cinnamon
  Pinch of salt (optional)
2 cups sliced, peeled apples, cut in
  ½-inch dice
1 teaspoon lemon juice
½ cup presoaked raisins

Preheat oven to 375 degrees. Cream tofu, bananas, egg substitute, oil and honey with a hand blender or food processor. Combine flours, baking powder and baking soda, 1 teaspoon cinnamon, and salt in a large bowl. Make a well in center and fold in creamed mixture with a spatula until moistened. Combine apples, remaining teaspoon cinnamon, lemon juice, and raisins. Add to batter. Oil muffin cups, then spoon batter into cups and bake 25 to 30 minutes. Muffins are ready when toothpick inserted in center comes out clean. Cool briefly and turn out on wire rack to finish cooling. Makes 12 muffins.

DyAnna Giltner

No-Fat Eggless Muffins

Basic Recipe:

1½ cups all-purpose flour
¾ cup sugar
2 teaspoons baking powder
¼ teaspoon baking soda (optional)

½ teaspoon salt
⅔ cup plain nonfat yogurt
⅔ cup skim milk
½ cup blueberries or grated apple

In large mixing bowl combine flour, sugar, baking powder, baking soda and salt. Gently stir in yogurt and milk, blending just until dry ingredients are moistened. Fold in fruit. Fill lightly greased (sprayed) non-stick muffin pan cups ¾ full. Bake at 400 degrees for 18 minutes or until well browned. Makes approximately 12 muffins. These freeze well. Optionally, use ⅓ cup skim milk and ⅓ cup undiluted orange juice and ½ cup dried cranberries.

Variation:

1½ cups whole-wheat flour
½ cup brown sugar
¼ teaspoon allspice
1 teaspoon cinnamon
1 tablespoon baking powder
½ teaspoon salt

¼ cup raisins
2 cups carrots or zucchini, shredded
2 teaspoons vanilla
⅔ cup plain nonfat yogurt
⅔ cup skim milk

Prepare as above. For those who don't like the baking soda taste, these rise beautifully without it. Top baked muffin with nonfat cream cheese to which 1 packet of sweetener has been added.

Edie Gottschall

Date Muffins

3 eggs
¾ cup sugar
1 package chopped dates

2 tablespoons flour
1 cup nuts, chopped

Mix eggs and sugar. Add other ingredients and mix well. Bake in small muffin tins 25 to 30 minutes at 250 degrees.

Gayla Ross

BROWN SUGAR BREAKFAST BARS

1 cup butter or margarine
1 cup brown sugar
¾ cup granulated sugar
2 teaspoons vanilla
2 large eggs
1 tablespoon white corn syrup
2 cups all-purpose flour

1 cup quick cooking oats
1 teaspoon baking soda
¼ teaspoon salt
½ teaspoon baking powder
½ cup raisins
1 cup nuts
1½ cups angel flake coconut

Beat butter, sugars and vanilla together until creamy. Mix in eggs and syrup. Combine flour, oats, baking soda, baking powder and salt. Add to butter mixture and blend well. Stir in raisins, nuts and coconut. Spread dough into a buttered 10×15-inch pan. Bake at 350 degrees about 40 minutes or until center feels firm when lightly touched. Cool, then cut into bars. Serve warm or cool. Freezes well. Serves 8 to 10.

Glenna Clayton

CREAM CHEESE BANANA BREAD

1 cup sugar
½ cup margarine
2 eggs
3 bananas, mashed
1 teaspoon salt

1 teaspoon soda
3 tablespoons sour cream
2 cups flour
1 cup nuts, chopped

Cream Cheese Mixture:
8 ounces cream cheese
⅓ cup sugar

1 egg
1 tablespoon flour

Mix 1 cup sugar, margarine, and 2 eggs. Add bananas, salt, the soda dissolved in the sour cream, and 2 cups flour. Mix well and add nuts. Divide ⅔ of this mixture into 2 greased and floured loaf pans. Combine cream cheese mixture ingredients and add to first mixture in pans. Put the rest of the first mixture on top. Bake at 350 degrees for 1 hour. Test for doneness.

Peggy Ernst

BANANA NUT BREAD

3/4 cup margarine
1 1/2 cups sugar
3 eggs
3 3/4 cups flour
1 1/2 teaspoons baking powder
1 teaspoon baking soda

1 teaspoon salt
1 teaspoon vanilla
3 bananas, overripe, mashed
1 cup nuts, chopped
6 tablespoons buttermilk (or mix sweet milk with 1 teaspoon lemon juice)

Cream margarine and sugar. Add eggs. Sift together flour, baking powder, baking soda and salt and add to mixture. Add vanilla, bananas, nuts and buttermilk. Mix well and divide equally into 2 greased 5×9-inch loaf pans. Bake at 350 degrees for one hour.

Ralph Livengood

BANANA TEA BREAD

1/4 cup walnuts or pecans, chopped
3 tablespoons buttermilk
1 teaspoon baking soda
2/3 cup sugar
1/3 cup canola oil

2 ripe bananas, mashed
3 egg whites, beaten
1 cup unbleached flour
1 cup whole wheat flour

Preheat oven to 350 degrees. Toast nuts in 350 degree oven 10 minutes and let cool. Spray loaf pan with vegetable oil spray. Combine buttermilk and soda; set aside. Cream sugar and oil; add mashed banana. Add flours and toasted nuts alternately with buttermilk mixutre. Pour into prepared loaf pan. Bake 45 to 50 minutes. Makes 1 loaf (about 20 slices). Freezes well.

Pat Yanigan

LEMON BREAD

1 cup margarine
2 cups sugar
4 eggs
½ teaspoon salt
½ teaspoon baking soda

3 cups flour, sifted
1 cup buttermilk
Grated rind of 1 lemon
1 cup pecans, chopped

Glaze:

Juice of 2 lemons

1 cup confectioners' sugar

Cream margarine and sugar. Blend in eggs. Sift together salt, soda and flour. Add alternately with buttermilk. Add lemon rind and nuts. Grease two 9×5-inch loaf pans. Line bottom with wax paper. Bake at 300 degrees for 40 minutes. Bread is done when straw poked in center comes out clean. If not done, reduce temperature and cook until done. For glaze, mix lemon juice and confectioners' sugar. Punch holes in bread with toothpick and pour glaze over bread while still warm.

Madalynne Callahan

STRAWBERRY NUT BREAD

3 cups sifted flour
1 teaspoon baking soda
1 teaspoon salt
1 tablespoon cinnamon
2 cups sugar

4 eggs, beaten
1¼ cups vegetable oil
2 cups frozen sliced strawberries, thawed
1¼ cups pecans, chopped

Sift dry ingredients together into a large mixing bowl. Combine remaining ingredients, mixing well. Make well in center of dry ingredients. Add liquid mixture, stirring just enough to moisten dry ingredients. Pour into 2 greased 9×5×3-inch pans or 6 greased 6×3×2-inch pans. Bake in 350 degree oven 1 hour for large pans or 40 minutes for small pans. Remove from oven and let cool 5 minutes before removing from pans. Remove from pans and finish cooling on wire racks. Makes 2 large or 6 small loaves.

Doris Westermeier

ORANGE SLICE BREAD

16 ounces orange slice candy
2 cups nuts, chopped
8 ounces dates, chopped
½ cup flour
1 cup margarine
2 cups brown sugar
5 eggs

¾ cup buttermilk
1 teaspoon vanilla
3 cups flour
1 teaspoon baking powder
1 teaspoon soda
½ teaspoon salt

Cut orange slice candy into small pieces with scissors. Put the dates, nuts and candy in a bowl and coat them with ½ cup flour. Beat together margarine and brown sugar, then add the eggs and remaining ingredients and mix. Stir in the date, nut, candy mixture. Put batter into 3 greased and floured loaf pans. Bake at 350 degrees about 1 hour (or less).

Glaze:

¼ cup lemon juice
½ cup orange juice

1½ cups confectioners' sugar

Mix well and pour over warm loaves after poking holes in the top of them. Use all of the mixture.

Peggy Ernst

PUMPKIN BREAD

3 cups sugar
1 cup liquid oil
4 eggs, beaten
2 cups pumpkin, cooked, mashed or
   one 16-ounce can pumpkin
3½ cups all-purpose flour
1 teaspoon baking powder
2 teaspoons salt

2 teaspoons soda
½ teaspoon ground cloves
1 teaspoon ground cinnamon
1 teaspoon ground nutmeg
1 teaspoon ground allspice
⅔ cup water
1 to 1½ cups chopped pecans (optional)

Combine sugar, oil and eggs; beat until light and fluffy. Stir in pumpkin. Combine dry ingredients and stir into pumpkin mixture. Add water and nuts, mixing well. Spoon batter into 2 well-greased 9¼×5¼×2¾-inch loaf pans. Bake at 350 degrees for 65 to 75 minutes. Makes 2 loaves.

Sarah Gardenhire

GRANDMOTHER'S GINGERBREAD

½ cup brown sugar
½ cup vegetable shortening
2 eggs
¼ cup molasses
1¼ cups sifted flour
¼ teaspoon salt

1 teaspoon baking soda
¼ teaspoon baking powder
1¼ teaspoons ginger
1 teaspoon cinnamon
¼ teaspoon ground cloves
½ cup hot water

Citrus Fluff:

1 egg
½ cup sugar
1 teaspoon grated orange rind
1 teaspoon grated lemon rind

2 tablespoons lemon juice
1 cup whipping cream, whipped
Twist of orange

In large bowl, combine sugar, shortening, eggs and molasses; blend well. Combine flour, salt, soda, baking powder and spices, gradually blend into molasses mixture. Blend in hot water. Pour batter into greased and floured 9×9×2-inch baking pan. Bake at 350 degrees for 25 to 30 minutes. Serve warm with Citrus Fluff. Make fluff by beating egg, sugar, rind and lemon juice in a small pan. Cook and stir over low heat until thickened (about 5 minutes). Cool thoroughly, then fold in whipped whipping cream. Chill. Spoon onto squares of warm gingerbread. Garnish with twist of orange.

Kala Casebolt

CARROT BREAD

1 cup sugar
⅔ cup salad oil (scant)
1½ cups flour
1 teaspoon baking powder
¾ teaspoon soda
1 teaspoon cinnamon

1 teaspoon salt
1 cup carrots, grated
2 eggs
½ cup pecans, chopped
1 (small) can crushed pineapple,
  drained (optional)

Mix sugar and salad oil in bowl. Sift flour, baking powder, soda, cinnamon and salt together and add to first mixture. Add carrots, eggs and pecans. Add pineapple if desired; it does enhance it. Pour in loaf pan and bake at 350 degrees for 1 hour.

Chris Sefcik

ZUCCHINI BREAD

2 cups unpeeled zucchini, grated
2 cups sugar
1 cup vegetable oil
3 eggs, slightly beaten
2 teaspoons vanilla
3 cups flour

1 teaspoon baking soda
1 teaspoon salt
½ teaspoon cinnamon
1 cup nuts, chopped
½ teaspoon grated lemon rind
1 cup raisins (optional)

Drain zucchini well; combine with sugar, oil, eggs and vanilla in large bowl. Add flour, baking soda, salt and cinnamon. Stir in nuts, rind and raisins. Divide batter into 2 well-greased 9×5×3-inch loaf pans. Bake at 350 degrees for 70 minutes. Cool in pans 10 minutes; turn out on rack. Can also be baked in muffin tins. Makes 2 loaves.

Joyce Doyle Murphey

MELT IN YOUR MOUTH SOUR CREAM ROLLS

1 cup sour cream
1½ packages dry yeast
⅓ cup warm water
1 cup butter

½ cup sugar
½ teaspoon salt
4 cups flour
2 eggs, well beaten

Heat sour cream in a double boiler until slightly yellow around the edges. Soften yeast in warm water and let stand for 15 minutes. Place butter, sugar and salt in a large bowl. Add sour cream and stir until butter melts. Cool to lukewarm. Blend 1 cup flour into the sour cream mixture and beat until smooth. Stir in yeast until well mixed. Add second cup of flour and beat until smooth. Add beaten eggs. Add remaining 2 cups of flour, one at a time. Cover and refrigerate at least 6 hours (overnight is best). Roll out dough on a floured surface and cut into desired shapes. Brush with melted butter and let rise about 1 hour. Bake at 375 degrees for 10 to 15 minutes or until golden brown.

Lynda Sanders

POTECA (CZECH SWEET BREAD)

1 package yeast
3 tablespoons warm water
2 eggs, beaten
¼ cup sugar

½ cup melted shortening
1 teaspoon salt
1 cup warm water
4 cups flour

Dissolve yeast in 3 tablespoons warm water. Set aside. Add sugar, shortening and salt to beaten eggs in a large bowl. Add yeast mixture and 1 cup warm water. Add flour. Mix and knead and place in refrigerator, covered, overnight. Take dough out of refrigerator and divide into two parts. Roll each part out on floured board. Spread ½ the filling on rolled out dough. Roll up and seal edges. Pull gently into 15- to 18-inch length. Form into spiral, circle, or crescent. Place on greased baking sheet. Slash across top and mash down. Repeat with other half. Cover and let rise to double (about 1 hour). Bake at 325 degrees until light brown. Remove from oven and ice with confectioner's sugar glaze, flavored with any flavor.

Pecan Filling:
¼ cup margarine
¾ cup firmly packed brown sugar
1 egg, beaten

2 tablespoons milk
1 teaspoon orange extract
2 cups pecans, finely chopped

Mix margarine, sugar and egg. Stir in the milk and orange extract. Blend in pecans. Can be frozen and used later. Warm before using.

Mary Nuuttila

WHOLE WHEAT BREAD

1 cake yeast
2½ cups warm water
3 tablespoons honey

3 tablespoons unrefined oil
6 cups whole-wheat flour
2 teaspoons sea salt

Dissolve the yeast in the water and add the honey and oil. Blend the flour and sea salt, and add to the liquid mixture. Knead a few minutes and cover; allow to rise until double in size. Punch down, and place into oiled loaf pans. Let rise again. Bake at 350 degrees about 30 minutes.

Jarrel W. Calhoun

JEWISH CHALLAH BREAD

2 tablespoons sugar	1/8 teaspoon powdered saffron
1 package active dry yeast	3 to 3 1/2 cups all-purpose flour
1/2 cup milk	2 eggs, slightly beaten
2 tablespoons butter	Vegetable oil
1 teaspoon salt	1 tablespoon poppy or sesame seeds

Combine 1/4 cup warm water (110 to 115 degrees), sugar and yeast in large mixing bowl. Let stand until bubbly, about 5 minutes. Heat milk, butter, salt and saffron in small saucepan over low heat just until warm. Add to yeast mixture. Beat 1 1/2 cups flour into yeast mixture until smooth, about 2 minutes on medium speed of electric mixer or 300 strokes by hand. Measure 1 1/2 tablespoons beaten egg into small bowl, cover with plastic wrap and reserve. Beat in remaining egg and enough flour to make moderately stiff dough. Turn dough onto lightly floured surface. Knead until smooth and satiny, 8 to 10 minutes. Shape into ball and place in lightly greased bowl, turning to grease all sides. Cover and let rise in warm place (80 to 85 degrees) until doubled in bulk, about 1 1/2 hours. Punch dough down. Cover and let rest 10 minutes. Divide into 3 equal parts. Shape each into rope about 20 inches long. Braid ropes loosely together on greased baking sheet. Tuck ends under and pinch to seal. Brush lightly with oil and let stand in warm place until almost doubled, 30 to 40 minutes. Brush braid with reserved egg. Sprinkle with poppy seeds. Bake in preheated 375 degree oven until golden brown, 25 to 30 minutes. Transfer to wire rack and cool completely.

Charlene Woods

SOURDOUGH STARTER

1 package active dry yeast	2 tablespoons sugar
1 quart lukewarm water	4 cups sifted flour

In a large crock (at least 3 quart capacity) soften yeast in lukewarm water. Add sugar and flour; beat to mix. Cover and let rise until light and slightly aged, 24 to 48 hours. Starter may be kept in refrigerator 7 to 10 days without attention. Then it should be stirred and equal amounts of flour and water added. To keep starter, pour off amount needed for recipe, then add equal amounts of flour and water to remainder. Amount will depend on amount of starter left. Bring it back to approximately the original level. Wait at least 24 hours before using again.

Virginia Salter

SOURDOUGH FRENCH BREAD

1 package dry yeast	2 tablespoons butter, melted
1½ cups warm water (110 degrees)	2 teaspoons salt
5 to 5½ cups all-purpose flour	½ teaspoon baking soda
1 cup sourdough starter	1 teaspoon yellow cornmeal
3 tablespoons sugar	1 egg white, slightly beaten

In a large mixing bowl, soften yeast in water. Blend in 2 cups of the flour, sourdough starter, sugar, butter and salt. Combine one cup of the flour and baking soda. Stir into flour-yeast mixture. Add enough remaining flour to make a moderately stiff dough. Turn out onto floured surface and knead 5 to 8 minutes or until smooth. Place in greased bowl, turning once. Cover with a cloth. Set in warm place, free from any drafts and let rise for 1 to 1½ hours or until doubled in size. Punch down dough and divide in half. Cover and let rest 10 minutes. Shape into two loaves (or better, 4 small ones). Place in greased pans sprinkled with cornmeal. Cover. Let rise in warm place about 1 hour or until almost doubled in size. Brush with egg white and make diagonal slashes across tops with a sharp knife or single-edge razor blade. Bake at 375 degrees for 30 to 35 minutes. Remove from pans and cool.

Jarrel W. Calhoun

BLUEBERRY BANANA-NUT SOURDOUGH BREAD

1 cup sugar	1 teaspoon baking soda
½ cup butter	3 tablespoons milk
2 eggs, beaten	1 cup mashed banana
1 cup sourdough starter	½ teaspoon vanilla
1½ cups all-purpose flour	½ cup nuts, chopped
½ teaspoon salt	¾ cup blueberries

Blend sugar and butter until creamy. Beat in eggs. Add sourdough starter. Mix flour with salt and baking soda. Add to sourdough mixture. Combine milk, banana, and vanilla. Mix well and add to mixture. Beat batter well after each addition. Add nuts. Fold in blueberries. Pour bread batter into a well greased loaf pan. Bake at 350 degrees for one hour or until done. Cool 10 minutes before removing from pan. Makes one loaf. (If smaller loaves are made, adjust time down).

Jarrel W. Calhoun

VIRGINIA SALLY LUNN BREAD

1 cup milk	1/2 cup warm water (105° to 115°F)
2 tablespoons sugar	1 package active dry yeast
1 teaspoon salt	3 eggs
1/3 cup butter or regular margarine	4 cups sifted all-purpose flour (sift before measuring)

In small saucepan, heat milk until bubbles form around edge of pan. Remove from heat. Add sugar, salt and butter, stirring until butter is melted; let cool to lukewarm. If possible, check temperature of warm water with thermometer. Sprinkle yeast over water in large bowl of electric mixer; stir to dissolve. Add milk mixture, eggs and all of flour. Beat at medium speed until smooth, about 30 seconds. Cover with waxed paper and towel; let rise in warm place (85 degrees), free from drafts, until double in bulk and bubbly (about 1 hour). Grease a 10×5×2½-inch angel-food pan. With wooden spoon, beat batter vigorously ½ minute. Pour batter evenly into prepared pan. Cover with towel; let rise in warm place (85 degrees), free from drafts, to within 1 inch of pan top (about 45 minutes). Meanwhile, preheat oven to 350 degrees. Bake 35 to 40 minutes or until golden brown. Remove from pan to wire rack. Serve hot, slicing with a serrated knife.

Deborah Grant

DINNER ROLLS

1 cup milk	1 cake or package of yeast
2 tablespoons shortening	1/4 cup lukewarm water
2 tablespoons sugar	1 egg, well beaten
1 teaspoon salt	3½ cups flour

Combine milk, shortening, sugar and salt. Heat to lukewarm. Cool and add yeast, softened in water. To the above add the egg and gradually stir in the flour; let rise to double in bulk. Brush dough with shortening before rising. (The softer the dough the lighter the rolls.) When doubled, knead down and form into rolls. Let rise again to double and bake at 375 degrees for 20 to 25 minutes. Use an 8×8-inch pan, well oiled.

Dorothy Lovett

HEAVENLY HOT ROLLS

1 cup shortening
1 cup sugar
1½ teaspoons salt
1 cup boiling water

2 eggs, beaten
2 packages dry yeast
1 cup warm water
6 cups white flour, sifted

Pour boiling water over shortening. When it is dissolved, add sugar and salt and let cool. Add eggs and mix well. Add yeast which has been dissolved in warm water. Gradually add flour and blend well. Cover and place in refrigerator for at least 4 hours. Put in container that will be large enough to give it room to rise. The dough will keep well in refrigerator for a week and can be used as desired. When ready to use, pinch off dough and put in pan to rise (about 3 hours). Bake at 375 degrees until brown.

Ruth Cave

POTATO WATER ROLLS

1 package yeast
1 cup warm water
1 cup potato water, warm*
4 tablespoons vegetable oil

4 tablespoons sugar
1½ teaspoons salt
4 to 6 cups flour

Sprinkle yeast over warm water; let stand 10 minutes. Add the potato water, oil, sugar, and salt. Stir thoroughly. Stir in the flour, about 2 cups at a time, until the dough is sticky and fairly stiff. It will take about 5 cups of flour. Save the remaining flour to use when kneading the dough. Scrape the sides of the mixing bowl so all the dough is together. Cover and let rise in a warm place until doubled in bulk. Punch the dough down, turn out onto floured surface and knead a few minutes. Roll out as for biscuits; cut with a biscuit cutter and place in greased baking pan with sides. Cover and let rise again until about doubled. Bake in 400 degree oven until tops are brown and sound a bit crusty when tapped with finger. Remove from oven and brush tops with butter.

*Reserve the water when boiling potatoes to mash. It will keep in the refrigerator for several days.

Betty Lou Winslow

MINI CRESCENT ROLLS

1 package dry yeast
¼ cup warm water (105° to 115°F)
¼ cup warm milk
⅓ cup sugar

1 teaspoon salt
1 egg, slightly beaten
¼ cup butter or margarine, softened
3½ to 4 cups all-purpose flour, divided

Dissolve yeast in warm water. Stir in sugar, milk, salt, egg, butter, and 2 cups flour. Beat until smooth. Add enough of the remaining flour so that dough can be handled. Turn onto lightly floured surface. Knead about 5 minutes, or until smooth and elastic. Place in greased bowl, turning to grease surface of dough. Cover and let rise in warm place until double. Punch down dough. Divide into three parts (or halves for larger rolls). Roll one part into a circle, about 10 inches and brush with soft butter. Cut into 16 wedges. Starting at outside roll each wedge toward the point. Place on greased baking sheet with point down, slightly curving ends to form crescent. Brush with butter and let rise in warm place 20 to 30 minutes. Preheat oven to 400 degrees. Bake 15 to 20 minutes. Repeat with remaining dough.

Virginia Salter

EASY CHEESY ROLLS

1 package yeast
⅔ cup Cheese-Whiz
2 tablespoons sugar
1 teaspoon salt

1 unbeaten egg
2 tablespoons butter, melted
1 cup sifted flour plus
1¼ to 1½ cups flour

Mix first 7 ingredients and beat 2 minutes until cheese is well blended (low speed on electric mixture). Gradually add enough of additional flour to form a dough. Mix well after each addition. Fill well greased muffin cup about ½ full of dough. Cover and let rise 1 to 1½ hours in warm place until doubled in size. Bake at 375 degrees for 12 to 15 minutes until golden brown. Makes 1 dozen.

Pamela Easter

ANGEL BISCUITS

1 package active dry yeast
2 tablespoons warm water
5 cups all-purpose flour
1 teaspoon soda
3 teaspoons baking powder

2 tablespoons sugar
1½ teaspoons salt
1 cup vegetable shortening
2 cups buttermilk

Dissolve yeast in warm water. Sift all dry ingredients into a large bowl. Cut in shortening with pastry blender. Add buttermilk, then yeast mixture. Stir until thoroughly moistened. Turn on to floured board and knead a minute or two. (No rising is required.) Roll out to ½-inch thickness and cut into rounds. Brush with melted butter and bake on ungreased pan at 400 degrees for 15 minutes, or until browned. Baked biscuits freeze nicely.

Note: After mixing, dough may be refrigerated in a plastic bag or covered bowl until ready to use, a week or more. If using plastic bag, leave space for dough to expand slightly. Dough may be used just as it comes from the refrigerator or readied for baking the day before and kept refrigerated until an hour before baking, allowing time to attain room temperature.

Chloye Whitson

FLUFFY BISCUITS

4 cups self-rising flour
⅔ cup solid vegetable shortening

1 cup milk (approximately)

Preheat oven to 450 degrees. In a large bowl, mix the flour and shortening with a wooden spoon until blended. Add the milk, a little at a time, until a soft dough forms. Do not overbeat. Spread a piece of waxed paper on the counter and sprinkle with flour. With a rolling pin or the palms of your hands, pat the dough out until it is about ½-inch thick. Cut with a small glass or biscuit cutter. Bake for 10 to 12 minutes or until just beginning to color. Makes 2 dozen.

Peggy Dawson

SCONES

2 cups sifted all-purpose flour	4 tablespoons shortening
4 teaspoons baking powder	2 egg yolks
2 tablespoons sugar	2 egg whites (do not mix together) divided
½ teaspoon salt	⅓ cup half-and-half (or milk)

Preheat oven to 450 degrees. Sift flour and measure out 2 cups. Add baking powder, sugar and salt, and sift into a bowl. Cut in shortening until crumbly. Beat 1 egg white slightly. Add slightly beaten egg yolks and beat well. Add the egg mixture and milk to the flour mixture. Stir carefully until all of the flour is moistened. Turn the dough onto a slightly floured board and knead for 30 seconds. Roll to a thickness of ½ inch. Cut into squares and then into triangles. Place on an ungreased baking sheet. Slightly beat other egg white and brush onto triangles. Sprinkle with sugar. Bake for 12 to 15 minutes. Serve hot. Good buttered, served with tea.

Susan Rumble

ORANGE CURRANT SCONES

2 cups all-purpose flour	1 cup currants or raisins
2 teaspoons baking powder	Sugar
½ teaspoon baking soda	¾ cup buttermilk
¼ teaspoon salt	1 large egg, separated
¼ teaspoon nutmeg	½ teaspoon grated orange peel
½ cup cold butter or margarine, cut up	

Preheat oven to 375 degrees. Stir flour, baking powder, baking soda, salt and nutmeg together in large bowl. With 2 knives, cut in butter until mixture resembles coarse crumbs. Stir in currants and 2 tablespoons sugar. Whisk buttermilk, egg yolk and orange peel together in bowl. Stir into flour mixture on lightly floured surface. Knead dough gently about 5 times or until it holds together. Shape into 2 equal balls; place on cookie sheet. Pat balls into 6-inch circles and cut each into 6 wedges. Whisk egg white until frothy; brush over scones. Sprinkle with sugar. Bake 20 to 22 minutes, until golden. Transfer to wire rack. Makes 1 dozen.

Lucy Martin

CORNBREAD

2 cups yellow corn meal
2 cups all-purpose flour
1 teaspoon salt
2 tablespoons sugar

8 teaspoons baking powder
3 eggs
⅔ cup melted margarine
2 cups milk

Grease and coat with corn meal a 13×9-inch pan. Preheat oven to 425 degrees. Sift together the first 5 ingredients. Add eggs, margarine and milk. Stir just until blended. Pour in prepared pan and bake for 30 minutes.

Noreen Collins

COUNTRY STYLE CORNBREAD

¼ cup vegetable oil
¼ cup bacon grease (optional)
1 cup cornmeal (stone ground)
½ cup all-purpose flour
1 teaspoon salt
2 tablespoons sugar

1 teaspoon baking powder
½ teaspoon baking soda
1 cup buttermilk
¼ cup sweet milk
1 egg, beaten

Preheat oven to 375 degrees. Heat oil in a 10-inch skillet in oven until hot. Combine all dry ingredients and mix well. Combine buttermilk, milk and egg. Add to dry ingredients and mix until moistened. Remove skillet from oven. Pour cornbread batter into hot grease. Bake 15 to 20 minutes until golden brown on top. Cut into 12 pieces.

Ruth Barnard

LOW CHOLESTEROL CORNBREAD

1 cup all purpose flour
1 tablespoon sugar (optional)
¾ cup yellow or white corn meal
2 teaspoons baking powder

2 egg whites, lightly beaten
1 cup skim milk
2 tablespoons vegetable oil

Spray baking pan with vegetable oil spray. Mix ingredients and bake at 425 degrees for 15 to 20 minutes.

Tina Lewis

HOT WATER CORNBREAD

2 cups yellow cornmeal
4 teaspoons flour
2 teaspoons sugar

3 teaspoons butter or margarine, melted
2 cups very hot water

Mix together all ingredients, then pour in hot water. Stir and make into patties with hands. It will be hot to handle so keep hands rinsed under running cold water. Fry on each side until brown in vegetable shortening or clean bacon drippings.

Dallas Deputy Mayor Pro-Tem
Charlotte Mayes

JALAPEÑO CORNBREAD

2 eggs, slightly beaten
8 ounces sour cream
1 8¼-ounce can cream style corn
⅔ cup salad oil
1½ cups cornmeal
3 teaspoons baking powder
½ teaspoon salt (or to taste)

2 to 3 whole canned jalapeños, seeded
  and chopped
¼ cup green bell pepper, chopped
¼ cup red bell pepper, chopped
¼ cup onion, chopped
1 tablespoon oil
2 cups (or more) sharp cheddar cheese

Preheat oven to 350 degrees. Sauté green and red bell pepper and onion in 1 tablespoon oil. Cool. Mix all ingredients except cheese. Heat well-greased iron skillet in oven. Pour half of mixture in heated skillet. Top with half of cheese. Pour on remaining mixture and spread to cover cheese. Sprinkle on remaining cheese. Bake at 350 degrees for 1 hour.

Linda Ritchey Chesley

GRANDMA'S PANCAKES

1 cup plus 2 tablespoons flour
1 teaspoon baking powder
2 teaspoons baking soda
¼ teaspoon salt
⅓ cup sugar

½ cup oatmeal
¼ cup cornmeal
2½ cups buttermilk
2 eggs
¼ cup oil

Mix all dry ingredients together. Mix buttermilk, eggs and oil together and add dry ingredients. Stir until just mixed. Drop by large spoonfuls on hot griddle.

Charlotte Stoltz

HEART-HEALTHY OATMEAL PANCAKES

(Low Cholesterol)

1½ cups regular *rolled oats*
1½ cups skim milk
½ cup whole-wheat flour
1 teaspoon baking powder

½ teaspoon ground cinnamon
1 tablespoon canola oil
1 teaspoon honey
2 egg whites

Place oats and milk in blender and let stand 1 minute. Add flour, baking powder, and cinnamon. Blend. Add canola oil, honey, and egg whites, and blend again, scraping down sides if necessary. Heat griddle pan until a drop of water spatters. Pour batter onto griddle, enough to make a 3-inch griddle cake, about ⅛ cup. Cook each cake until puffed, turn, brown other side. Serve with butter flavoring and applesauce. Will keep in refrigerator.

Jeanette Kloppe

PANCAKE NONPAREIL

½ cup flour
½ cup milk
2 eggs, slightly beaten
Pinch of nutmeg

¼ cup butter
2 tablespoons confectioners' sugar
Juice of ½ lemon

Preheat oven to 425 degrees. In a mixing bowl, combine flour, milk, eggs and nutmeg. Beat lightly. Leave the batter a little lumpy. Melt butter in a 12-inch skillet with a heatproof handle. When very hot, pour in batter. Bake 15 to 20 minutes or until golden brown. Sprinkle with sugar and return briefly to oven. Remove from oven, sprinkle with lemon juice, then serve with jam or marmalade. This baked pancake is a breakfast, brunch, or afternoon delight.

Ruth Kopplin

DIPS FOR STRAWBERRIES

Romanoff Dip:
- *1 cup sour cream*
- *¼ cup brown sugar*

- *Dash of cinnamon*
- *2 tablespoons bourbon*

Mix all ingredients together.

Fraiche a la Creme:
- *1 pint strawberries*
- *½ cup whipping cream*
- *¼ cup sugar*

- *¼ teaspoon almond extract*
- *½ cup sour cream*

To make Creme Fraiche, beat whipping cream with sugar and almond extract in a chilled bowl until stiff. Then fold in sour cream until evenly blended. Wash and hull strawberries. Mix with creme fraiche and refrigerate until serving time. Serve in champagne or sherbet glasses with a sprig of mint.

Stella Klein

CARAMEL SAUCE

- *1 cup butter*
- *2⅓ cups brown sugar*
- *1 cup light corn syrup*

- *1 15-ounce can sweetened condensed milk*
- *Dash of salt*

In a saucepan, melt butter; add brown sugar and salt. Stir in corn syrup. Mix well, gradually add sweetened condensed milk. Cook over medium heat, stirring constantly for 15 to 20 minutes. Serve as a dip for apple wedges, ice cream topping or spooned over apple pie.

Edie Gottschall

COCONUT SYRUP FOR PANCAKES

- *1½ cups white corn syrup*
- *½ cup butter*

- *1 cup cream of coconut*

In a saucepan, heat all ingredients. Serve warm.

Gerald Ramsey

PESTO

3 cups fresh basil, loosely packed
¾ cup olive oil
¼ cup pine nuts
3 garlic cloves

1 teaspoon salt
½ cup Parmesan cheese, freshly grated
3 tablespoons Romano cheese (or
   additional Parmesan cheese)

Put basil, oil, pine nuts, garlic and salt into a blender or food processor. Process until smooth. Pour sauce into a small bowl. Add cheeses. Mix to blend. Taste and adjust for seasoning. Makes 1 cup of pesto. If you plan to freeze the pesto, add the cheese after the pesto has thawed.

Edie Gottschall

BACON AND TOMATO PASTA SAUCE

1 pound bacon
3 tablespoons olive oil
3 large onions, coarsely chopped
5 garlic cloves, sliced thin
1 can crushed tomatoes
1 can stewed tomatoes, chopped
   (combined tomatoes should
   total 44 ounces)

1 tablespoon tarragon
2 teaspoons sugar
   Pinch cayenne pepper
¼ cup fresh parsley, minced
1½ pounds pasta, cooked
   Butter or margarine
   Parmesan cheese

Fry bacon until crisp. Drain bacon. Pour out all grease except 1 tablespoon from skillet. Add olive oil and onions to skillet. Sauté onions until wilted, about 5 minutes. Stir in garlic, tomatoes, tarragon, sugar and pepper. Simmer 30 minutes to reduce liquid. Crumble bacon and add along with the parsley. Remove from heat. Toss cooked pasta with butter to taste. Serve sauce on top of pasta. Sprinkle with Parmesan cheese.

Meri Ann Lawson

WHITE MEATBALL SAUCE

8 tablespoons margarine
5 beef bouillon cubes
¼ cup flour
4 cups whipping cream
1 large onion, chopped

8 cups milk (any kind)
1 tablespoon dill weed
Pepper to taste
5 pounds meatballs

Melt margarine, add bouillon cubes and flour; cook 5 minutes. Add other ingredients. Cook over medium heat until thick. Add meatballs. Keep warm until served.

Suzanne Betterley

FAT-FREE SAUCE FOR FISH

½ cup Bloody Mary Mix or
  Snappy Tom
2 cloves garlic, minced

1 teaspoon fresh rosemary, finely minced
1 dash Worcestershire sauce
Juice of 1 lemon

Mix all ingredients. Baste halibut (or other fish) steaks with sauce on charcoal grill — about 5 minutes on a side. Serve remainder of warm sauce on top of fish.

Mary Jane Hinnant

CRANBERRRY-ORANGE CHUTNEY

2 oranges, peeled, seeded and
  sectioned
16 ounces whole berry cranberry sauce
16 ounces pear halves, drained and
  chopped
1 apple, unpeeled, cored, chopped

1 cup sugar
½ cup raisins
¼ cup pecans, chopped
1 tablespoon white vinegar
½ teaspoon ground ginger
½ teaspoon ground cinnamon

Combine all ingredients in a saucepan; bring to a boil over medium heat. Reduce heat and simmer 5 minutes. Cool and store in refrigerator. Yields 5 cups.

Alecia Gentile

SWEET HOT MUSTARD

16 ounces Coleman's dry mustard
4 cups white vinegar
4 cups sugar
1 tablespoon cornstarch

4 whole eggs
3 shakes salt
4 cups (32 ounces) yellow mustard

Mix dry mustard and vinegar; soak overnight. Add sugar and cornstarch; add beaten eggs and salt. Cook until thickened (15 to 20 minutes), stirring often. Remove from heat and add yellow mustard. Store in refrigerator. Makes 2 quarts. Great gift for giving in small jars.

Alecia Gentile

DADDY'S HOT SAUCE

8 cups tomatoes
1 cup crushed garlic (pulverized)
3 cups onions, finely chopped

3½ cups hot peppers, finely chopped
⅙ to ¼ cup salt

Peel, core and cut tomatoes into 1 inch pieces. Prepare and measure all other ingredients. Put in large pot at the same time and mix thoroughly. Add salt to taste, starting with ⅙ cup. Bring mixture to a boil fairly rapidly. Simmer for 1 hour with pot covered. Taste frequently. (Tasting goes very well with a "cold beer"). Remove lid and let some water cook off. Sterilize containers and lids in boiling water. Put into containers while hot, but not boiling. After cooling, refrigerate and keep refrigerated until used. Makes 6½ pints.

Willard Baker

FRESH PEACH SALSA

2 peaches, ripe but firm
½ small red onion, peeled and
    ends trimmed
½ cup canned pineapple juice
¼ cup lime juice, freshly squeezed

1 tablespoon fresh ginger, minced
1½ teaspoons ground coriander
1 teaspoon light brown sugar
½ teaspoon salt
¼ teaspoon cayenne pepper

Peel peaches and slice fruit away from pit. Dice peaches. Mince red onion. Combine with remaining ingredients. Mix lightly. Let sit for 20 minutes at room temperature and serve. Makes 3½ cups.

Debbie Ross

POPPY SEED DRESSING

1½ cups sugar
2 teaspoons dry mustard
2 teaspoons salt
⅔ cup vinegar

3 tablespoons onion juice
2 cups salad oil
3 tablespoons poppy seeds

Mix first 4 ingredients. Add onion juice and blend thoroughly in electric blender. Add oil slowly, blending constantly and continue to beat until thick. Add poppy seeds and blend just until mixed. Makes 3½ cups.

Pearl Scott

CAESAR SALAD DRESSING

½ cup light olive oil
1 to 3 garlic cloves
1 raw egg
½ cup Parmesan cheese

¼ cup lemon juice
1 teaspoon Worcestershire sauce
½ inch anchovy paste

Press garlic into oil. Let stand for 1 to 2 hours. Add remaining ingredients. Shake vigorously. Serve over romaine lettuce. Add croutons.

Pat Hill

CREAMY FRENCH DRESSING

½ cup white vinegar
¾ cup sugar
2 teaspoons salt
2 teaspoons paprika

½ teaspoon seasoning salt
⅛ teaspoon garlic salt
1 cup salad oil
2 tablespoons salad dressing

Mix all ingredients. Makes 1 pint plus.

Joyce Kirkland

ROQUEFORT DRESSING

1 cup mayonnaise
1 large garlic clove, minced
½ cup sour cream
1 tablespoon vinegar

4 ounces crumbled Roquefort cheese
  (about 1 cup)
¼ teaspoon salt
¼ teaspoon black pepper

Crumble cheese into mixing bowl. Add mayonnaise and sour cream; stir. Add vinegar, salt, pepper and garlic. Blend well. Store covered in refrigerator. Makes 2 cups.

Jo Boyd

SESAME SEED SALAD DRESSING

½ cup sesame seeds
1 tablespoon butter
¼ cup Parmesan cheese
1 cup sour cream
½ cup mayonnaise
1 tablespoon tarragon vinegar
1 tablespoon sugar

1 teaspoon salt
  Dash of white pepper
1 clove garlic
¼ cup bell pepper, diced
¼ cup cucumber, diced
2 tablespoons onion, minced

Brown the sesame seeds in the butter. Add to the rest of the ingredients. Mix well.

Greta Rees

BARBECUE SEASONING MIX

1 tablespoon celery seeds
1 tablespoon green or black peppercorns
1½ teaspoons dried thyme
1½ teaspoons dried marjoram
1½ teaspoons cayenne

2 tablespoons paprika
3 tablespoons mustard powder
1 teaspoon ground coriander
1½ teaspoons salt
3 tablespoons brown sugar

Pulverize celery seeds and peppercorns with mortar and pestle. Combine all ingredients and mix well.

Dedicated to Tare Mirelez

MANZANILLO SUN DILLS

6 cups water	2 or 3 hot peppers
⅔ to ¾ cup salt	½ teaspoon alum
1 pint apple cider vinegar	5 cloves garlic
30 small cucumbers (about 4.4 pounds)	2 tablespoons dill weed (or seed)
	1 tablespoon pickling spices

Sterilize a 1-gallon glass jar or four 1-quart jars (divide amounts listed for small jars). In a saucepan, mix water, salt and vinegar and heat to boiling. Set aside to cool. Pack previously washed cucumbers in jar(s). Add remaining ingredients. Pour cooled liquid over cucumbers, place lid on jar and set in sun for 10 days. Chill before serving.

Bettye McLaughlin

14-DAY DILL PICKLE

Brine:

9 cups water	1 cup salt

Mix and stir until dissolved. To each quart of cucumber, okra, cauliflower, etc.

Add:

½ jar of brine water	1 teaspoon dill weed
½ jar of white vinegar	½ teaspoon onion flakes
(sour pickling vinegar)	⅛ to ¼ teaspoon garlic flakes

Seal jars. Set in sunny window ledge 14 days. Refrigerate before opening.

Tom Rush

DESSERTS

—■—

GARDEN GOURMET COOKBOOK

COUNTRY FRENCH APPLE CRESCENT CASSEROLE

2 tablespoons sugar
½ to 1 teaspoon cinnamon
1 large apple, peeled, cored, sliced
   in eighths

1 8-ounce can refrigerated quick
   Crescent dinner rolls

Sauce:
½ cup sugar
½ cup whipping cream
1 tablespoon almond extract or
   Amaretto

1 egg
½ cup almonds, sliced
   Cinnamon

Heat oven to 375 degrees. In small bowl, combine 2 tablespoons sugar and ½ teaspoon cinnamon; blend well. Separate dough into 8 triangles; sprinkle sugar mixture evenly over each. Gently press sugar mixture into each triangle, flattening each slightly. Place an apple slice on wide end of each triangle. Tuck in edges around apple slice. Roll up, starting at wide end; roll to opposite point. Seal all seams. Place tip side down, in ungreased 9-inch round baking dish or pie pan, placing long side of 7 filled crescents around outside edge of dish and 1 in center. Bake at 375 degrees for 15 to 20 minutes or until golden brown.

For sauce, combine sugar, whipping cream, almond extract and egg in a small bowl and whisk until well blended. Spoon sauce mixture evenly over partially baked rolls. Sprinkle with almonds and cinnamon. Bake an additional 13 to 18 minutes or until deep golden brown. Cover top of pan with foil during last 5 minutes of baking time if necessary to prevent excessive browning. Serve warm. Makes 8 servings.

Maurice Buchanan

MOUSSE AU CHOCOLAT BASQUE

8 ounces sweet chocolate
5 eggs, separated

5 tablespoons water

Melt chocolate in double boiler. Add the water. Stir over fire until dissolved. Slide yolks into mixture. Beat well. Beat egg whites in a mixer. Add chocolate mixture. Mix well with wire whisk. Pour into bowls or cups. Refrigerate for 6 or 7 hours. Garnish with whipped cream and grated chocolate. Makes 6 cups.

Martha Baker

FLAN

1½ cups sugar, divided
3 tablespoons water
1 quart milk
6 eggs

2 egg yolks
⅓ cup dark rum
½ cup whipping cream

Combine ½ cup sugar with 3 tablespoons water in small saucepan over moderate heat until syrup turns a light golden color. When golden pour into a 2-quart soufflé dish. Tip dish back and forth until bottom is coated. Refrigerate. Bring milk and remaining sugar to simmer over moderately high heat. Combine whole eggs and yolks and beat only until well mixed. Gradually add hot milk, whipping constantly. Strain through cheesecloth-lined sieve. Stir in rum and cream until well blended. Pour into soufflé dish and set in large pan as deep as the dish. Add hot water to half way up the side of the dish. Bake in preheated 350 degree oven for one hour. Lift from pan, cool and refrigerate. To serve, run thin spatula around edge and turn onto serving plate. Prepare the day before. Serves 10.

Connie Klemow

BAKED CUSTARD

3 eggs, slightly beaten
½ cup sugar
¼ teaspoon salt

2 cups milk, scalded
1 teaspoon vanilla

In a double boiler, combine eggs, sugar and salt. Slowly stir in slightly cooled milk and vanilla. Pour into six 5-ounce custard cups. Set cups in shallow pan. Pour hot water around them 1-inch deep. Bake at 325 degrees for 40 to 45 minutes until knife inserted off-center comes out clean. Serve warm or chilled.

Susan Rumble

BREAD PUDDING

5 cups French bread	1½ cups sugar
6 eggs	2 tablespoons butter or margarine
1 cup white raisins	1 teaspoon vanilla
4 cups milk	1 teaspoon rum flavoring
⅛ teaspoon salt	1½ teaspoons nutmeg

Break bread into small chunks. Beat eggs and mix with remaining ingredients. Pour over bread chunks. Stir well and let set 1½ hours or until moistened in refrigerator, stirring occasionally. Pour into a 9×13-inch baking dish sprayed with vegetable oil and bake at 350 degrees for about 1 hour, or until knife inserted in center comes out clean. Serve with rum sauce.

Rum Sauce:

¾ cup margarine	2 eggs, beaten
1½ cups sugar	⅓ cup rum

Melt margarine in top of double boiler. Mix sugar and eggs; add to margarine, stirring occasionally until sauce is slightly thickened, about 4 minutes. Remove from heat and add rum.

Jo Boyd

WATALAPPAN

(Steamed Coconut Custard)

1 cup dark brown sugar	¼ teaspoon ground cardamon
6 eggs	Pinch ground cloves
1 cup coconut milk	Pinch ground nutmeg
½ cup water	¼ teaspoon rose essence

In a saucepan, dissolve sugar in water over low heat; cool. Beat eggs slightly and add sugar syrup. Stir in coconut milk. Add remaining ingredients. Pour into greased individual custard cups or a greased bowl. Cover with waxed paper or baking parchment and steam for 1 to 1½ hours at 250 degrees. Chill before serving.

Betty Josey

EGGNOG BREAD PUDDING

¾ pound loaf egg bread, cut in cubes
1 cup candied cherries, coarsely
  chopped
½ cup light brown sugar, packed
½ cup raisins
6 large eggs

½ teaspoon nutmeg
4 cups eggnog
2 cups half-and-half
2 tablespoons brandy or rum
2 tablespoons butter or margarine

Grease 9×13-inch baking dish. Place bread cubes in roasting pan. Bake at 325 degrees for 10 minutes, stirring occasionally, until toasted. Place in prepared baking dish; stir in cherries and raisins. In large bowl, whisk sugar and eggs until blended. Stir in nutmeg, eggnog, half-and-half and brandy. Pour over bread cube mixture. Dot with butter. Set baking dish in roasting pan filled with enough hot water to come halfway up the side of the dish. Bake 50 minutes, or until knife inserted in center comes out clean. If desired, serve with whipped cream or ice cream and sprinkle with additional ground nutmeg. Serves 12.

Cookbook Committee

EASY BREAD PUDDING

6 slices bread
2 eggs
2½ cups skim milk
½ cup raisins

1 cup brown sugar
½ teaspoon allspice
½ teaspoon cinnamon
½ teaspoon nutmeg

Mix eggs, milk, sugar and spices in a glass baking dish. Add 6 slices of bread, torn up, and the raisins. Bake 35 minutes at 325 degrees or until set. Serve warm or cold.

Shirley Moseley

ORANGE TAPIOCA PUDDING

Grated rind of 1 orange
3 oranges, peeled and cut up
5 cups water
½ teaspoon salt
1 cup baby pearl tapioca

2 cups sugar
1 teaspon vanilla
1 8-ounce carton prepared whipped
   topping

Grate rind of one orange in a 3 to 4 quart pan; add water and salt; bring to a boil. Add the tapioca; let boil 2to 3 minutes. Remove from heat and let stand until tapioca is clear. Add 1½ cups sugar and vanilla; cool. Meanwhile, to the cut up oranges, add the remaining sugar and set aside until ready to serve. Mix the oranges and juice in the cooled tapioca, stirring well, then add the prepared whipped topping. Serve.

Cookbook Committee

HOT FUDGE PUDDING

1 cup cake flour
2½ teaspoons baking powder
¾ cup sugar
¼ teaspoon salt
5 tablespoons plus ⅔ cup cocoa,
   divided use

½ cup milk
4 tablespoons butter, melted
1 cup walnuts, chopped
1 cup brown sugar, packed
2 cups hot water
1 teaspoon vanilla

Combine flour, baking powder, sugar, salt and 5 tablespoons cocoa; set aside. Blend milk and melted butter. Combine with flour mixture. Add walnuts. Spread in a greased 8-inch square baking pan. Combine brown sugar, remaining cocoa, hot water and vanilla. Pour over batter in pan. Do not mix. Bake at 350 degrees for 45 minutes or until top springs back when lightly touched. Do not overbake. Makes 12 servings.

Faye Swindell

CHOCOLATE KAHLÚA DELECTABLE

Batter:

- 1 package brownie mix
- 2 tablespoons water
- 3 eggs
- 1 teaspoon vanilla

Lightly oil an 11×15-inch pan and line it with waxed paper. Oil and flour paper. Blend all ingredients in electric mixter on medium speed until batter is smooth. Spread evenly in pan and bake at 350 degrees for 10 minutes. Turn cake onto wire rack to cool and peel off waxed paper. Lightly oil an 8-inch springform pan and line with cooled cake pieces. Cut strip for sides. Spoon filling into mold. Cover top of filled mold with circle of cake. Chill for at least four hours until firm. Unmold and cover top of cake with Chocolate Glaze. Let drizzle down sides. Chill and serve in thin slices.

Filling:

- 24 ounces semisweet chocolate
- ½ cup strong prepared coffee
- 3 eggs, separated
- ½ cup Kahlua
- ⅓ cup sugar
- ½ cup whipping cream, whipped

Melt chocolate with coffee in double boiler. Remove from heat. Beat egg yolks until pale yellow and stir into chocolate. Gradually stir in Kahlúa. Allow to cool. In a separate bowl, beat egg whites, gradually adding sugar until stiff peaks form. Fold whipped cream into cooled chocolate mixture. Fold in egg whites.

Chocolate Glaze:

- 8 ounces semisweet chocolate
- ⅓ cup water
- ½ cup mini marshmallow (optional)

Melt chocolate with water in double boiler over simmering water. Stir in marshmallows until smooth.

Mary Ann Edwards

STANDING PROUD CHOCOLATE TRUFFLE LINZER HEART

Crust:

5 ounces hazelnuts, toasted
2/3 cup sugar
1¼ cups sifted all purpose flour
1¼ teaspoons ground cinnamon
¼ teaspoon salt
¼ teaspoon ground cloves
¼ teaspoon ground ginger
½ cup plus 2 tablespoons chilled, unsalted butter, in small pieces

1 ounce cream cheese, cut into small pieces, frozen
1 large egg, beaten to blend
½ ounce bittersweet chocolate, finely Chopped (not unsweetened or semisweet)
1 egg white, beaten to blend
1/3 cup seedless raspberry jam

Filling:

9 ounces bittersweet chocolate chopped (not unsweetened or semisweet)
5 tablespoons unsalted butter at room temperature
3 tablespoons whipping cream

1/3 cup plus 2 tablespoons seedless raspberry jam
1 basket fresh raspberries
1 basket blueberries
Lightly sweetened whipped cream

Crust: Finely chop nuts with sugar in processor. Add flour, cinnamon, salt, cloves and ginger. Process just to blend. Add butter and cream cheese to processor. Process until mixture resembles coarse meal. Add 1 egg and chocolate. Process, using on/off turns, until large moist clumps form. Use 10½×9½-inch heart shape tart pan with removable bottom. Press dough onto bottom and 3/4-inch up sides of pan, using plastic wrap if necessary to prevent dough from sticking to hands. Freeze until dough is firm, about 10 minutes. Brush lightly with egg white. Set pan on heated cookie sheet and bake until crust is golden brown and sides are beginning to pull away from pan, about 23 minutes. Spread bottom crust evenly with 1/3 cup jam. Bake 3 more minutes. Cool crust completely on rack.

Filling: Stir chocolate, butter and cream in heavy medium saucepan over medium low heat until melted and mixture is smooth. Mix in 2 tablespoons jam. Cool slightly. Pour filling evenly into crust. Smooth top. Chill until firm. Spread remaining jam over filling and outer edge of crust. Cover with foil and refrigerate overnight.

Remove torte from pan. Transfer to platter. Let stand at room temperature 45 minutes. Place blueberries in left-hand corner. Arrange raspberries, and whipped cream (spoon into pastry bag fitted with small star tip) in rows across top, alternating rows. This achieves a "red, white and blue flag" effect.

Lynda Sanders

BLACK WALNUT TORTE

½ cup black walnuts, chopped
½ cup chocolate wafer crumbs or
   graham cracker crumbs
1 envelope unflavored gelatin
¼ cup cold water
1 6-ounce package semisweet chocolate chips

½ cup sugar (divided)
¼ teaspoon salt
½ cup milk
3 eggs, separated
1 cup whipped cream

Combine crumbs and nuts. Rinse out an 8-inch springform pan with cold water. Line bottom with waxed paper. Cover with half of crumb mixture. Soften gelatin in cold water. In a saucepan, cook chocolate, ¼ cup sugar, salt and milk until blended. Beat egg yolks and add to hot mixture slowly, stirring constantly. Cook, stirring until thickened. Remove from heat. Add gelatin and stir until dissolved. Chill until nearly thickened. Beat egg whites and add ¼ cup sugar. Fold into chocolate mixture; add whipped cream and pour into pan. Top with remaining crumb mixture. Chill until firm.

Dedicated to Nancy Bradford

PUMPKIN ROLL

1 cup sugar
⅔ cup flour
3 eggs

½ teaspoon soda
1 teaspoon cinnamon
⅔ cup pumpkin
   Confectioners' sugar for dusting

Filling:

1 cup confectioners' sugar, sifted
8 ounces cream cheese

6 teaspoons butter
1 teaspoon vanilla

Mix cake ingredients together and pour into lightly greased and floured wax paper-lined cookie sheet. Bake 15 minutes at 350 degrees. Remove immediately and place on tea towel that has been lightly dusted with confectioners' sugar. Roll up until cool. Meanwhile mix filling ingredients. Unroll and spread with filling and roll up again. Refrigerate several hours to set. May be frozen. Before serving, dust completed pumpkin roll lightly with confectioners sugar. Looks lovely served on a silver tray.

Gloria Schwartz

PUMPKIN SQUARES

Crust:
1½ cups graham crackers, crushed

⅓ cup sugar
½ cup butter, melted

Cream Cheese Mixture:
2 eggs, beaten

8 ounces cream cheese, softened
½ cup sugar

Pumpkin Mixture:
1 16-ounce can pumpkin
3 eggs, separated
½ cup sugar
½ cup evaporated milk
½ teaspoon salt
2 teaspoons cinnamon

½ teaspoon nutmeg
½ teaspoon ginger
1 envelope unflavored gelatin
¼ cup cold water
1 cup heavy cream, whipped
1 tablespoon sugar
1 teaspoon vanilla

Mix graham crackers, sugar and butter and press into 9×13-inch pan. Mix 2 beaten eggs, sugar and cream cheese and pour over crust. Bake at 350 degrees for 20 minutes. Beat egg yolks and mix with pumpkin, sugar, evaporated milk, salt and spices. Cook in top of double boiler until thick, about 5 minutes. Remove from heat; add gelatin dissolved in ¼ cup water. Cool. Beat 3 egg whites to soft peaks. Add ¼ cup sugar gradually and beat until stiff. Fold into pumpkin mixture and pour over crust. Chill. Top with whipped cream to which sugar and vanilla have been added.

Margaret Lievsay

TRUE TRIFLE

3 9-inch cake layers, ½-inch thick
2 cups sherry
4 cups boiled custard
6 ounces almonds, blanched, chopped

1 pint preserves (strawberry or raspberry)
1 dozen almond macaroons, crushed
1 cup cream, whipped

Place one cake layer on bottom of deep dish. Pour ⅓ of sherry over layer. Spread ⅓ custard on top. Sprinkle with ⅓ of almonds. Spread ½ of preserves. Sprinkle ⅓ of macaroon crumbs. Repeat procedure with second cake layer. Repeat again with third layer except omit preserves. Top with whipped cream. Chill in refrigerator. May be made a day ahead.

Carol Russell

OLDE ENGLISH TRIFLE

1 prepared 10¾-ounce pound cake
½ cup seedless raspberry jam
1 cup Amaretti cookies, coarsely
    broken
1 cup Marsala
3 tablespoons sugar
1½ tablespoons cornstarch
3 egg yolks

2½ cups milk
1 teaspoon vanilla
2 cups whipping cream
3 tablespoons confectioners' sugar
½ teaspoon almond extract
1 cup almonds, sliced and toasted
    Candied cherries or fresh strawberries

Cut cake into ¼-inch slices and spread out flat to dry for several hours. Spread a thin layer of jam on half the cake slices. Top with remaining cake slices. Cut into 1-inch cubes and scatter in a large glass bowl. Add amaretti crumbs and toss together. Sprinkle with Marsala and toss to coat. Whisk the granulated sugar, cornstarch and egg yolks together in a saucepan; whisk in milk in thin steady stream. Cook, stirring constantly, over medium heat until thickened. Remove from heat and whisk in vanilla; cool. Pour cooled custard over cake mixture. Whip cream in a chilled bowl until soft peaks form; beat in confectioners' sugar and almond extract and continue beating until stiff. Pipe cream over the top of the trifle using a pastry bag. Scatter almonds over the top. Refrigerate, covered with plastic wrap until ready to serve, up to 3 days. Garnish with candied cherries. Serves 8 to 10.

Frank J. Macaluso

BEIGNETS SOUFFLES

1 stick (½ cup) butter
1 cup water
½ teaspoon salt

2 teaspoons sugar
1 cup flour
3 eggs
    Fat for frying

Cut butter in 5 or 6 pieces. Heat water in heavy saucepan. Add butter, salt and sugar. When butter melts and the water boils, add flour all at one time. Beat vigorously with wooden spoon until the mixture breaks away from the sides of the pan and forms a ball. Add 1 whole egg, mixing thoroughly. Add 2 more eggs, one at a time, beating thoroughly. The dough should be firm and waxy. Pipe or drop spoonfuls into deep hot fat (360 degrees). Fry until rich golden brown. Drain on paper towels. Serve sprinkled with powdered sugar. Serve with watermelon basket filled with fruit: grapes, strawberries, blueberries, melon balls, etc.

Peggy Dawson

ALMOND CRUSTED KEY LIME DESSERT

Crust:

¾ cup margarine or butter
1½ cups flour

¾ cup blanched almonds, chopped
⅓ cup sugar

Filling:

6 eggs, separated
2 14-ounce cans sweetened
Condensed milk

2 teaspoons grated lime rind
⅔ cup fresh lime juice (4 limes)

In large skillet melt margarine or butter. Lightly spoon flour into measuring cup, level off. Add flour and remaining ingredients to melted butter, blend well. Cook over medium high heat for 5 to 6 minutes or until mixture is golden brown and crumbley, stirring constantly. Reserve ⅓ cup of crumb mixture for topping. Using back of spoon, press mixture firmly into bottom of ungreased 13×9-inch pan. Cool completely. Beat egg whites until stiff. Set aside. In small bowl beat egg yolks. Gradually add condensed milk; mix well. Add lime rind. Gradually add lime juice, beating well after each addition. Fold mixture into beaten egg whites. Pour into crust, top with reserved crumb mixture. Freeze about 3 hours or until firm. For longer storage cover with foil. Allow to stand at room temperature a few minutes before serving.

Bettie Campbell

STRAWBERRY SUPREME

1 cup flour
½ cup pecans, chopped
¼ cup brown sugar
½ cup butter, melted
2 egg whites
1 cup sugar

2 teaspoons lemon juice
1 teaspoon vanilla
1 10-ounce package frozen
strawberries, thawed
1 12-ounce container whipped topping

Mix flour, brown sugar, nuts and butter. Spread in 9×13-inch pan. Bake in 300 degree oven for 20 minutes. Remove from oven and break up into small chunks. Reserve ⅓ of crumbs for topping. Spread remaining crumbs in bottom of pan. Put egg whites, sugar, lemon juice, vanilla and strawberries in a large bowl and beat 10 to 15 minutes at high speed. Fold in whipped topping. Spread strawberry mixture over crumbs in pan. Sprinkle remaining crumbs on top. Cover and freeze. Remove and let stand at room temperature about 20 minutes before cutting and serving. Serves 12 to 16. (Can be frozen for 1 month.)

Neva Muller

SUMMER'S BEST HOMEMADE ICE CREAM

4 eggs
2½ cups sugar
6 cups half and half

2 cups whipping cream
3 tablespoons vanilla
½ teaspoon salt

Beat eggs until light. Add sugar gradually, beating until thick. Add remaining ingredients. Mix well. Pour into ice cream freezer. Surround it with ice and rock salt. Crank until done.

Mary Curtis

ICE CREAM CAKE

1½ pints raspberry sherbet
1½ pints lime sherbet
1½ pints orange sherbet
3 quarts vanilla ice cream

2 cups pecans, toasted, chopped
4 or 5 ounces semisweet baking
   chocolate, grated
2 cups whipping cream
Green food coloring

Use a 10×4-inch 2-part angel food cake pan. Make 8 balls from each of the 3 sherbets (24 in all). Place on cold cookie sheets in freezer until firm. Chill cake pan. In large bowl mix vanilla ice cream with nuts and chocolate. Spoon in bottom of pan to make a 1-inch layer. Arrange half of sherbet balls on ice cream layer. Cover with softened ice cream. Then add another layer of balls. Cover with remaining ice cream. Freeze overnight. Remove from pan. Frost with whipped cream, tinted with food coloring. Put back in freezer. Serve with flowers in the center.

Dollie Bleuler

PEACH CUSTARD

4 tablespoons flour, heaping
1 egg
1 cup sugar
6 fresh peaches, peeled and sliced

1½ cups water
Pinch of salt
½ teaspoon vanilla

In a saucepan, cook flour, egg, sugar, water and salt until thick. Add vanilla. Cool. Place peaches in large mixing bowl; pour sauce over and place in refrigerator, covered for 12 hours. Top with whipped cream to serve.

Suzanne Townsend

FROZEN MOCHA TORTE

1 cup crisp macaroon cookie crumbs
2 tablespoons butter, melted
3 cups chocolate ice cream, softened

½ cup hot fudge sauce
3 cups coffee ice cream, softened
4 ounces chocolate-coated toffee bars, coarsely chopped

Stir together cookie crumbs and butter; press onto bottom of 9- or 10-inch spring form pan. Bake at 350 degrees for 8 minutes, or until lightly browned. Cool. Spread chocolate ice cream over cooled crust; drizzle evenly with ¼ cup hot fudge sauce (cooled) and freeze until firm. Top with layer of coffee ice cream. Sprinkle evenly with crushed candy and drizzle with remaining hot fudge sauce. Cover and freeze until firm. Makes 10 to 12 servings.

Pat Davis

BUSTER BAR DESSERT

1 15-ounce package chocolate
    sandwich cookies, crushed
½ cup butter, melted (for crust)
1 15½-ounce can evaporated milk
½ cup butter (for topping)

⅔ cup chocolate chips
2 cups confectioners' sugar
½ gallon vanilla ice cream, softened
½ cup pecans, chopped
8 ounces prepared whipped topping

For crust, mix crushed cookies with ½ cup butter. Reserve ¾ cup; press the rest into a 9×13-inch pan. For topping, mix milk, ½ cup butter, chocolate chips and sugar in saucepan. Melt and boil for 8 minutes, stirring constantly. Set aside. Spread ice cream over crust and sprinkle pecans over ice cream. Add topping and freeze one hour. Spread prepared whipped topping on top and sprinkle with reserved crust. Freeze.

Mildred Britton

BANANAS FOSTER

½ cup butter
1½ cups brown sugar
4 bananas, sliced
1 to 2 tablespoons banana extract

Dash cinnamon
¼ cup rum
Vanilla ice cream

Melt butter. Add sugar and cook until bubbly. Add bananas. Heat 2 to 3 minutes. Stir in extract and cinnamon. Heat rum. Ignite and pour over bananas. Serve over ice cream.

Lucy Martin

BAKED BANANAS

4 firm, ripe bananas with skins
3 tablespoons unsalted butter
1/3 cup sugar

3 tablespoons lime juice
1/2 cup orange juice, freshly squeeze

Preheat oven to 375 degrees; place bananas on baking sheet and bake 15 to 20 minutes until skins are blackened. Set aside to cool slightly. Melt butter in large skillet over medium heat. Add sugar and lime juice. Cook, stirring occasionally until light caramel color, about 5 minutes. Stir in orange juice and cook until mixture is thick, bubbly and glossy, about 5 minutes. Slit banana skins and remove whole bananas to sauce in skillet. Cook bananas, basting often with sauce, for 5 minutes or until bananas are heated through and well coated. Serve warm. Makes 4 servings.

Carla Singer

MAINE BLUEBERRY BUCKLE

4 cups flour
1 cup sugar
4 teaspoons baking powder
1 1/2 teaspoons salt

2/3 cup shortening
1 1/2 cups milk
2 eggs
2 cups blueberries (if frozen, do not thaw)

Sift dry ingredients together. Add shortening, milk and eggs. When mixed thoroughly, fold in blueberries. Sprinkle topping on batter. Bake in greased 9×13-inch pan at 350 degrees for 35 to 40 minutes or until cake tester comes out clean.

Topping:
1 cup sugar
2 teaspoons cinnamon

4 tablespoons flour
4 tablespoons butter

Mix ingredients together and sprinkle on top of batter before baking.

Great coffee cake or good as a dessert served with ice cream. Preferable to use frozen Maine blueberries, if possible.

Ellie LeTourneau

EASY FRUIT COBBLER

1 cup sugar	1 teaspoon baking powder
⅔ cup flour	½ cup butter
⅔ cup milk	2 cups any fruit, sweetened to taste

Melt butter in an 8×8-inch square pan. Mix remaining ingredients, except fruit, and pour into pan. Add fruit. Bake at 375 degrees for 45 minutes. Pastry will come to top when baked.

Helen Wood

APPLE/CRANBERRY CRISP

2 cups fresh cranberries	1 cup quick-cooking rolled oats
3 cups red apple, unpeeled and sliced	½ cup flour
¾ cup sugar	½ cup brown sugar, firmly packed
½ cup butter	½ cup nuts, chopped

Combine cranberries, apple slices and ¾ cup sugar in bottom of 2-quart casserole. Melt butter; stir in remaining ingredients. Spread over berries and apples. Bake in 350 degree oven for 1 hour. Makes 6 servings. (This dessert is slightly tart ; a scoop of ice cream on top provides a sweet touch.)

Jarrel W. Calhoun

CURRIED FRUIT

1 16-ounce can peach halves, drained	⅓ cup butter, melted
1 16-ounce can pineapple slices, drained	¾ cup light brown sugar
1 16-ounce can pear halves, drained	4 teaspoons curry powder
	Maraschino cherries

Dry fruit thoroughly on paper towels. Arrange in 1½-quart shallow casserole, reserving 5 pineapple slices for top layer. Place a cherry in center of each pineapple slice. Mix melted butter, sugar and curry powder together and sprinkle over fruit. Bake uncovered at 325 degrees for 1 hour. Serves 6.

Mrs. Frank Cass

APPLE~BLACKBERRY CRISP

2 cups flour
2½ cups sugar, divided
¼ teaspoon salt
1 cup unsalted butter, chilled and
    cut in pieces

5 pounds golden delicious apples,
    peeled, cored, sliced thinly
1½ cups fresh or frozen blackberries,
    thawed and drained
¼ cup flour

Topping: Mix flour, 1½ cups sugar and salt in food processor. Add butter and blend in using on/off turns until mixture resembles coarse crumbs. (Can be prepared one day ahead. Cover and chill.)

Fruit: Toss apples, blackberries, remaining sugar and flour in a large bowl. Transfer to a buttered 9×13-inch baking dish, mounding slightly. Crumble topping over fruit. Bake at 350 degrees until fruit bubbles and topping is golden brown. Cool at least 15 minutes. Scoop into bowls and serve warm. Serves 12.

Dorothy Emmons

RHUBARB CRUNCH

Topping:
1 cup flour, sifted
¾ cup rolled oats
1 cup brown sugar, packed

½ cup butter or margarine, melted
1 teaspoon cinnamon

Fruit Mixture:
1 16-ounce package frozen
    rhubarb, thawed
1 cup sugar

2 tablespoons cornstarch
1 cup water
1 teaspoon vanilla

Mix crumb topping ingredients together until crumbly. Press half of crumb mixture into greased 9-inch round cake pan. Cover with rhubarb. In small saucepan, pour remaining fruit mixture ingredients. Cook until thick and clear, stirring often. Pour over rhubarb. Top with remaining crumbs. Bake at 350 degrees for 1 hour. Serve warm, cut into squares. May be served plain, with ice cream or whipped topping. Makes 8 servings.

Sarah Diamond

RICE PUDDING

4 cups milk
1 egg, well beaten
1 4-serving package vanilla
   pudding (not instant)
½ teaspoon cinnamon (optional)

1 cup minute rice, dry
2 1½-ounce boxes raisins
1 teaspoon vanilla extract
½ teaspoon nutmeg (optional)

Mix all ingredients in order given. Bring just to full boil over medium heat. Cool 30 minutes, stirring twice. If desired, add nutmeg and cinnamon to warm pudding. Stir well. Pour into serving dishes and sprinkle with nutmeg and cinnamon. Serves 6.

Virginia Lutskus

MILLIONAIRE'S PIE CRUST

2 cups sifted flour, bleached or
   unbleached
1 pinch of salt
12 tablespoons butter

1 tablespoon extra fine granulated sugar
1 egg yolk, slightly beaten
3 to 4 tablespoons ice water

Combine flour and salt. Cut in butter with pastry blender until mixture resembles breadcrumbs. Add sugar, egg yolk and water to barely bind the dough. Mix lightly. Form dough into a ball, wrap in plastic-wrap and refrigerate for 30 minutes before rolling. This rich pastry dough may be frozen for several months and left to defrost at room temperature prior to using.

Dedicated to Pat Farmer

PRALINE APPLE CREAM PIE

1 15-ounce package pie crust
Filling:
   2 teaspoons sugar
   1 teaspoon flour
Topping:
   ½ cup sugar
   ½ cup brown sugar, firmly packed
   ¼ cup cornstarch
   ¼ teaspoon salt
   2 cups half-and-half

¼ teaspoon cinnamon
1½ cups peeled, thinly sliced apple

3 tablespoons butter or margarine
1 teaspoon vanilla
8 to 10 pecan halves
   Nutmeg

Heat oven to 450 degrees. Prepare pie crust according to package directions for unfilled one-crust pie, using 9-inch pie pan. (Reserve remaining crust for later use.) Bake for 6 to 8 minutes or until very light golden brown. Cool completely. Reduce oven to 350 degrees. In 2 quart microwave-safe bowl, combine sugar, flour and cinnamon for filling. Blend well. Add apple slices; toss lightly to coat. Microwave on HIGH for 3 to 5 minutes or until apples are tender, stirring halfway through cooking. Spoon mixture evenly into cooled crust. For topping, combine sugars, cornstarch and salt in saucepan. Blend well. Gradually stir in half-and-half. Add margarine. Cook over medium heat until mixture beings to thicken, about 10 minutes, stirring constantly. Stir in vanilla. Carefully pour topping over apple filling. Arrange pecan halves over topping. Sprinkle with nutmeg. Bake at 350 degrees for 35 to 40 minutes or until filling has puffed areas and crust is golden brown. Cool completely. Refrigerate until ready to serve. Serves 8.

Maurice Buchanan

FRUIT PIE

½ cup butter	1 cup flour
2 tablespoons	Sugar

Cream butter and sugar; add flour. Press into pie pan and bake at 400 degrees for about 7 minutes.

Filling:

1 8-ounce package cream cheese, softened	2 tablespoons lemon juice
½ cup sugar	2 tablespoons cream or milk
1 teaspoon lemon rind, grated	

Mix filling ingredients together and line baked pie crust. Layer sliced fresh peaches or blueberries over the top.

Glaze:

Mash 3 cups strawberries or blueberries, with 1 cup sugar. Let stand for 30 minutes. Mix in 3 tablespoons cornstarch. Cook over medium heat until thick and juices are clear. Cool. Pour over cheese and fruit. Refrigerate. May be topped with whipped cream.

Donda Drake

CARAMELIZED APPLE TART

Pastry:

1 cup flour	3 tablespoons sugar
⅛ teaspoon salt	½ cup butter or margarine
	3 tablespoons ice water

Filling:

6 tablespoons butter or margarine divided	½ cup sugar
	3 cups apples, peeled and sliced
	2 tablespoons brown sugar

Make pastry as for pie crust and chill 1 hour. In a 9-inch deep-dish pie pan, melt 3 tablespoons butter. Sprinkle 3 tablespoons of sugar over butter. Arrange apples in layers, sprinkling each layer with sugar. Dot with butter. Roll out pastry to fit pan and cover apples. Bake at 375 degrees for 30 minutes. Cool 5 minutes. Carefully invert onto ovenproof plate. Sprinkle with brown sugar and place under broiler until sugar melts and top browns.

Betty Josey

OUT OF THIS WORLD CHERRY PIE

2 large pie shells, baked
1 can prepared cherry pie filling
¾ cup sugar
1 16-ounce can crushed pineapple,
    undrained

1 tablespoon cornstarch
1 3-ounce box raspberry gelatin
6 bananas, sliced
1 cup nuts, chopped

In saucepan, combine cherry pie filling, sugar, pineapple and cornstarch. Cook over medium heat until thick. Remove from heat and add gelatin, stirring to blend. Cool. Add bananas and nuts. Pour into crusts and top with whipped cream.

Eleanore Nelson

PEACH CREAM PIE

1 prepared unbaked deep dish pie shell
6 to 8 large peaches
1 cup sugar
3 heaping tablespoons flour

1 cup whipping cream, unwhipped
Nutmeg, to taste
Almond flavoring, to taste
Vanilla, to taste

Peel and slice peaches. Place in bottom of pie shell. Mix remaining ingredients together and pour over peaches. Bake at 325 degrees for approximately 1 hour.

Renee Morris

AMAZING AMBROSIA PIE

1¾ cups milk
¾ cup sugar
⅓ cup biscuit mix
4 eggs

Rind of ½ orange
¼ cup margarine
1½ teaspoons vanilla
1 cup flaked coconut

Combine milk, sugar, biscuit mix, eggs, orange rind, margarine and vanilla in electric blender. Cover and blend on low speed for 3 minutes. Pour into greased 9-inch pie pan. Let stand about 5 minutes; sprinkle with coconut. Bake at 350 degrees for 40 minutes. Serve warm or cool. Store in refrigerator.

Lilah Ovard

STRAWBERRY PIE

1 9-inch pie shell, baked
8 ounces cream cheese
1 cup sugar, divided
1 teaspoon lemon rind, grated
2 tablespoons lemon juice

4 cups fresh strawberries
2 10-ounce packages frozen
   strawberries, thawed
¼ cup cornstarch
   Whipped cream, sweetened

Blend ½ cup sugar with cream cheese. Add grated lemon rind and lemon juice. Spread in pie shell. Top with fresh strawberries. In a saucepan, combine thawed strawberries, remaining sugar and cornstarch and cook until bubbly. Cook 2 minutes more. Cool completely. Pour over fresh strawberries in pie shell. Chill. Top with sweetened whipped cream. Serves 8.

Dedicated to Betty Costello

BUMBLEBERRY PIE

(Served during the Calgary, Alberta Stampede)

   Pastry for 2 crust pie
1⅓ cups sugar
⅓ cup flour
1 teaspoon cinnamon
1 cup blackberries

1 cup raspberries
1 cup strawberries
1 cup rhubarb (can use frozen)
1 cup apples, sliced

Make your own favorite crust or use ready-made crust. For filling, stir flour, sugar and cinnamon and toss with all fruit. Fill 9-inch pie shell. Put on top crust. Crimp edges and cut vents to allow steam to escape. Sprinkle with 1 teaspoon sugar on top crust. Bake at 400 degrees for 20 minutes. Reduce heat to 325 degrees for an additional 20 minutes.

Our Canadian Friends

FRESH PEACH PIE

Baked pie shell
3½ cups fresh peaches, sliced
¾ cup sugar
2 tablespoons cornstarch

2 tablespoons butter or margarine, melted
Juice of 1 lemon
Small amount of orange juice

Sprinkle peach slices with sugar and allow to absorb for 30 minutes. Drain juice and add enough orange juice to make 1½ cups liquid. Stir liquid into cornstarch and cook over low heat until thickened. Add lemon juice and melted butter and cool to room temperature. Spoon small amount into cooled pie crust. Add sliced peaches and pour the balance of glaze over peaches. Chill.

Susan Krutz

COUNTRY LEMON TART

Butter Pecan Crust:
1¼ cups flour
1 egg yolk
⅓ cup pecans, finely chopped

3 tablespoons confectioners' sugar
½ cup butter or margarine
¼ teaspoon salt

Combine all ingredients in mixing bowl. Blend with fork; form dough into a ball. Dust fingertips with flour; press dough evenly into bottom and up sides of greased 9-inch pie plate. Bake at 350 degrees for 10 minutes.

Filling:
3 eggs, beaten
1 cup sugar
1 tablespoon flour

3 tablespoons lemon juice
1½ teaspoons lemon rind, grated
Confectioners' sugar

Combine eggs, sugar, flour, lemon juice and rind in a mixing bowl; stir until smooth. Pour mixture into baked crust. Bake 20 to 25 minutes more, or until filling is set. Cool on a wire rack; dust with confectioners' sugar. Store, covered, in the refrigerator. Makes 10 to 12 servings.

Dedicated to Velma McShan

NUTTY COCONUT CREAM PIE

1 pie shell, baked and cooled
1 15-ounce can cream of coconut, divided
2 3-ounce packages vanilla pudding and pie filling mix

1¾ cups milk
3½ ounces macadamia nuts, chopped
1½ cups whipping cream
½ cup coconut, toasted

Reserve 3 tablespoons cream of coconut and set aside. In saucepan, cook remaining cream of coconut, pudding mix and milk according to package directions. Stir in half of nuts. Pour in pie shell. Beat whipping cream with 3 tablespoons of cream of coconut until stiff. Spread over pie; top with coconut and remaining nuts. Serves 10.

Dedicated to Lettie Moore

BOB HOPE'S FAVORITE LEMON PIE

1 pie shell, baked and cooled
1 cup plus 2 tablespoons sugar
3 tablespoons cornstarch
1 cup boiling water

4 egg yolks
2 tablespoons butter
Grated rind of 1 lemon
4 tablespoons lemon juice
Pinch of salt

Meringue:
3 egg whites

2 tablespoons sugar

Combine corn starch and sugar, add water slowly, stirring constantly until thick and smooth. Add slighly beaten egg yolks, butter, lemon rind, juice, and salt. Cook 2 or 3 minutes. Pour into baked shell. Beat egg whites and 2 tablespoons sugar until stiff. Cover filling with meringue. Bake in slow oven 15 minutes or until light brown.

Bob Hope

LUSCIOUS LEMON COCONUT PIE

1¼ cups sugar
2 tablespoons flour
⅛ teaspoon salt
¼ cup soft butter
3 eggs
1 cup coconut

½ cup cold water
2 teaspoons grated lemon rind
¼ cup lemon juice
1 teaspoon sugar and cinnamon
1 teaspoon egg white

Mix sugar, flour and salt. Blend in butter. Beat eggs in separate bowl. Add sugar mixture and blend well. Add coconut. Mix in water, lemon rind and juice. Pour into shell. Moisten edge of crust. Add top crust. Cut slits for steam. Brush with egg white, sprinkle with sugar and cinnamon. Bake at 400 degrees for 35 minutes.

Buttermilk pie crust dough:
2½ cups unbleached flour
2 tablespoons sugar
1 teaspoon salt

½ cup unsalted butter, chilled, sliced
½ cup solid shortening, chilled
¼ cup plus 2 tablespoons buttermilk

Combine flour, sugar and salt in large bowl. Add butter and shortening. Cut in using fork or pastry blender until mixture resembles coarse meal. Add buttermilk and stir with fork until moist clumps form. Dough can be prepared in processor. Using on/off turns, cut butter and shortening into dry ingredients until coarse meal forms. Add buttermilk and process just until moist clumps form. Press together to form dough. Divide in half. Gather dough into balls; flatten into disks. Wrap separately and chill 1 hour. (Can be prepared ahead. Refrigerate 1 week or freeze 1 month. Let dough stand at room temperature to soften slightly before using.) Makes enough for 2 crusts.

Lynda Sanders

CHOCOLATE ANGEL PIE

Meringue Shell:

2 egg whites

⅛ teaspoon salt

⅛ teaspoon cream of tartar

½ cup sugar

½ cup pecans, chopped

½ teaspoon vanilla

Combine egg whites, salt and cream of tartar; beat until foamy. Add sugar gradually, beating until very stiff peaks form. Fold in nuts and vanilla. Spread in greased 8-inch pie pan; build sides up to ½-inch above pan. Bake at 300 degrees for 50 to 55 minutes. Cool.

Filling:

2 ounces German sweet chocolate

3 tablespoons water

1 teaspoon vanilla

1 cup whipping cream

Melt chocolate in water over low heat, stirring constantly. Cool until mixture thickens. Add vanilla. Whip cream and fold into chocolate. Pour into cooled shell. Chill. Serves 6. (Small meringue tarts can be made by placing 1 teaspoon of meringue on cookie sheet and baking as above.)

Stella Klein

MRS. TOWNLEY'S CHOCOLATE PIE

1 package German sweet chocolate

¼ cup butter or margarine

1 14½-ounce can evaporated milk

1½ cups sugar

3 tablespoons cornstarch

⅛ teaspoon salt

1 10-inch pie shell, unbaked

1⅓ cups coconut, flaked

⅓ cup pecans, chopped

2 eggs

1 teaspoon vanilla

Mix chocolate with butter over low heat and stir until blended. Gradually add milk. Mix sugar, cornstarch and salt. Beat in eggs and vanilla. Add chocolate mixture. Pour into pie shell. Mix coconut and nuts and sprinkle over filling. Bake at 375 degrees for 45 minutes, or until top is puffed. Cool at least 4 hours. Pie will not be firm until it cools. Store in refrigerator.

Dedicated to Kate Townley

GRASSHOPPER PIE

24 plain chocolate wafers, crushed
4½ tablespoons margarine, melted
25 large marshmallows
¾ cup milk

½ pint heavy cream
2 ounces green creme de menthe
2 ounces white creme de cacao

Mix wafers and margarine together and press into bottom and sides of a 9-inch pie plate. Melt marshmallows and milk in a double boiler. Chill until cool; then beat with electric mixer. Beat heavy cream and fold into chilled mixture. Fold in creme de menthe and creme de cacao. Pour into pie crust and freeze. Remove for a few minutes before serving to soften a little. May be decorated with grated chocolate, if desired.

Kay Damms

SOUR CREAM PIE

(This is an old Kentucky recipe from the early 1900s)

2 cups sour cream
2 cups sugar (may be reduced to
    1½ cups)
½ cup raisins, ground after
    scalding and draining

½ teaspoon cinnamon
¼ teaspoon cloves
3 eggs, separated
1 unbaked pie shell

Drained cherries from canned prepared pie filling may be used to substitute for raisins.

Mix all ingredients except egg whites. Pour into an unbaked pie shell. Bake in 375 degree oven for 20 to 25 minutes. Filling may not be completely set, but will do so upon cooling. Make meringue of the egg whites, and sweeten to taste. Spread on top of pie and brown in 350 degree oven. Refrigerate until serving time. Prepared whipped topping may be used instead of meringue.

Anne Walker

LOIS' PECAN PIE

3 eggs, slightly beaten
1 cup sugar
½ cup light corn syrup
3 tablespoons butter or margarine

1 teaspoon vanilla
1 cup pecans, broken
9-inch pie shell, unbaked

Mix all ingredients except pecans and pie shell. Add pecans. Pour into pie shell and bake at 450 degrees for 10 minutes; then reduce temperature to 350 degrees and continue baking for 30 minutes. (An egg substitute may be used in place of the eggs.)

Lois Duncan

PECAN DELIGHT OR MYSTERY PIE

3 egg whites
1 cup sugar
1 cup nuts, broken

23 Ritz crackers, crushed
1 teaspoon vanilla
½ pint whipping cream, whipped

Beat egg whites until stiff peaks form, gradually beating in sugar. Fold in nuts, cracker crumbs and vanilla. Pour into buttered 9-inch pie pan and bake at 325 degrees for 30 minutes. Cool. Top with whipped cream and chill. (Pie is better if baked a day ahead.)

Kala Casebolt

CHOCOLATE KARO PECAN PIE

1 cup dark corn syrup
3 eggs, slightly beaten
1/8 teaspoon salt
1 teaspoon vanilla
1 cup sugar

2 tablespoons margarine, melted
1 cup pecan halves
1 9-inch pie shell, unbaked
1 cup semisweet mini chocolate chips

Cover bottom of pie shell with chocolate chips. Mix remaining ingredients, adding pecan halves last. Pour into pie shell over chips. Bake at 375 degrees for 10 minutes and then reduce heat to 350 degrees and bake 30 to 35 minutes. When pie is done, outer edges of filling should be set, center slightly soft; filling will continue to cook after the pie is removed from the oven.

Susan Rumble

OSGOOD PIE

This is a very old recipe which has been in the family for generations. It's believed to have originated in England. It came down to my mother from my grandmother, the late Mrs. Maude Montgomery Clough of Fort Worth.

Bring a pan of water to a boil and pour in 2 cups of raisins; remove from heat and cover, allowing raisins to soak about 1/2 hour. Pour off water and rinse raisins well with hot water. Drain.

2 cups sugar
3/4 cup butter, softened,
   (not margarine)
2 unbaked pie shells

1 cup pecans, chopped
5 eggs, separated
1 teaspoon vanilla

Mix raisins with remaining ingredients, except egg whites. Beat egg whites until stiff and fold into mixture. Pour into 2 unbaked pie shells and bake at 300 degrees for 45 minutes, or until firm and golden brown. Top with whipped cream.

Kathi Clough Miller

AUNT ZULA'S EXCELLENT EGG CUSTARD PIE

3 eggs
¾ cup sugar
2 cups milk

3 tablespoons butter
1 teaspoon vanilla
Nutmeg to taste

Unbaked pie shell

1 egg white, slightly beaten

Brush shell with slightly beaten egg white. Scald milk and add butter. Beat eggs and blend in sugar, vanilla and nutmeg. Quickly stir the egg/sugar mixture into the hot milk. Pour into prepared crust. Bake for 10 minutes at 475 degrees and 10 minutes more at 375 degrees.

Virginia Duncan

EGGNOG PIE

3 eggs, separated
½ cup sugar
2 cups light cream or milk
Dash salt

Dash nutmeg
½ teaspoon vanilla
1 9-inch unbaked pie shell

Beat egg yolks, sugar and cream/milk. Add salt, nutmeg and vanilla. Fold in stiffly beaten egg whites. Pour into pie shell and bake at 400 degrees for 25 to 30 minutes. (Sherry or rum flavoring to taste may be substituted for vanilla.)

Susan Rumble

APPLE "PIE" CAKE

¼ cup butter, softened
1 cup sugar
1 egg
1 cup flour
1 teaspoon salt
1 teaspoon cinnamon

2 tablespoons hot water
1 teaspoon vanilla
3 cups cooking apples, peeled, cored and diced
½ cup pecans, chopped
   Rum Butter Sauce (below)
   Whipped cream (below, optional)

Cream butter; gradually add sugar, beating well at medium speed. Add egg; beat until blended. Combine flour, salt and cinnamon, mix well. Add to creamed mixture. Beat on low speed until smooth. Stir in water and vanilla. Fold in apples and pecans; spoon into a greased and floured 9-inch pie plate. Bake at 350 degrees for 45 minutes or until a toothpick inserted in center comes out clean. Cut this cake into pie-shaped wedges. Serve warm with Rum Butter Sauce and whipped cream.

Rum Butter Sauce:
   ½ cup brown sugar, firmly packed
   ½ cup sugar
   ¼ cup butter, softened

   ½ cup whipping cream
   2 tablespoons rum, if desired

Combine ingredients, except rum, in a small saucepan; mix well. Bring to a boil, and cook 1 minute. Stir in rum.

Whipped cream:
   1 pint whipping cream
   ⅓ cup brown sugar

   1 teaspoon vanilla

Whip together and serve a dollop over each serving.

Lynda Sanders

FRESH APPLE CAKE

Cake:

   2 cups apples, finely diced
   1 cup sugar
   1 egg

   1 teaspoon cinnamon
   1 teaspoon baking soda
   1 cup flour

Mix all ingredients together. Pour into well-greased 8×8-inch baking pan. Bake at 375 degrees for 40 minutes. Serve with sauce.

Sauce:

   ½ cup sugar
   ½ cup brown sugar
   2 tablespoons flour

   ¼ cup butter
   1 teaspoon vanilla
   1 cup cold water

Combine all ingredients and boil until thick. Pour over warm cake.

Zelma Klingman

GLAZED APPLE CAKE

   ⅔ cup cooking oil
   1 teaspoon vanilla
   2 eggs
   2 cups flour
   1 cup sugar

   1 teaspoon salt
   1½ teaspoons baking soda
   ½ teaspoon cinnamon
   1 21-ounce can apple pie filling or
      2½ cups fresh apples, chopped
   ½ cup pecans, chopped

Combine oil, vanilla and eggs and stir until blended. Add remaining ingredients and stir until blended. Pour into a 9×13-inch greased and floured pan. Bake at 350 degrees for 25 to 35 minutes, or until wooden pick inserted comes out clean. Pierce cake every inch with a long-tined fork and spread with glaze.

Glaze:

   ½ cup sugar
   ½ cup sour cream

   ¼ teaspoon baking soda
   ¼ nuts, chopped.

Blend well.

Chris Coker

MERINGUE WREATH CROWNED CAKE

Meringue:
- 4 egg whites (room temperature)
- ¼ teaspoon cream of tartar
- ½ teaspoon almond extract
- Pinch of salt
- 1 cup confectioners' sugar

Butter Cake:
- 1½ cups cake flour
- 2 teaspoons baking powder
- ¼ teaspoon salt
- ⅓ cup butter
- ½ teaspoon almond extract
- ¾ cup granulated sugar
- 6 egg yolks
- ½ cup milk
- ½ teaspoon vanilla

Filling:
- 2 cups whipping cream
- 1 teaspoon vanilla
- 1 cup confectioners' sugar

Raspberry sauce: (optional)
- 10 ounces frozen raspberries with juice
- 12 ounce jar raspberry jam
- ½ cup sugar
- 2 to 3 tablespoons cornstarch
- ⅓ cup sherry or Grand Marnier

Meringue: In large bowl, beat together egg whites, cream of tartar and salt until soft peaks form. Gradually add sugar, beating until stiff shiny peaks form. Beat in almond extract. Draw a 9-inch circle on foil-covered baking sheet. Spoon meringue in wreath shape inside circle. Bake at 275 degrees for about 1½ hours until slighly colored. Turn off oven and leave for several hours. (Meringue can be prepared ahead and stored in airtight container for up to 1 week.)

Butter cake: Sift together flour, baking powder and salt, set aside. In large bowl, cream together butter and sugar until very light and fluffy. Add egg yolks, one at a time, beating well after each addition. Blend in flour mixture in 3 parts, alternating with milk and beating well after each addition. Beat in vanilla and almond extract. Pour batter into buttered and lightly floured 10-inch round layer cake pan. Bake at 350 degrees for about 20 minutes or until tester comes out clean. Cool 5 minutes in pan, then remove and let cool on rack. (Cake can be prepared ahead, wrapped and stored for up to 2 days).

Filling: Whip cream until stiff; fold in sugar and vanilla.

Raspberry sauce: Place all ingredients except liqueur in a large saucepan. Cook over low heat, stirring constantly until smooth and thick. Cool and add sherry or Grand Marnier. Press through a strainer for a smooth, clear liquid. Can be served warm or cold. It can be stored in the refrigerator for a month.

(continued on page 244)

(continued from page 243)

MERINGUE WREATH CROWNED CAKE

Assembly: Place cake upside down on large cake plate. Cover with raspberry sauce and half the filling. Place meringue on top of cake. Transfer 1 cup of remaining filling to piping bag. Pipe rosettes around outside where meringue joins cake. Spoon remaining filling into hole in center of meringue. At serving time, spoon fresh sliced strawberries into center of wreath. Spoon raspberry sauce over strawberries. Reserve remaining sauce for future use. Serves 16.

Faye Dudley Brooks

LEMON ANGEL FOOD CAKE WITH STRAWBERRIES

Cake:
1 cup cake flour	½ teaspoon cream of tartar
1¼ cups sugar	3 tablespoons fresh lemon juice
½ teaspoon salt	2 teaspoons lemon rind, grated
10 large egg whites	½ teaspoon almond extract

Position rack in lowest third of oven and preheat to 350 degrees. Sift flour, ¼ cup sugar and salt into medium bowl. Resift flour mixture. Using electric mixer, beat egg whites and cream of tartar in large bowl until foamy. Gradually beat in 1 cup sugar until stiff and glossy peaks form. Beat in lemon juice, rind and almond extract. Sift ¼ of flour mixture over and gently fold into whites. Repeat with remaining flour in 3 more batches. Spoon batter into 10-inch diameter straight-sided tube pan. Bake until cake is golden brown and toothpick inserted near center comes out clean, about 50 minutes. Immediately invert cake over neck of a bottle. Cool completely in pan. Run knife around pan sides to loosen cake. Transfer cake to serving plate.

Topping:
2 pints fresh strawberries, sliced	2 tablespoons honey

Combine strawberries and honey in medium bowl and let stand 30 minutes. Slice cake into wedges and serve with strawberries.

DyAnna Giltner

PINEAPPLE UPSIDE-DOWN CAKE

Topping:
- 1/4 cup butter or margarine
- 1 cup brown sugar
- 4 pineapple slices, drained
- 4 maraschino cherries

Cake:
- 1 1/4 cups flour, sifted
- 3/4 cup sugar
- 1 1/4 teaspoons baking powder
- 1/2 teaspoon salt
- 1 egg
- 1/4 cup shortening
- 1/2 cup minus 1 tablespoon pineapple Syrup
- 1/2 teaspoon lemon rind, grated

Melt butter and stir in brown sugar. Pour into an 8-inch square baking dish. Place pineapple slices in mixture and place maraschino cherry inside each pineapple slice. Sift dry ingredients together over softened shortening. Add remaining ingredients. Beat 2 minutes. Pour over pineapple mixture and bake at 350 degrees for 30 minutes. Remove from oven and let stand 5 minutes. Turn upside down onto serving plate.

Susan Rumble

MEXICAN WEDDING CAKE

2 cups flour
2 cups sugar
1 teaspoon baking soda

1 teaspoon vanilla
1 20-ounce can crushed pineapple
½ cup nuts, chopped

Combine all ingredients. Bake at 350 degrees for 30 to 35 minutes in a 9×13 greased and floured pan.

Frosting:
8 ounces cream cheese
½ cup margarine, melted
¾ cup sugar

½ cup nuts, chopped
1 teaspoon vanilla

Beat all ingredients until light and fluffy. Pour over cake while hot.

Pauline Steele

TEXAS CHOCOLATE CAKE

2 cups flour
2 cups sugar
1 cup water
½ cup margarine
½ cup oil
3 tablespoons cocoa

2 eggs
2 tablespoons vinegar
½ cup buttermilk
1 teaspoon vanilla
1 teaspoon baking soda
1 teaspoon cinnamon

Mix flour and sugar together; set aside. Combine and bring to a boil: water, margarine, oil and cocoa. Pour over flour mixture. Add eggs, one at a time. Stir vinegar into buttermilk and add to mixture. Add remaining ingredients and bake at 350 degrees in a 10×15-inch pan for 25 minutes. Frost while hot. Makes 48 bars.

Frosting:
3½ tablespoons cocoa
½ cup butter or margarine
6 tablespoons milk

1 16-ounce box confectioners' sugar
Chopped nuts, if desired

In a saucepan, bring to a boil the cocoa, butter and milk; boil for 2 minutes. Add confectioners' sugar and nuts. If too thick, add a bit more milk.

Ruth Roan and Martha Baker

WACKY CHOCOLATE CAKE

1½ cups flour
1 cup sugar
¼ cup cocoa
1 teaspoon baking soda
½ teaspoon salt
½ cup chopped pecans

1 tablespoon white vinegar
1 teaspoon vanilla
½ cup oil
1 cup water
1 cup chocolate chips

Mix flour, sugar, cocoa, baking soda and salt in bowl; add remaining ingredients except chips and nuts, and beat until smooth. Pour into 9- or10-inch square pan. Bake at 350 degrees for 30 to 35 minutes. Place on wire rack. Immediately sprinkle chocolate chips on top and let stand until melted. Spread evenly. Sprinkle with chopped nuts.

Bette Schroer

FLOURLESS CHOCOLATE CAKE

Cake:
7 eggs, separated
1 cup confectioners' sugar

½ cup cocoa
1 teaspoon vanilla

Sift sugar and cocoa. Add to well beaten egg yolks and vanilla. Beat egg whites until stiff. Fold in cocoa mixture. Bake in ungreased springform pan at 350 degrees for 35 minutes.

Filling:
1 pint whipping cream
3 heaping tablespoons
    confectioners' sugar

2 heaping tablespoons cocoa
½ teaspoon vanilla

Whip cream; as cream is whipping, add sugar and cocoa. Add vanilla. After cake has cooled and center falls in, fill cavity and frost sides with filling. Refrigerate 4 hours.

Barbara Bigham

MISSISSIPPI MUD CAKE

2 cups flour	5 ounces unsweetened chocolate
1 teaspoon baking soda	1 cup butter, cut into pieces
Pinch of salt	2 cups sugar
1¾ cups coffee	2 eggs, lightly beaten
¼ cup bourbon	1 teaspoon vanilla

Sift flour, baking soda and salt in bowl; set aside. Heat coffee and bourbon over low heat for 5 minutes. Add unsweetened chocolate and butter and heat mixture, stirring until chocolate and butter are melted and mixture is smooth. Remove from heat and stir in sugar; let mixture cool for 3 minutes and transfer it to the bowl of an electric mixer. Add flour mixture ½ cup at a time, beating at medium speed, and continue to beat the mixture for 1 minute more. Add egg and vanilla and beat until smooth. Butter a 9-inch tube pan, 3½-inches deep and dust it with cocoa. Pour in batter and bake at 275 degrees for 1 hour and 30 minutes. Let cool completely in pan on a rack and turn out onto a serving plate. Serve with whipped cream sweetened and flavored with white creme de cocoa to taste or with hot fudge.

Jacque Schuster

CHOCOLATE PECAN TORTE

(with Strawberry Buttercream)

¾ cup unsalted butter, softened
2 cups sugar
8 eggs
2 tablespoons vanilla
¼ teaspoon salt

12 ounces bittersweet or semisweet
chocolate, melted
3½ cups pecans, finely ground
Strawberry buttercream
Easy chocolate glaze
6 to 8 strawberries, halved

Butter four 9-inch round cake pans; line bottoms with parchment; butter parchment. Using electric mixer, cream butter until light. Add sugar and beat until fluffy. Beat in eggs one at a time. Add vanilla and salt. Stir in chocolate and pecans. Divide batter among pans. Bake at 375 degrees about 22 minutes, or until tester inserted in center comes out fudgy but not wet (top may crack). Cool in pans 5 minutes. Invert onto racks. Discard parchment. Cool layers completely. (Can be prepared up to 2 days ahead. Wrap each layer separately with plastic and refrigerate.) Arrange one cake layer bottom side up on platter. Spread ⅔ cup Strawberry Buttercream over layer. Repeat with remaining layers and buttercream, ending with cake, bottom side up. Cover and refrigerate torte for at least 6 hours. Pour glaze over cake; smooth over sides and top. Can be prepared 1 day ahead and refrigerated. Arrange strawberries around top edge of torte, cut side down. Let stand at room temperature 1 hour before serving.

Strawberry Buttercream:
1¼ cups unsalted butter, softened slightly
2 cups confectioners' sugar, sifted
4 egg yolks

½ cup pureed fresh strawberries
3 tablespoons strawberry preserves

Cream butter and sugar until light and fluffy. Mix in yolks, then pureed berries and preserves. Cover tightly and refrigerate until set. (Can be prepared 2 days ahead.) Soften buttercream at room temperature until spreadable. Makes about 2½ cups.

Easy Chocolate Glaze:
3 ounces semisweet chocolate,
coarsely chopped
½ cup water
6 tablespoons unsalted butter

3 tablespoons oil
¾ cup cocoa
½ cup plus 2 tablespoons sugar

Heat chocolate, butter, water and oil in top of double boiler until chocolate melts. Remove from heat. Add cocoa and sugar and stir until sugar dissolves and glaze is smooth. Let cool until thickened slightly but still pourable. Makes about 2 cups.

Dedicated to Winnie Brieden

POOR MAN'S CAKE

(Contains no milk, butter or eggs)

2 cups sugar	1 teaspoon cloves
1 cup shortening	3 cups flour
2 cups boiling water	2 teaspoons baking soda
2 cups raisins	1 teaspoon salt
2 teaspoons cinnamon	1 cup nuts

In a saucepan, blend sugar, shortening, water, raisins and spices. Cook 3 minutes. Cool to lukewarm. Stir in remaining ingredients. Bake in a greased and floured 8×12-inch pan at 300 degrees (yes, 300 degrees) for 45 minutes, or until cake shrinks from sides of pan. Cool in pan. May be frosted, if desired or served with whipped cream (also good as is).

Kay Damms

T-BAR TEMPTATION CAKE

3 cups flour	1¾ cups sugar
1½ teaspoons baking soda	¾ cup butter or margarine, softened
1½ teaspoons cinnamon	3 eggs
1 teaspoon salt	1½ cups applesauce
¾ teaspoon nutmeg	2 cups semisweet chocolate chips
¼ teaspoon ground cloves	2 tablespoons confectioners' sugar
1¼ cups pecan halves	

Grease and flour a 10-inch tube or Bundt pan. In large bowl, combine flour, soda, cinnamon, salt, nutmeg and cloves; set aside. Chop ¾ cup pecan halves; reserve remaining ½ cup for top. In large bowl, at medium speed, cream sugar and butter until light and fluffy, scraping bowl occasionally. Add eggs, one at a time. Reduce speed to low. Add flour mixture alternately with applesauce, beating after each addition, just until smooth. Fold in 1 cup chocolate chips and chopped pecans. Pour into prepared pan. Sprinkle remaining chocolate chips and pecan halves on top of batter. Bake at 350 degrees for 1 hour, or until toothpick inserted in center comes out clean. Place on wire rack; cool 20 minutes. Loosen edges and turn onto wire rack and cool completely. Sprinkle with confectioners' sugar.

Pamela Easter

MARTHA'S CHRISTMAS CAKE

1 *pound box muscat raisins*
2 *cups sugar*
2 *heaping tablespoons cocoa*
¾ *teaspoon cloves*
¾ *teaspoon cinnamon*
¾ *teaspoon allspice*

¾ *teaspoon nutmeg*
½ *cup vegetable oil*
1 *cup English walnuts*
3 *cups boiling water*
2½ *cups flour*
¼ *teaspoon salt*
2 *teaspoons soda*

Boil everything *except* flour, soda and salt. Let cool. Stir in flour, soda and salt. Grease and flour tube pan. Bake at 375 degrees for 50 minutes. This cake keeps well and is moist.

Marhta Weisend

DATE-MINCEMEAT CAKE

1 *9-ounce package mincemeat*
½ *cup water*
1 *cup walnuts or pecans, broken*
1 *8-ounce box chopped dates*
1 *15-ounce can sweetened condensed milk*

1 *egg, beaten*
¾ *cup unsifted flour*
½ *teaspoon baking powder*
½ *teaspoon vanilla extract*

Break mincemeat into small pieces in large sauce pan. Add water. Stir until smooth. Boil briskly one minute. Remove from heat and cool. Add nuts, dates, milk, egg and vanilla; blend well. Stir in flour and baking powder until just blended. Pour into one large loaf pan, or four mini loaf pans which have been greased, waxpaper lined, and greased again. Bake at 300 degrees for 1½ hours or until top is golden brown (45 minutes for mini pans). Toothpick inserted in center should come out clean. If desired, drizzle hot cake with cherry brandy. Store in refrigerator.

Virginia Lutskus

DALLAS'S BEST BANANA NUT CAKE

(My mother's maiden name is Dallas,
descendent of George M. Dallas, vice president of the United States under James K. Polk)

½ cup butter
1½ cups sugar
2 whole eggs
4 tablespoons milk
1 teaspoon lemon juice

1 teaspoon soda
4 bananas, mashed
1½ cups flour
1 cup nuts

Make sour milk by combining milk with lemon juice. Set aside. Cream together butter and sugar. Beat vigorously adding eggs one at a time. Dissolve soda in milk and stir into mixture. Gradually add flour. Beat well and add bananas and nuts. Pour into greased Bundt pan. Bake for 50 minutes at 350 degrees. Check for doneness.

Icing:
1½ cups sugar
¾ cup evaporated milk

½ cup butter
½ teaspoon vanilla

Slowly bring to boil stirring constantly. Boil 5 minutes being careful to stir to prevent scorching. Take off heat. Let cool. Beat to thick consistency to spread on cake.

Lynda Sanders

ITALIAN CREAM CAKE

2 cups sugar
½ cup butter
½ cup shortening
5 egg yolks
1 teaspoon vanilla
½ cup Angel Flake coconut

2 cups sifted flour
1 teaspoon soda
1 cup buttermilk
1 cup chopped pecans
5 egg whites

Grease and flour three 9-inch round pans. Cream together sugar, butter and shortening. Add egg yolks, one at a time. Add vanilla, and coconut. Mix well. Sift flour and soda together and add to the first mixture, alternating with buttermilk, beginning and ending with flour mixture. Add nuts. Beat egg whites until stiff and fold into the batter. Bake at 350 degrees for 25 minutes.

Icing:

8 ounces cream cheese, softened
½ cup margarine
1 pound confectioners' sugar

1 teaspoon vanilla
1 cup chopped pecans

Beat cream cheese and margarine until creamy. Add vanilla, then sugar, and mix well. Fold in pecans and spread on cooled layers. Stack layers and ice sides of cake. Cake should be kept refrigerated after it is iced.

Joan Fleeker

HUMMINGBIRD CAKE

Cake:

- 3 cups flour
- 2 cups sugar
- 1 teaspoon salt
- 1 teaspoon soda
- 1 teaspoon cinnamon

- 3 eggs, beaten
- 1½ cups vegetable oil
- 1½ teaspoons vanilla extract
- 1 8½-ounce can crushed pineapple
- 2 cups pecans, chopped (divided use)
- 2 cups bananas, mashed

Frosting:

- 8 ounces cream cheese, softened
- ½ cup butter, softened

- 1 1-pound box confectioners' sugar
- 1 teaspoon vanilla extract

Combine dry ingredients for cake in a large mixing bowl. Add eggs and oil, stirring until dry ingredients are moistened, but do not beat. Stir in vanilla, pineapple, 1 cup nuts and bananas. Spoon batter into 3 well-greased and floured 9-inch cake pans. Bake at 350 degrees 25 minutes or until cake tests done. Cool in pans 10 minutes, then remove and cool.

For frosting, combine cream cheese and butter in a small bowl and mix until smooth. Add confectioners' sugar and beat until light and fluffy. Stir in vanilla. Spread frosting between layers and on top and sides of cake. Sprinkle with remaining pecans.

Dorothy Jones

PRUNE NUT CAKE

2 cups flour, sifted
1 teaspoon soda
½ teaspoon salt
1 teaspoon cinnamon
1 teaspoon allspice
2 cups sugar

1 cup cooking oil
3 eggs
1 cup buttermilk
1 cup pecans, chopped
1 cup prunes, chopped

Mix together flour, soda, salt, cinnamon and allspice. Cream together sugar, oil and eggs. Beginning and ending with dry ingredients, add alternately with buttermilk to creamed mixture. Stir in pecans and prunes. Pour into greased and floured Bundt or 10-inch tube pan. Bake at 350 degrees 1 hour and 10 minutes. Remove from oven and let cool 5 minutes. Remove and place in shallow pan. Immediately spoon buttermilk glaze over cake until it is absorbed.

Buttermilk Glaze:
1 cup sugar
½ cup buttermilk
1 tablespoon light corn syrup
¼ teaspoon soda

¼ teaspoon salt
1 teaspoon vanilla
1 tablespoon butter or margarine

Combine all ingredients in a saucepan and bring to a boil over low heat. Continue cooking 4 to 5 minutes, stirring constantly. Spoon over hot cake.

Gail Thomas

FIG PRESERVE CAKE

2½ cups sugar
¾ cup butter or margarine
4 eggs
1 cup buttermilk
1 tablespoon baking soda
3 cups flour

1 teaspoon nutmeg
1 teaspoon cloves
1 teaspoon cinnamon
2 cups fig preserves
1 teaspoon vanilla
1 cup pecans, chopped

Cream butter and sugar. Add well beaten eggs. Mix soda with buttermilk and add to above mixture. Gradually add flour sifted with spices. Add fig preserves, vanilla and nuts. Bake in a loaf pan at 300 degrees for 1 hour. Spoon with sauce while hot, if desired.

Sauce:

1 cup sugar
½ cup margarine
1 tablespoon corn syrup

1 tablespoon vanilla
½ cup buttermilk
½ teaspoon baking soda

In a saucepan, mix all ingredients and boil 3 minutes.

Ginny Woods

RHUBARB PUDDING CAKE

1 cup sugar
1 egg
2 tablespoons butter, melted
1 cup buttermilk
1 cup fresh rhubarb, diced

½ teaspoon salt
½ teaspoon baking soda
1 teaspoon baking powder
2 cups flour

Topping:
2 tablespoons melted butter   ½ cup sugar

Blend together sugar, egg and butter; beat in buttermilk until smooth. Stir together salt, baking soda, baking powder and flour. Stir dry ingredients into buttermilk mixture; mix well. Stir in rhubarb. Pour into greased 9-inch square baking pan. Combine topping ingredients and sprinkle on top of batter. Bake at 350 degrees for 45 minutes or until cake tests done.

Vanilla Sauce:
½ to 1 cup sugar
½ cup evaporated milk

½ cup margarine
1 teaspoon vanilla

Mix sugar, margarine and milk. Bring to a boil and cook 1 minute, stirring constantly. Remove from heat; stir in vanilla. Serve over cake.

Dawna Zunino

ORANGE DATE CAKE

1 cup butter, softened
2 cups sugar, divided
2 eggs
1 cup sour cream
1 teaspoon baking soda
2 cups flour
1 teaspoon baking powder

1 cup chopped dates
1 cup nuts, chopped
¼ teaspoon salt
Grated rind of 2 oranges
1 teaspoon vanilla
½ to ⅔ cup orange juice

Cream butter and 1 cup sugar; add eggs and mix well. Combine sour cream and soda; mix with creamed mixture. Add flour, baking powder, and orange rind. Mix well. Add dates, nuts, vanilla and salt. Bake at 350 degrees for 45 minutes in greased and floured tube pan. Let stand 10 minutes. Combine orange juice and remaining sugar. Pour over cake in pan.

Jane Reed

BUTTERMILK CAKE

¼ teaspoon baking soda	4 eggs
1 cup buttermilk	1 teaspoon vanilla
3 cups sugar	3 cups flour
1 cup solid vegetable shortening	⅛ teaspoon salt

Stir baking soda into buttermilk. Cream sugar and shortening until smooth. Add eggs one at a time; beat until creamy. Add vanilla. Add flour and salt alternately with the buttermilk mixture. Pour into greased and floured angel food cake pan. Bake at 350 degrees for 1 hour and check for doneness with a toothpick. A wonderful crust will form on the top. Great served warm with strawberries and cream.

Debbie (Mrs. John) Carona

DUMP CAKE

1 can (20 ounces) crushed pineapple, undrained	1 yellow cake mix (dry)
1 16-ounce can cherry pie filling	1 cup nuts
	½ cup butter or margarine, cut into thin slices

Layer the above ingredients in a 9×13-inch greased cake pan. Bake at 350 degrees for 48 to 53 minutes.

Mayor Steve Bartlett

CREAM CHEESE FUDGE RIPPLE POUND CAKE

8 ounces cream cheese, softened	2 teaspoons vanilla
1½ cups butter or margarine	3 cups flour
3 cups sugar	2 ounces baking chocolate, melted
6 eggs	

Cream butter, cream cheese and sugar; add eggs one at a time. Add vanilla. Stir in flour. Grease and flour a Bundt pan. Pour ¾ cake batter into pan. Mix chocolate into remaining batter and drop by spoonfuls over vanilla batter. Swirl with knife. Bake at 325 degrees for 1 hour and 15 minutes, or until a toothpick inserted comes out clean. Cool slightly and invert on plate to cool.

Noreen Collins

BROWN SUGAR POUND CAKE

3 cups flour, sifted
1 teaspoon baking powder
¼ teaspoon salt
¾ cup butter, room temperature
¾ cup shortening
1 pound dark brown sugar

1 cup sugar
5 eggs
1 cup milk
1½ teaspoons vanilla
2 cups pecans, chopped

Sift together flour, baking powder and salt; set aside. Cream butter and shortening until very light; add brown sugar gradually, creaming until fluffy. Add granulated sugar gradually, also creaming until fluffy. Beat in eggs one at a time. Add sifted dry ingredients alternately with milk, beginning and ending with dry ingredients and beating each addition only enough to blend. Stir in vanilla and nuts. Pour into a well-greased and floured 10-inch tube pan and bake at 325 degrees about 45 minutes.

Jane H. Cox

CARAWAY POUND CAKE

1½ cups butter, or margarine, softened
1 pound confectioners' sugar
6 eggs
1 teaspoon vanilla

2¾ cups cake flour, sifted
1 teaspoon orange zest, grated
2 tablespoons caraway seeds
¼ teaspoon mace

Butter and flour a 10-inch (12 cup) tube pan. In large bowl, beat butter with electric mixer until creamy. Sift confectioners' sugar; gradually add to butter, beating until mixture is light and fluffy. Beat in eggs, one at a time, beating well after each addition. Add vanilla. Gradually beat in cake flour. Stir in orange zest, caraway seeds and mace. Pour into prepared pan, smooth top. Bake at 300 degrees for 1½ hours; cool in pan 5 minutes. Remove from pan and cool completely.

Anna Bradberry

SOUR CREAM POUND CAKE

1 cup butter
3 cups sugar
6 egg yolks
3 cups flour, sifted
¼ teaspoon baking soda

1 cup sour cream
1 teaspoon almond flavoring
1 teaspoon vanilla
6 egg whites, beaten stiffly

Cream butter and sugar until smooth. Add egg yolks one at a time. Alternate flour and sour cream. Add baking soda and flavorings; mix until smooth. Fold in beaten egg whites gently. Bake at 300 degrees for 1½ hours in an ungreased tube or Bundt pan.

Renee Morris

SEVEN-UP POUND CAKE

½ cup vegetable shortening
1 cup butter
3 cups flour
3 cups sugar

Pinch of salt
5 eggs
1 teaspoon vanilla
¾ cup 7-Up

Cream together shortening, butter, flour and sugar. Add eggs one at a time and beat well after each addition. Add salt, vanilla and 7-Up. Bake at 350 degrees in a deep pan for about 45 minutes.

Dallas Deputy Mayor Pro-Tem
Charlotte Mayes

TINY CHEESE CAKES

Graham cracker crumbs
3 8-ounce packages cream cheese,
    softened
1 cup sugar

4 eggs
1 teaspoon vanilla
1 cup sour cream plus 1 tablespoon sugar

Grease miniature muffin tins heavily. Fill each cup with graham cracker crumbs; pour out excess, saving crumbs for additional tins. Beat together cream cheese, sugar, eggs and vanilla until creamy. Fill each cup with cheese mixture. Bake at 350 degrees for 8 to 10 minutes. Remove from oven and cool slightly (5 minutes). Frost with sour cream and sugar mixture; bake 5 minutes more to set. To remove from pans, run a thin-bladed knife gently around the edge of each cake. Makes 5 dozen. (Freezes well.)

Alice Swanberg

ALMOND CHEESECAKE

Crust:

1½ cups graham cracker crumbs   ⅓ cup sugar
⅓ butter, melted

Combine ingredients and press evenly on bottom and sides of a lightly buttered 10-inch springform pan. Bake at 350 degrees for 7 to 10 minutes. Cool completely.

Filling:

4 8-ounce packages cream cheese,   2 eggs
   softened   ½ teaspoon vanilla
1 cup sugar   ½ teaspoon almond extract

Mix all ingredients together. Pour into cooled crust. Place in cold oven and turn to 350 degrees. Bake 30 minutes.

Topping:

1 pint sour cream   ¾ teaspoon almond extract
¾ cup sugar   ½ teaspoon lemon juice

Combine all ingredients. Pour over baked cheesecake. Bake 8 minutes longer. Chill overnight.

Lorine Six

GERMAN STYLE CHEESECAKE

5 8-ounce packages cream cheese,   1½ teaspoons lemon juice
   softened   5 eggs
¾ to 1 cup sugar   2 to 3 egg yolks
2 teaspoons vanilla   ¼ to ½ cup heavy cream
3 tablespoons flour   Graham cracker crumb crust

Mix cream cheese, sugar, vanilla, flour and lemon juice. Add eggs and egg yolks one at a time. Then add heavy cream. Pour into graham cracker crumb crust in springform pan. Bake at 350 degrees approximately 50 minutes. This makes one 5-pound cheesecake. If baking 2 or 3 smaller ones, bake 30 minutes or until golden on top.

Dedicated to Jodi Sohl

JEWISH CHEESECAKE

Graham Cracker Crust:

    1 cup graham cracker crumbs   *6 tablespoons butter, melted*

    1 cup walnuts, finely chopped   *1½ teaspoons cinnamon*

Mix all together and press firmly into bottom and sides of buttered large springform pan. Set aside.

Filling:

    6 8-ounce packages cream cheese,   *6 eggs, room temperature*

      softened   *2 teaspoons vanilla*

    1 pint sour cream, room temperature   *1¾ cups sugar*

Mix all together with mixer until well blended. Pour into prepared pan and bake at 450 degrees for 10 minutes; lower temperature to 350 degrees and bake for 50 minutes. Chill overnight in pan. Remove outer rim of springform pan and top with fresh or frozen strawberries.

Joyce Doyle Murphey

HEAVENLY CHOCOLATE CHEESECAKE

    2 cups vanilla wafers, crushed   *1 envelope unflavored gelatin*

    1 cup almonds, toasted and ground   *2 8-ounce packages cream cheese,*

    ½ cup butter, melted   *softened*

    ½ cup sugar   *½ cup sour cream*

    2 cups milk chocolate morsels   *½ teaspoon almond extract*

    ½ cup milk   *½ cup heavy cream, whipped*

Crust: In large bowl, combine wafer crumbs, almonds, butter and sugar; mix well. Pat firmly into 9-inch springform pan, covering bottom and 2 inches up sides. Set aside.

Cake: Melt over hot (not boiling) water, milk chocolate morsels; stir until smooth. Set aside. Pour milk into small saucepan; sprinkle gelatin on top. Set aside for 1 minute. Cook over low heat, stirring constantly, until gelatin dissolves. Set aside. In large bowl, combine cream cheese, sour cream and melted chocolate; beat until fluffy. Beat in gelatin mixture and almond extract. Fold in whipped cream. Pour into prepared pan. Chill until firm (about 3 hours). Run knife around edge of cake to separate from pan; remove sides. Garnish as desired.

Dedicated to Peggy Michaels

CHOCOLATE CHEESECAKE

2 cups graham cracker crumbs
¼ cup sugar
7 tablespoons melted butter or
   margarine
4 eggs, separated
⅔ cup sugar, divided

16 ounces cream cheese, softened
12 ounces chocolate chips
½ cup very strong hot coffee
2 tablespoons light rum
1½ teaspoons vanilla

Combine crumbs, sugar and melted butter and mix thoroughly. Butter a 9- or 10-inch spring-form pan generously. Pat crumbs onto bottom and halfway up sides. Set aside. Beat yolks and half the sugar in large bowl until very thick and lemon-colored (about 4 to 5 minutes). Cut the cheese into small pieces and beat into egg mixture until completely smooth. Heat chocolate and coffee together until chocolate is melted. Add rum and vanilla. Add this to cream cheese mixture and beat until smooth. In another bowl beat egg whites until soft peaks form, slowly adding remaining sugar and beating until very stiff peaks form. Fold into cheese mixture. Pour into pan. Bake at 350 degrees for 55 minutes. Turn off oven but leave in until lukewarm, about 1 hour. Cool. Remove from rack. Decorate with whipped cream and chocolate curls. *Do not overbake!* Serves 10.

Zelma Klingman

CUISINE D'OR OREO CHEESECAKE

1¼ cups graham cracker crumbs
⅓ cup unsalted butter, melted
¼ cup brown sugar, packed
4 8-ounce packages cream cheese, at room temperature
1½ cups sugar, divided
2 tablespoons flour
4 eggs
2 egg yolks

3 teaspoons vanilla, divided
1½ cups Oreo cookies, chopped
2 cups sour cream
1⅓ cups whipping cream, divided
8 ounces semisweet chocolate, chopped
5 Oreo cookies, halved crosswise
1 maraschino cherry, halved

Crust: Blend cracker crumbs, butter and brown sugar in bottom of 9- or 10-inch springform pan; then press onto bottom and sides. Refrigerate until firm, about 30 minutes.

Filling: Beat cream cheese in large bowl of electric mixer on lowest speed until smooth. Beat in 1¼ cups sugar and flour until well blended. Beat in eggs and yolks until smooth. Stir in ⅓ cup cream and 1 teaspoon vanilla. Pour half of batter into prepared crust. Sprinkle with chopped cookies. Pour remaining batter over, spreading evenly. Bake at 425 degrees for 15 minutes. Reduce oven to 225 degrees and bake 50 minutes more, covering top loosely with foil, if top browns too quickly. Increase oven temperature to 350 degrees. Blend sour cream, remaining ¼ cup sugar and 1 teaspoon vanilla in small bowl. Spread over cake. Bake 7 minutes. Refrigerate immediately. Cover cake with plastic wrap and chill overnight.

Glaze: Scald 1 cup cream in heavy medium saucepan over high heat. Add chocolate and remaining 1 teaspoon vanilla and stir 1 minute. Remove from heat and stir until chocolate is melted. Refrigerate glaze 10 minutes. Set cake on platter and remove springform. Pour glaze over top of cake. Using pastry brush, smooth top and sides. Arrange cookie halves, cut side down, around outer edge of cake. Place cherry halves in center. Refrigerate cake until ready to serve. Serves 10.

Pamela Easter

PUMPKIN CHEESECAKE WITH FRANGELICO

24 gingersnaps
3 tablespoons sugar
1/4 cup unsalted butter, melted
16 ounces cream cheese, room
    temperature
16 ounces solid pack pumpkin
5 eggs

3/4 cup brown sugar, firmly packed
1/2 cup Frangelico
1 teaspoon cinnamon
1 teaspoon vanilla
1/2 teaspoon ground ginger
1/4 teaspoon grated nutmeg
1/4 teaspoon ground cloves

Crust: Grind gingersnaps with sugar in processor to fine crumbs. With machine running, slowly add butter. Press mixture into bottom of 9-inch springform pan. Freeze for 15 minutes. (Can be prepared 3 days ahead).

Filling: Position rack in center of oven and preheat to 350 degrees. Blend all ingredients in processor until smooth, stopping once to scrape down sides of work bowl. Pour filling into crust-lined pan. Bake until edges of cake begin to pull away from sides of pan and cake begins to brown, about 45 minutes; center will not be firm.

Topping:
16 ounces sour cream
1/4 cup sugar

1/4 cup Frangelico
10 hazelnuts

Whisk together sour cream, sugar, and Frangelico. Without removing cake from oven, pour topping evenly over hot cake starting at edges. Spread evenly. Continue baking cake until edges begin to bubble, about 10 minutes. Cool on rack. Refrigerate at least 12 hours. (Can be prepared 2 days ahead.) Lightly press hazelnuts into top edge of cake. Let stand at room temperature for 30 minutes before serving.

Dedicated to Annette Davis

ARMAGNAC PRUNE CAKE

12 ounces pitted prunes	1 tablespoon baking soda
2 cups water	2½ teaspoons ground cinnamon
¼ cup Armagnac or Cognac	1 teaspoon ground nutmeg
¾ cup vegetable oil	1 teaspoon ground allspice
2¼ cups sugar	½ teaspoon ground cardamon
5 large eggs	½ teaspoon ground cloves
2 tablespoons vanilla extract	1 teaspoon salt
3 cups all purpose flour	1½ cups nonfat buttermilk

Glaze:

1½ cups sugar	2 tablespoons light corn syrup
½ cup unsalted butter	2 tablespoons fresh lemon juice
½ cup Armagnac or Cognac	1 teaspoon baking soda
Vanilla nonfat frozen yogurt (optional)	

Cake: Position rack in center of oven and preheat to 350 degrees. Butter and flour 12-cup Bundt pan. Combine prunes, water and Armagnac in heavy medium saucepan. Simmer until prunes are tender, about 15 minutes. Drain prunes, reserving ¼ cup cooking liquid for glaze. Coarsely chop prunes. Beat oil, sugar, eggs and vanilla in large bowl until well blended. In medium bowl, mix flour, baking soda, spices and salt to blend. Mix dry ingredients into oil mixture. Add buttermilk, beating just until batter is smooth. Fold in chopped prunes. Transfer batter to prepared pan. Bake cake until tester inserted near center comes out clean, about 1 hour 5 minutes. Transfer to rack in pan.

Glaze: Combine reserved ¼ cup prune cooking liquid, sugar, butter, Armagnac, corn syrup, lemon juice and baking soda in heavy large saucepan. Bring to boil over medium heat, stirring occasionally. Boil 2 minutes. Pierce cake in several places with long toothpick or wooden skewer. Slowly pour 1¼ cups glaze over hot cake. Reserve extra glaze. Let glazed cake cool in pan 30 minutes. Turn cake out onto platter. Cool completely. Cut cake into wedges. Serve with frozen yogurt, passing additional glaze separately as sauce. Makes 16 servings.

DyAnna Giltner

CHOCOLATE PHANTASMAGORIA

Cake:

8 squares semi-sweet chocolate	½ cup sour cream
1 stick butter	3 cups cake flour
1¾ cups superfine sugar	1 teaspoon baking soda
½ teaspoon vanilla	1 teaspoon baking powder
2 eggs, separated	

Filling:

12 squares semisweet chocolate	3 tablespoons Kahlúa
¾ cup butter	

Truffles for top of cake:

12 squares semisweet chocolate	3 tablespoons Kahlúa
¾ cup butter	

Ganache:

1 cup whipping cream	2 tablespoons granulated sugar
2 tablespoons unsalted butter	12 squares semisweet chocolate

Cake: Grease a 10-inch spring form pan. Break the chocolate into small pieces. Place in a double boiler with the butter over ½ cup water. Heat slowly until melted, stirring occasionally. Beat in the sugar and the vanilla, then leave to cool. Beat in the egg yolks, then fold in the sour cream and flour (that has been combined with the soda and baking powder). Beat egg whites until stiff, then fold into the mixture. Pour the mixture into the prepared pan. Bake in the oven at 350 degrees for 1 hour or until firm to the touch and set in the middle. Turn out onto a wire rack and leave to cool.

Filling: Break the chocolate into small pieces. Place in double boiler with the butter. Heat until melted. Stir in 2 tablespoons Kahlúa. Leave until slightly thickened. Cut the cake into two layers and sprinkle the remaining Kahlúa on each cut half. Place the top half in the base of the springform pan, cut side up. Pour in the truffle filling. Place the second half of sponge on top. Chill until set. When the cake is set, un-mold and stand on a wire rack placed over a cookie sheet.

Frosting (Ganache): Place the whipping cream, butter and sugar in a saucepan over medium high heat. Stir to dissolve sugar. Bring the mixture to a boil. Place the chocolate in a stainless steel bowl. Pour the boiling cream over the chocolate and allow to stand for 5 minutes. Stir until smooth. Allow to cool to room temperature. Frost cake, covering completely.

Truffles: Mix ingredients and shape into small balls with melon baller. Roll in cocoa powder. Place truffles around perimeter of iced cake. This should allow each piece of cake to have 1 to 2 truffles, depending on size of cake slice.

Lynda Sanders

BENNE WAFERS

½ cup sesame seed, toasted
½ cup butter or margarine
1 cup sugar
1 egg

½ teaspoon vanilla
½ cup flour, sifted
¼ teaspoon baking powder
Dash salt

Toast sesame seeds at 325 degrees for 15 minutes or until light brown. Line ungreased cookie sheets with foil. Mix butter, sugar, egg and vanilla. Sift flour, baking powder and salt. Add sesame seeds to dry ingredients and combine with butter mixture. Drop ¼ teaspoon of dough onto foil covered cookie sheet. Place cookies 2 inches apart. Bake at 325 degrees for 8 minutes or until golden brown. Cool. Makes 10 dozen.

Linda Smith

SOUR CREAM SUGAR COOKIES

1½ cups sugar
1 cup vegetable shortening
2 eggs
4 tablespoons sour cream

3 cups flour
1 teaspoon baking soda
1 teaspoon salt
1 teaspoon vanilla

Mix sugar and shortening together until creamy. Stir in eggs and sour cream until well blended. Sift together flour, soda and salt. Add dry ingredients and vanilla to sugar mixture. Mix into a stiff dough. If possible, refrigerate dough for 8 to 12 hours. Drop by tablespoonsful onto greased and floured cookie sheets. Bake in preheated 375 degree oven for 12 to 14 minutes until light golden brown. Makes 2½ dozen cookies.

Laura S. Gibson

GOOEY BUTTER SQUARES

1 box yellow cake mix (not pudding)
1 8-ounce package cream cheese
3 eggs

½ cup margarine, melted
1 16-ounce box confectioners' sugar

Grease 9×13-inch cake pan. Mix cake mix, margarine and 1 egg; press firmly into bottom of pan. Mix confectioners' sugar, remaining eggs and cream cheese with electric mixer until smooth. Pour over dough. Bake at 350 degrees for 35 to 40 minutes. Crust will be puffy but will fall when cool. Serves 24.

Max Hardesty

COCONUT-ALMOND COOKIES

1 cup sugar	2 cups flour
½ cup brown sugar	1 teaspoon soda
1 cup solid shortening	1 teaspoon cream of tartar
1 egg	¾ cup coconut
1½ teaspoons almond flavoring	

Cream together first 5 ingredients. Add flour, soda and cream of tartar. Stir and add coconut. Form into balls and roll in granulated sugar. Place on cookie sheet and bake at 375 degrees for 6 to 10 minutes. *Do not overbake* — they will become crisp rather than chewy. These should be *light* in color, *not* brown.

Lynda Sanders

COFFEE COOKIES

1 cup sugar	1 teaspoon cinnamon
1 cup molasses	1 teaspoon ginger
1 cup solid vegetable shortening	½ cup nuts, chopped
2 eggs	1 teaspoon soda
4½ cups flour	1 cup hot coffee

Mix first 4 ingredients together. Sift flour with spices. Mix with first 4 ingredients. Add chopped nuts. Dissolve soda in coffee. Mix all together and form into flattened balls on an ungreased cookie sheet. Bake about 10 minutes at 350 degrees.

Caryn Roscoe

CARAMEL BROWNIES

1 box German chocolate cake mix	⅔ cup evaporated milk, divided
¾ cup margarine, melted	1 6-ounce package chocolate chips
49 caramels (yes, 49!)	1 cup pecans, chopped

Melt caramels in ⅓ cup evaporated milk in top of double boiler. Stir occasionally. Mix cake mix, melted margarine and ⅓ cup evaporated milk. Batter will be thick. In a 9×13-inch greased glass baking dish, spread half of cake mixture. Bake for 6 minutes at 350 degrees. Remove from oven, pour caramel mixture over the partially baked batter. Spread chocolate chips and chopped pecans on top of caramel mixture. Drop remaining cake batter by spoonfuls on top of caramel mixture. This will not completely cover, but it all blends while baking. Bake another 14 to 15 minutes. Cool and cut into squares.

Brenda Wright

SOUR CREAM COOKIES

1 cup margarine, softened	Dash of salt
2 cups sugar	½ teaspoon baking soda
2 eggs	4 teaspoons baking powder
1 cup sour cream	1 teaspoon vanilla
4½ cups flour	1 teaspoon almond extract

Cream margarine and sugar. Add eggs and sour cream. Combine flour, salt, baking soda and baking powder. Add to creamed mixture. Add vanilla and almond flavoring. Chill for 10 minutes. Drop by teaspoonfuls onto greased cookie sheet. Bake at 400 degrees for 10 minutes (barely browned). Cool.

Icing:

1 pound box confectioners' sugar	4 tablespoons milk
½ cup shortening	½ teaspoons almond extract
1 egg white	Food coloring (if desired)
1 teaspoon vanilla	

Mix ingredients with electric mixer until smooth. Makes 6 to 8 dozen cookies.

Patsy Beene

GINGERSNAPS

¾ cup shortening	¼ teaspoon salt
1 cup sugar	2 teaspoons baking soda
¼ cup light molasses	1 teaspoon cinnamon
1 egg, l n	1 teaspoon cloves
2 cups flour	1 teaspoon ginger

Cream shortening and sugar; add molasses and egg. Sift dry ingredients and add to above mixture. Mix well and roll into walnut-sized balls. Dip into sugar and place on greased cookie sheet 2 inches apart. Bake at 375 degrees for 15 minutes or at 350 degrees for 9 minutes for chewy texture. Cool slightly and remove from cookie sheet.

Sarah Gardenhire

ROSEMARY COOKIES

¾ cup butter or margarine
1 cup sugar
1 egg
¼ cup molasses
2 teaspoons ground dried rosemary

1¾ cups sifted flour
1 teaspoon baking soda
½ teaspoon salt
¼ teaspoon ground cloves
½ teaspoon ginger

Cream butter and sugar; add egg and molasses. Stir in remaining ingredients and mix well. Drop by scant teaspoonfuls on greased cookie sheet. Bake at 325 degrees for 10 to 12 minutes. Makes 2 dozen.

Anna Bradberry

CHOCOLATE CHIP COOKIES

½ cup butter or margarine
½ cup sugar
½ cup brown sugar, packed
1 egg
½ teaspoon vanilla
1 cup flour
1¼ cups rolled oats

¼ teaspoon salt
½ teaspoon baking powder
½ teaspoon baking soda
1 6-ounce package chocolate chips
2 ounces milk chocolate, grated
¾ cup nuts, chopped

Mix rolled oats in a blender until it turns to powder; measure before blending. Cream butter and sugar. Add egg and vanilla. Mix together flour, oats, salt, baking powder and soda. Combine wet and dry ingredients and add chocolate chips, grated chocolate and nuts. Batter will be very stiff. Shape cookies about the size of golf balls and bake on ungreased cookie sheet for 6 to 10 minutes at 375 degrees. Makes about 2 dozen.

Dorothy Jones

PEANUT BUTTER CHOCOLATE CHIPPERS

½ cup sugar
⅓ cup brown sugar
½ cup margarine
½ cup peanut butter
½ teaspoon vanilla
1 egg

1 cup flour
½ cup quick-cooking oats
1 teaspoon baking soda
¼ teaspoon salt
1 cup chocolate chips

Cream sugars, margarine and peanut butter; add vanilla and egg and mix well. Blend in dry ingredients and stir in chocolate chips. Drop by rounded tablespoonfuls onto ungreased cookie sheet. Bake at 350 degrees for 12 minutes. (Can also be baked in a greased 9×9-inch pan for 30 minutes. Cool and cut into bars.)

Marjorie Kimmel

COTTAGE CHEESE CHIP COOKIES

1 cup margarine
1¾ cups sugar
2 eggs
2 teaspoons vanilla
½ teaspoon soda
1 teaspoon baking powder
1 cup cottage cheese

½ teaspoon salt
2⅔ cups flour
½ cup cocoa
½ cup nuts, chopped
6 ounces mini chocolate chips
½ cup coconut

Beat together margarine, sugar and eggs. Add remaining ingredients and mix well by hand. Make into walnut size balls; then roll in powdered sugar. Flatten on cookie sheet. Bake at 325 degrees 15 minutes or more. Remove from pan immediately. The cookies will be soft.

Peggy Ernst

DAD'S COOKIES

1 cup butter or margarine, softened	1 teaspoon baking powder
1½ cups light brown sugar	½ teaspoon baking soda
1 egg	½ teaspoon salt
1 teaspoon vanilla	1 cup flaked coconut
2 cups flour	1 cup rolled oats

Cream butter in large mixing bowl. Add brown sugar and mix well. Blend in egg and vanilla. Sift together flour, baking powder, baking soda and salt. Add to mixture. Add coconut and rolled oats and blend thoroughly. Lightly grease cookie sheet and place small balls of dough 2 inches apart. Flatten with fork dipped in cold water to ½ inch. Bake at 375 degrees for 8 to 10 minutes. Let cool on cookie sheet for 2 minutes. Remove and let cool on rack. Makes 6 to 7 dozen.

Margot Winspear

"CRISPY" OATMEAL COOKIES

1 cup butter or margarine	1 teaspoon baking soda
1 cup brown sugar	1 cup flaked coconut
1 cup granulated sugar	1½ cup rolled oats
2 eggs, beaten	2½ cups Rice Krispies
1 teaspoon vanilla	1 cup nuts (optional)
2 cups flour	

Cream butter and sugars. Add eggs. Sift together flour and baking soda and add to creamed mixture. Add remaining ingredients and drop by teaspoonfuls onto greased baking sheet and flatten with fork. Bake at 350 degrees for 10 to 12 minutes. Makes 7 to 8 dozen.

Sally Junkins

NO~BAKE COOKIES

2 cups sugar
¼ cup butter or margarine
½ cup milk
½ cup cocoa
2 cups quick-cooking oats

½ cup peanut butter
1 teaspoon vanilla
½ cup nuts, chopped (optional)
½ cup raisins (optional)

Mix sugar, butter, milk and cocoa in large saucepan. Bring to a boil over medium heat and boil 2 minutes. Add oats, peanut butter, vanilla, nuts and raisins. Mix thoroughly. Drop by teaspoonfuls onto waxed paper.

Gayla Ross

POTATO CHIP COOKIES

1 cup butter or margarine, softened
½ cup sugar
1¾ cups flour

¾ cup potato chips, crushed
1 teaspoon vanilla

Cream butter and sugar until fluffy. Add flour, potato chips and vanilla. Drop by rounded teaspoonsful onto ungreased cookie sheet. Bake at 350 degrees for 10 to 15 minutes or until edges are lightly browned. Cool 5 minutes. Remove to wire racks. Dust with confectioners' sugar. Makes 4 dozen.

Edna Talty

LEMONADE COOKIES

1 cup butter or margarine
1 cup sugar
2 eggs
3 cups sifted all-purpose flour

1 teaspoon baking soda
1 6-ounce can frozen lemonade
   concentrate, thawed
Sugar

Cream together butter and 1 cup sugar. Add eggs; beat until light and fluffy. Sift together flour and baking soda. Add alternately to the creamed mixture with ½ cup of the lemonade concentrate. Drop dough from a teaspoon 2 inches apart onto ungreased cookie sheet. Bake cookies in a 400-degree oven about 8 minutes or until lightly browned around the edges. Brush hot cookies lightly with remaining lemonade concentrate. Sprinkle with sugar. Remove cookies to cooling rack. Makes about 4 dozen small cookies.

Karen Bradshaw

GRANDMA LENA'S HEALTH COOKIES

1 cup shortening
1 egg
2 cups sugar
3 cups flour
1 teaspoon baking soda
2 teaspoons baking powder
1 teaspoon vanilla

½ teaspoon salt
½ teaspoon cinnamon
½ teaspoon nutmeg
1 cup sour milk or buttermilk
3 cups rolled oats
1 cup muscat raisins

Beat shortening, egg and sugar; mix flour with baking soda , baking powder, salt, cinnamon and nutmeg. Add alternately with milk to sugar mixture. Stir in oats, raisins and vanilla. Drop by teaspoonsful onto cookie sheet. Bake at 400 degrees about 12 minutes, or until light brown. Nuts can be added, if desired.

Noreen Collin

HAZELNUT OATMEAL COOKIES

½ cup margarine, softened
1 cup brown sugar, packed
¼ cup sour cream
1 egg
1 teaspoon vanilla

1 cup flour
¾ teaspoon baking powder
½ teaspoon baking soda
1½ cups rolled oats
1 cup hazelnuts, chopped

Cream margarine and sugar. Add sour cream, egg and vanilla. Set aside. Sift together flour, baking powder and baking soda. Add rolled oats; stir. Add dry ingredients to margarine and sugar mixture and stir until blended. Stir in hazelnuts. Drop by rounded teaspoonsful on a greased cookie sheet. Bake at 400 degrees for 8 minutes or until golden brown. Cool on a wire rack. When cool, frost with Hazelnut Icing. Makes 36 cookies.

Icing:

¼ cup margarine
3 tablespoons milk

½ teaspoon Frangelico
2 cups confectioners' sugar

Brown margarine in pan over medium-high heat. Remove from heat and add milk and Frangelico. Stir in confectioners' sugar; blend until smooth.

Pamela Easter

ORANGE DROP COOKIES

¾ cup shortening
¼ cup butter or margarine, softened
1½ cups brown sugar, packed
2 eggs
1 cup buttermilk
2 tablespoons orange rind, grated
¼ cup orange juice

1 teaspoon vanilla
3½ cups flour
2 teaspoons baking powder
1 teaspoon baking soda
¼ teaspoon salt
1 cup pecans, chopped
Pecan halves

Cream first 3 ingredients; beat in eggs. Slowly beat in buttermilk, rind, juice and vanilla. Stir together flour, baking powder, soda and salt; blend into batter. Stir in chopped pecans. Drop from teaspoon onto greased cookie sheet. Place pecan half on each cookie. Bake at 350 degrees about 15 minutes. Makes 96.

Dedicated to Carolyn Stricker

FRUIT CAKE COOKIES

½ cup butter or margarine
1½ cups dark brown sugar, packed
4 eggs
3 tablespoons milk
1 cup whiskey
½ pound candied pineapple
½ pound candied cherries
3 cups pecans, chopped

3½ cups plus ½ cup flour
3 teaspoons baking soda
1 teaspoon cinnamon
1 teaspoon nutmeg
1 teaspoon cloves
1 teaspoon allspice
½ pound raisins, white or dark

Cut fruit into small chunks. Chop pecans and add with raisins to fruit mixture. Dredge in the extra ½ cup of flour. Set aside. Mix all dry ingredients and sift 2 to 3 times. Cream butter and sugar; add eggs one at a time. Add liquids and then dry ingredients. Combine all with fruit in a large bowl and mix well. Drop by teaspoonfuls onto greased cookie sheet. Bake at 350 degrees for 12 to 15 minutes. Remove from cookie sheet and let cool. They may be crunchy after cooling, but will soften up overnight when stored in an airtight container. Makes about 6 dozen cookies.

Dedicated to Rutha Poe

MINCEMEAT COOKIES

1 9-ounce package mincemeat
½ cup water
1 cup shortening
2 cups brown sugar
2 eggs, well beaten

3½ cups flour
1 teaspoon baking soda
½ teaspoon instant coffee powder
1 teaspoon salt

In saucepan, mix mincemeat and water. Stir over low heat for 3 minutes. Set aside to cool. Cream shortening and add sugar gradually. Stir in eggs and add mincemeat. Beat well with wooden spoon. Add dry ingredients. Drop by teaspoonfuls onto greased cookie sheets. Bake at 400 degrees for 10 to 12 minutes.

Rosemary LaQuey

PUMPKIN COOKIES

2 cups shortening
2 cups sugar
1 16-ounce can pumpkin
2 eggs
2 teaspoons vanilla
4 cups flour
2 teaspoons baking powder

2 teaspoons cinnamon
1 teaspoon baking soda
1 teaspoon nutmeg
½ teaspoon allspice
1 teaspoon salt
2 cups raisins
1 cup nuts, chopped

Cream shortening and sugar. Add pumpkin, eggs and vanilla; beat well. Stir together flour, baking powder, cinnamon, baking soda, nutmeg, allspice and salt. Add to batter; mix well. Stir in raisins and nuts. Drop by rounded teaspoonfuls 2 inches apart on greased cookie sheet. Bake at 350 degrees for 12 to 15 minutes. Cool on rack. If desired, frost with vanilla icing. Makes 84.

Pamela Easter

DOUBLE PEANUT BUTTER COOKIES

1½ cups sifted all-purpose flour
½ cup granulated sugar
½ teaspoon soda
¼ teaspoon salt

½ cup shortening
½ cup creamy peanut butter
¼ cup light corn syrup
1 tablespoon milk
Additional peanut butter

Sift together dry ingredients. Cut in shortening and peanut butter until mixture resembles coarse meal. Blend in syrup and milk. Blend by hand. Shape into 2-inch roll; chill. Slice ⅛ to ¼-inch thick. Place half the slices on ungreased cookie sheet: spread each with ½ teaspoon peanut butter. Cover with remaining slices; seal edges with fork. Bake at 350 degrees for about 12 minutes. Cool slightly; remove from sheet. Makes 2 dozen.

Karen Bradshaw

MEXICAN MOCHA BALLS

1 cup butter or margarine, softened
½ cup sugar
1 teaspoon vanilla
2 cups flour
¼ cup unsweetened cocoa

1 teaspoon instant coffee crystals
¼ teaspoon salt
1 cup walnuts, finely chopped
½ cup maraschino cherries, chopped
Sugar

Cream first 3 ingredients. Stir flour with cocoa, coffee and salt. Gradually beat into creamed mixture. Stir in nuts and cherries. Chill 1 hour. Form into 1-inch balls. Place on ungreased baking sheet. Bake at 325 degrees for 20 minutes. Cool on rack. While warm, but not hot, dust with sugar. Makes 72 balls.

Pamela Easter

MEXICAN WEDDING COOKIES

2 cups flour
1⅓ cups confectioners' sugar, sifted,
    divided
1 cup pecans, finely chopped

Pinch of salt
1 teaspoon vanilla
1½ cups unsalted butter, softened

In a medium bowl, combine flour, ⅔ cup of the sugar, nuts and salt. Stir in vanilla. Work the butter into the mixture until it forms a cohesive ball. For each cookie, pinch off about 1½ tablespoons dough and form it into a ball, using either your hands or two teaspoons. Place on a greased baking sheet and flatten slightly with a spoon. Bake at 350 degrees for about 30 minutes. Allow to cool on a wire rack and dust generously with confectioners' sugar. Makes 25 to 30 cookies.

Peggy Dawson

CHOCOLATE PIXIE COOKIES

½ cup butter
4 cups sugar
8 eggs, beaten
4 cups flour

1 teaspoon salt
4 teaspoons baking powder
8 squares semisweet chocolate, melted
1 cup pecans, chopped

Cream butter and sugar; add beaten eggs a little at a time. Combine flour, salt and baking powder gradually; add melted chocolate to butter mixture. Stir in pecans. Chill dough several hours. Shape into walnut-size balls; dip the top of each ball into confectioners' sugar. Bake at 300 degrees for 10 to 12 minutes on greased cookie sheet. Makes 6 dozen. Tops will be crackled looking.

Helen White

SCRUMPTIOUS SUGAR COOKIES

1 cup confectioners' sugar	4 cups flour
1 cup granulated sugar	1 teaspoon cream of tartar
1 cup butter or margarine	1 teaspoon baking soda
1 cup cooking oil, less 1 tablespoon	1 teaspoon salt
2 eggs	¼ teaspoon almond extract, optional
2 teaspoons vanilla	

Cream sugars and shortenings. Add eggs and vanilla and mix until creamy. Add dry ingredients and beat together by hand until smooth. *Do not use mixer.* Refrigerate overnight. Shape into balls the size of a walnut. Place on cookie sheet and press down with a glass dipped in sugar or use a meat mallet dipped in sugar. Bake at 350 degrees for 11 to 12 minutes. Makes 9 dozen. Cookies can be decorated with colored sugar.

Virginia Belcher

PECAN TASSIES

Crust:

¼ cup plus 3 tablespoons butter	1 cup flour
1 3-ounce package cream cheese	

Mix ingredients in mixer or by hand. Divide into 24 small balls. Put into small tart or muffin tins; press around side to form cups.

Filling:

1 egg	1 tablespoon butter or margarine
¾ cup brown sugar, packed	1 teaspoon vanilla
⅔ cup pecans, chopped	Dash of salt

Mix all ingredients and put about 1 tablespoon of filling into each crust cup. Bake at 375 degrees for about 30 minutes, or until golden brown. Makes 24.

Grace Smith, Mary Scoggins and Kala Casebolt

ALFAJORES

⅔ cup butter or margarine
1 cup sugar
1 egg
2 egg yolks
1 teaspoon vanilla

2 teaspoons lemon rind, grated
1½ cups cornstarch
1 cup flour
1 teaspoon baking powder
1 tablespoon brandy

Cream butter; add sugar and continue creaming. Add egg and egg yolks, beating until light and frothy. Add vanilla and lemon rind. Sift dry ingredients together and add to butter mixture, mixing well. Add brandy. Blend until dough is smooth. Chill for a few hours, or until dough is firm enough to roll out. Roll dough ½-inch thick on a floured surface and cut into rounds with a 1¾-inch floured cookie cutter. Place on buttered baking sheet. Bake at 325 degrees for 15 to 20 minutes, or until very lightly browned. Cool. Fill each pair of cookies with Dulce de Leche. Roll edges in coconut. Makes 24 filled cookies.

Dulce de Leche:
2 cups milk
¾ cup sugar
1 teaspoon vanilla

Dash of baking soda
1 cup dried or fresh coconut, grated

Combine milk, sugar, vanilla and baking soda in a saucepan. Bring to a boil. Cook over low heat 2½ hours or until the mixture forms a soft ball when a small amount is dropped into cold water. Stir occasionally; test once or twice to see whether desired stage has been reached. Spread the dulce de leche between the alfajores. Sprinkle coconut on a piece of waxed paper and roll each cookie on its side to pick up coconut. Makes ⅔ cup filling.

Alternate Method for Filling: Cover 1 can of sweetened condensed milk with water; bring to a boil and boil, covered, for 2½ hours.

Dulce de Leche can be found at Mexican or South American food stores.

Dolores Danna

SUGAR COOKIES

¾ cup shortening (part butter)
1 cup sugar
1 egg, well beaten
3 cups sifted flour

2 teaspoons baking powder
1 teaspoon flavoring
1 cup sweet milk

Cream shortening and sugar together. Then add well-beaten egg and flavoring (vanilla or lemon). Sift flour with baking powder and add with milk to cream mixture. Chill dough several hours before rolling to desired thickness. Cut and sprinkle with sugar. Bake at 375 degrees for 10 to 12 minutes. Can also be rolled into long rolls and refrigerated several hours. Cut into desired widths.

Ila Post

DATE~FILLED COOKIES

Filling:
16 ounces chopped dates
½ cup water

⅔ cup sugar

Combine all ingredients in a saucepan; cook over low heat until a smooth paste is made.

Dough:
1 cup shortening
1 cup sugar
1 cup brown sugar
3 eggs

1 teaspoon vanilla
1 tablespoon water
4 cups flour
1 teaspoon baking soda

Cream shortening and sugars. Add eggs, vanilla and water; add flour and baking soda and mix well. Separate dough into two parts. Roll dough out to about ⅛ inch thickness. Cut with decorative cutters and put a teaspoonful of filling in the center of each cookie; top with another cookie of the same shape and seal edges. Bake on lightly greased cookie sheet at 350 degrees for about 12 minutes or until light brown. Makes 3 to 4 dozen.

Second choice: Divide dough; roll dough out in a rectangle about ¼ to ½-inch thick. Spread filling over dough. Roll up like a jelly roll and chill well. Slice about ¼-inch thick and bake on lightly greased cookie sheet at 350 degrees for about 12 minutes. Makes 3 to 4 dozen.

Alta Foster and Kala Casebolt

BLAKE'S BROWNIES

1 cup butter
4 ounces unsweetened chocolate
4 eggs
2 cups sugar
1 cup flour

1 teaspoon vanilla
½ cup nuts, chopped
Pinch of salt
6 ounces chocolate chips (optional)

Grease and flour a 9×13-inch pan. Melt butter and chocolate in double boiler. Cool. Beat eggs and sugar together. Add vanilla. Fold cooled chocolate mixture into egg mixture. Fold flour and salt in gently and then add nuts and chocolate chips (if used). Pour into pan and bake for approximately 25 to 30 minutes at 325 degrees. Do not overbake. Cool before cutting into bars.

Pat Hill

CHOCOLATE LAYER BARS

First layer:
4 ounces unsweetened chocolate
1 cup butter
2 cups sugar
4 eggs, lightly beaten

1 cup flour
1 teaspoon vanilla
½ teaspoon salt
1 cup nuts, chopped

Melt unsweetened chocolate and butter. Add sugar and eggs; mix well. Add flour, vanilla, salt and nuts. Mix well and pour into a greased 9×13-inch pan. Bake at 325 degrees for 22 minutes. Cool.

Second layer:
3 cups confectioners' sugar
½ cup butter

3 tablespoons vanilla custard mix (instant)
3 tablespoons cream or milk

Mix together confectioners' sugar, butter, custard, and enough milk to make icing a spreadable consistency. Ice chocolate layer with this mixture.

Third layer:
1 6-ounce package semisweet
   chocolate chips

1½ tablespoons butter
3 tablespoons water, if needed

When second layer is set, melt chocolate with butter and water and spread over second layer. Freeze or refrigerate. Before serving, cut into bars. Serve at room temperature. Makes 24 to 36 bars.

Dedicated to Kelly Klein

GRAMMA-RAM MINT BARS

Base:
- ½ cup butter, melted
- ¼ cup granulated sugar
- ⅓ cup cocoa
- 1 egg
- 2 cups graham cracker crumbs
- 1 cup flaked coconut
- ½ cup chopped walnuts

Filling:
- ¼ cup butter
- 2 tablespoons custard powder
- 1 teaspoon mint extract
- 3 tablespoons milk
- 2 cups sifted confectioners' sugar
- Green food coloring

Icing:
- 3 ounces semisweet chocolate
- 1 tablespoon butter

Mix together all ingredients for base. Press into 9-inch square pan. Refrigerate while making filling. For filling, cream together butter, custard powder, mint extract, and green coloring for desired tint. Gradually blend in milk and confectioners' sugar alternately. Reserve ¼ cup for decorating, and spread remainder over base. Chill well before icing. For icing, melt chocolate and butter together. Spread on chilled mixture and chill until chocolate sets. Cut into bars, decorate with reserved filling. Store in refrigerator. Makes 48 bars.

Dedicated to all grandchildren

CHEWY BARS

- 1 16-ounce box light brown sugar
- ½ cup butter or margarine
- 4 eggs
- 1 teaspoon vanilla
- 1½ cups flour
- 1½ teaspoons baking powder
- 2 cups pecans, chopped

Cream butter and sugar well. Add eggs one at a time. Beat well. Mix flour and baking powder together; add pecans. Fold into sugar/butter mixture. Add vanilla; mix well. Pour into greased 9×13-inch pan. Bake at 325 degrees for 40 minutes. Top will not look done in places, but actually is when cooled. Cut into 1½- or 2-inch squares.

Lorine Six

CREAM CHEESE DREAMS

Crust:

1 cup flour	*½ cup pecans, chopped fine*
⅓ cup light brown sugar	*⅓ cup margarine, melted*

Combine above ingredients and reserve ⅓ cup for topping. Press remainder firmly into lightly greased 8-inch square cake pan. Bake at 350 degrees for 12 to 15 minutes until lightly browned.

Filling:

1 8-ounce package cream cheese, softened	*1 teaspoon lemon juice*
¼ cup sugar	*2 tablespoons milk*
1 egg	*1 teaspoon vanilla*

Combine ingredients and beat with electric mixer until smooth. Pour over baked crust and top with remaining crumb mixture. Bake at 350 degrees for 25 minutes. Cut into 16 squares and then cut each square diagonally into triangles. Makes 32 triangles.

Betty Ways

PTA BARS

1 cup margarine	*1¾ cups flour*
2 cups brown sugar, not packed	*1 cup flaked coconut*
2 eggs	*1 cup nuts*
	1 6-ounce package butterscotch morsels

Mix all ingredients except butterscotch morsels, and spread in 9×13-inch pan. Bake 25 to 30 minutes at 350 degrees. A few minutes before removing from oven, sprinkle butterscotch morsels over top. Let melt, remove from oven and spread evenly over bars. Let cool, then cut into squares. Makes 4 to 5 dozen.

Neva Muller
Pauline Steele

FILBERT BARS

2 cups flour	1 tablespoon water
1/3 cup granulated sugar	1 teaspoon vanilla
1 teaspoon baking powder	1 cup confectioners' sugar, sifted
1/2 teaspoon salt	2/3 cup filberts, pecans or black walnuts,
3/4 cup butter or margarine	finely chopped
1 egg yolk, beaten	1 tablespoon orange liqueur or juice
1 egg white	1 ounce unsweetened chocolate
1 tablespoon butter or margarine	1/2 cup confectioners' sugar

Stir together flour, sugar, baking powder and salt. Cut in butter until crumbly. Combine egg yolk, water and vanilla; mix into flour mixture. Pat half of dough into greased 9×13-inch pan. Mix confectioners' sugar, nuts, liqueur and egg white and spread over dough in pan. Between two sheets of waxed paper, roll remaining dough to 9×13-inch rectangle. Carefully peel off top paper. Invert dough and paper onto filling in pan; carefully remove paper. Pat dough to fit. Bake at 375 degrees about 25 minutes. Cool; sift confectioners' sugar over top. Melt together 1 ounce chocolate and 1 tablespoon butter. Blend in 1/2 cup confectioners' sugar and enough hot water to make of pouring consistency. Drizzle over cooled bars; let glaze set before cutting into bars.

Pamela Easter

APRICOT BARS

1 8-ounce package dried apricots	1/4 teaspoon salt
3/4 cup water	2 teaspoons grated orange rind
1 cup flour	2 tablespoons orange juice
6 tablespoons butter	2 eggs, beaten
1 1/2 cups brown sugar, divided	1 1/4 cups coconut, divided
1 tablespoon cornstarch	

Rinse and cut apricots into small pieces. Combine with water; cover and simmer for 20 minutes. Meanwhile, mix flour, butter and 1/2 cup brown sugar. Press crumb mixture into greased 8×10-inch pan. Bake at 350 degrees for 15 minutes. Mix 1 cup brown sugar, cornstarch and salt; stir into undrained apricots and cook until thickened. Remove from heat; stir in remaining ingredients, reserving a little coconut for topping. Fill crust and bake at 350 degrees for 25 minutes.

Dedicated to Rhonda Suderman

FRESH PRUNE BARS

1½ cups flour, sifted
1 tablespoon baking soda
¾ teaspoon salt
⅓ cup sugar and ¾ cup sugar,
    as called for

⅓ cup shortening
¾ cup milk
12 fresh Italian prunes
¼ teaspoon nutmeg
3 teaspoons butter

Sift flour, baking soda, salt and ⅓ cup sugar together. Cut in shortening until fine. Stir in milk; spread in bottom of a buttered 8×12-inch baking dish. Arrange pitted and quartered prunes over the top. Mix ¾ cup sugar and nutmeg; cut in butter to form crumbs. Sprinkle over prunes. Bake at 375 degrees for 45 to 50 minutes. Serve warm. Serves 6 to 8. (Scandinavian recipe.)

Anne Walker

MAZURKA

½ cup golden raisins
½ cup dried apricots, snipped
½ cup currants
½ cup regular rolled oats
½ cup Grape Nuts cereal

1 cup blueberry topping (recipe follows)
2 egg whites, slightly beaten
Grated rind of 1 lemon
1¼ cups whole wheat pastry flour

Combine all ingredients except flour. Sprinkle flour over fruit mixture; mix thoroughly. Spread dough into non-stick pan about ½ inch deep. Bake in a 300 degree oven about 35 minutes. Cut into squares or triangles while still in pan. If needed, return pan to oven for additional 5 minutes to dry out cookies.

Blueberry Topping:
1 cup apple juice concentrate
½ to ¾ cup blueberries, fresh or frozen

2 tablespoons cornstarch

Mix ingredients until cornstarch dissolves. Heat to boiling; boil until mixture thickens and clears.

Tonya Calhoun

MINCEMEAT BARS

2 cups flour
1 cup sugar
½ teaspoon baking soda
½ teaspoon salt

½ cup vegetable oil
¼ cup milk
1 28-ounce jar mincemeat
1 cup pecans, chopped

In large bowl, mix dry ingredients. Add oil and milk; stir until mixture is crumbly. Reserve 1 cup of mixture and press remaining in a 9×13-inch pan. Spread with mincemeat; sprinkle with reserved mixture and nuts. Bake at 400 degrees for 30 minutes, until brown. Cut into bars.

Dedicated to Pauline Cervantes

SOUR LEMON SQUARES

1 cup flour, sifted
2 tablespoons sugar
⅓ cup margarine, softened
2 eggs

1 cup brown sugar
½ cup pecans, chopped
½ cup coconut
½ teaspoon vanilla

Combine flour and sugar. Cut margarine into flour and sugar until coarse crumbs form. Press into bottom of greased 9×13-inch pan. Bake at 350 degrees for 15 minutes or until lightly browned. Meanwhile, mix eggs, brown sugar, pecans, coconut and vanilla. Pour over hot pastry. Bake 30 minutes or until firm. Cool 15 minutes. Top with glaze.

Glaze:
⅔ cup confectioners' sugar
1 tablespoon lemon juice

1 teaspoon grated lemon rind
¼ teaspoon lemon extract

Cool and cut into squares.

Noreen Collins

CARAMELS

2 cups sugar
1 cup brown sugar
1 cup light corn syrup
1 cup half and half

1 cup butter or margarine
1 cup milk
4 teaspoons vanilla

Combine all ingredients, except vanilla, in a saucepan. Cook over low heat until sugar is dissolved. Heat to 248 degrees on a candy thermometer, stirring frequently. Remove from heat and add vanilla. Pour into greased 9×9-inch pan and cut into pieces when firm. Cut waxed paper into 3×3-inch squares. Wrap each piece individually. Caramels should be frozen or refrigerated after wrapping, if they are to be kept more than a week or two.

JoAnna Almgren

AUNT MARY'S DIVINITY

2⅓ cups sugar
⅔ cup white corn syrup
½ cup water
¼ teaspoon salt

2 egg whites
1 cup chopped nuts
½ teaspoon vanilla

Stir first 4 ingredients together in a saucepan over low heat until sugar is dissolved. Boil without stirring to 265 degrees or until a little mixture dropped in cold water forms a hard, almost brittle, ball. (If sugar crystals form on side of pan, remove with a wet cloth wrapped around a fork.) Remove syrup from heat. Pour slowly over stiffly beaten egg whites. Beat by hand or with a beater until mixture loses its gloss and holds its shape. Add nuts and vanilla. Pour into greased 9×9×2-inch pan. Cool and cut into squares, or drop by teaspoon onto waxed paper. Cool and store in a tin.

Karen Bradshaw

JUST PLAIN FUDGE

2 tablespoons butter
2 squares baking chocolate
2 cups sugar

⅔ cup milk
Pinch of salt
1 teaspoon vanilla

Melt butter and chocolate together in a saucepan. Add sugar, milk and salt. Cook until it forms a soft ball, when dropped into cold water; then place pan in a large pan of cold water to cool. Add vanilla while cooling. Beat until thick and pour into greased pan or onto waxed paper.

Jarrel W. Calhoun

MILLION DOLLAR FUDGE

3 3¾-ounce plain chocolate bars
2 cups chocolate chips
1 7-ounce jar marshmallow creme
1 tablespoon butter or margarine

1 teaspoon vanilla
4½ cups sugar
1 14½-ounce can evaporated milk
12 ounces (or more) pecans, chopped

Mix together in a 6- to 8-quart bowl, chocolate bars broken into pieces, chocolate chips, marshmallow creme, vanilla and butter. In a large saucepan, mix sugar and milk; boil for 6 minutes. Pour over ingredients in bowl and blend until smooth and creamy. After mix is completely blended, add pecans. Drop by teaspoonfuls onto waxed paper. Let stand 4 to 6 hours or overnight to set. Makes 6 pounds.

Peggy Hasse

WHITE CHOCOLATE CREME FUDGE

3 cups sugar
1 cup half-and-half
6 tablespoons butter or margarine

1 7-ounce jar marshmallow creme
12 ounces white chocolate
1 cup pecans or walnuts, chopped

In heavy saucepan over low heat, bring sugar, half-and-half, and butter to a boil. Stirring frequently, cook to a medium soft ball stage (237 degrees on a candy thermometer). Remove from heat. Immediately add marshmallow creme, white chocolate, broken into small pieces, and nuts. Stir until melted. Beat until smooth and creamy. Spread into foil lined 9×13-inch pan. Cool. Cut into squares. Makes 3 pounds.

Pamela Easter

SOUTH DAKOTA BUTTERMILK FUDGE

2 cups sugar
¾ cup butter (not margarine)
1 cup buttermilk
1 teaspoon baking soda

2 tablespoons light corn syrup
2 tablespoons vanilla (yes, tablespoons)
1 cup pecans, chopped

In heavy 3¾ quart saucepan, combine sugar, butter, buttermilk, baking soda and corn syrup over low to medium heat. Cook, stirring occasionally, until mixture reaches hard ball stage (265 degrees on a candy thermometer). Remove from heat and stir in vanilla and pecans. Place in bowl of ice and beat with a wooden spoon — it will set up quickly. When candy thickens, pour into a buttered 8-inch square pan. Cool; then cut into 1-inch squares.

Gloria Ann Lyon

GLAZED NUTS

1 egg white
¾ cup brown sugar

½ teaspoon vanilla
2 cups pecan halves

Beat egg white until soft peaks form. Continue beating and gradually add vanilla and brown sugar. Fold in pecans. Place pecan halves (well coated in sugar mixture) on lightly greased baking sheet about 1 inch apart. Bake at 250 degrees for 30 minutes. Turn off oven and leave in oven an additional 30 minutes. Store in air-tight container. May be placed in freezer.

Pat Norvell

PEANUT BRITTLE

2 cups sugar
1 cup white corn syrup
½ cup water
1 teaspoon butter

2 cups raw peanuts
1 teaspoon vanilla
2 teaspoons soda

Boil sugar, syrup and water together to 260 degrees. Add butter and peanuts and cook on medium low to a light golden brown. Remove from heat and *quickly* add vanilla and soda. Stir and pour onto a buttered tin. Let stand until cold and then break into pieces.

Karen Bradshaw

BUTTERMILK PRALINES

2 cups sugar
1 cup buttermilk
1 teaspoon baking soda
1 teaspoon butter flavoring

1 teaspoon vanilla
1 tablespoon butter
2 cups chopped nuts

Combine first 3 ingredients in a heavy saucepan. (Coat inside edge of pan for about 1-inch with butter to prevent boiling over.) Cook over medium heat to a soft ball stage (235 degrees). Remove from heat and add butter, vanilla, butter flavoring and nuts. Beat until it loses its shine. Drop by spoonfuls onto waxed paper and cool. Makes about 20 to 22 pralines.

Kala Casebolt

MARTHA WASHINGTON CANDY

1 1-pound box confectioners' sugar
1 can sweetened condensed milk
½ cup margarine

2 cups pecans, chopped
2 teaspoons vanilla

Cream margarine and condensed milk. Add sugar; when thoroughly mixed, add vanilla and pecans. Drop by teaspoonfuls onto waxed paper-covered trays and place in freezer until hard enough to stay on toothpick.

Coating: Melt 4 squares unsweetened chocolate with a 2½-inch square of paraffin. Dip candy by sticking a toothpick into bottom of each hardened candy. Store in refrigerator. Easy and delicious!

Joyce Moore

PEANUT BUTTER CHOCOLATE TRUFFLES

½ cup whipping cream
8 ounces milk chocolate, cut up
⅓ cup creamy peanut butter

¾ teaspoon vanilla
Cocoa powder or crushed, unsalted roasted peanuts, as needed

Heat cream to just below boiling. Place chocolate in mixer bowl. Pour hot cream over and beat until chocolate is melted. Stir in peanut butter and vanilla. Chill at least 2 hours, or until firm enough to handle. Roll chocolate mixture into 1-inch balls, between palms of hands. Then roll in cocoa or peanuts before serving. Coconut or pecans can also be used.

Dedicated to Eileen Stover

CHOCOLATE TRUFFLES

⅓ cup almonds, sliced
⅓ cup sugar
1½ pounds semisweet chocolate,
    (or bittersweet) chopped
1 tablespoon strong coffee

⅓ cup butter, softened
2 tablespoons whipping cream
2 tablespoons liqueur (any flavor)
Cocoa powder

In a small saucepan, combine almonds and sugar. Over low heat, cook slowly until golden brown, stirring with a wooden spoon. Remove from heat and pour mixture onto an oiled plate. Allow to harden. In a food processor or blender, crush nut mixture to a coarse powder. Melt 8 ounces chocolate in a double boiler. Stir in coffee; cool slightly. Beat in butter; stir in cream and crushed nut mixture. Divide mixture in half. Flavor each half with 1 or 2 tablespoons of liqueur. Gently roll heaping teaspoonsful of mixture into balls. Work quickly, as chocolate sets fast. Set aside on waxed paper; refrigerate until firm. Melt remaining chocolate; dip some truffles and place on waxed paper to set. Roll others in cocoa when nearly set. Place in paper candy cups. Store, covered, in a cool place. Makes 1½ pounds.

Helen Tieber

DATE-PECAN BOURBON TRUFFLES

1 cup dates, pitted, coarsely chopped
2 tablespoons bourbon, divided
¼ cup whipping cream
2 tablespoons maple syrup

2 tablespoons unsalted butter
¼ teaspoon nutmeg
6 ounces chocolate, semisweet or bittersweet, chopped
1½ cups pecans, toasted and finely chopped

Line cookie sheet with foil. Mix dates and 1 tablespoon bourbon in bowl; set aside. Bring cream, maple syrup, butter and nutmeg to simmer in heavy medium saucepan, stirring frequently. Remove from heat. Add chocolate and whisk until smooth and melted. Stir in date mixture and remaining 1 tablespoon bourbon. Freeze mixture until firm enough to mound on spoon, about 20 minutes, stirring occasionally. Drop chocolate mixture by rounded tablespoon onto foil-lined sheet. Freeze until almost firm, about 10 minutes. Roll each mound in pecans. Chill until firm. (Can be prepared 2 weeks ahead; cover and keep refrigerated.) Serve cold.

Pamela Easter

CHOCOLATE TOFFEE MATZOS

½ pound matzos (approximately)	1 12-ounce bag chocolate chips
1 cup butter	1 cup chopped pecans (optional)
1 cup brown sugar	1 cup toffee candy pieces (optional)

Preheat oven to 450 degrees. Line a 15×10×1-inch jellyroll pan with aluminum foil. Fit matzos in pan in a single layer, covering entire pan. (Some may be left over.) In a small pan over medium-high heat, melt butter and brown sugar. Boil until mixture coats a spoon (about 3 to 5 minutes). Pour mixture over matzo layer. Bake 4 minutes; remove from oven. Sprinkle chocolate chips on top. Bake 1 minute more. Remove from oven and gently spread melted chocolate to cover as completely as possible. Sprinkle with chopped nuts or toffee candy, if desired. Cool completely in refrigerator. Break into pieces and store in covered tin in refrigerator. Makes about 2 pounds; 32 servings.

Bonnie Powers

CHOCOLATE COVERED CALORIES

1 12-ounce package chocolate chips	1 cup ripple potato chips, slightly crushed
1 6-ounce package peanut butter chips	1½ cups peanuts, dry roasted

Melt chips on medium setting in microwave until melted. Stir often. Add potato chips and nuts, mix well. Drop by teaspoonful onto wax paper.

Nancy Spicer

TRIPLE CHOCOLATE PEANUT CLUSTERS

2 pounds white chocolate	12 ounces milk chocolate chips
12 ounces semisweet chocolate chips	24 ounces dry roasted peanuts

Melt chocolates in electric skillet on lowest setting, or in double boiler, stirring constantly. Cool 5 minutes. Stir in peanuts. Drop mixture by tablespoonfuls onto waxed paper. Cool completely. Wrap individually in plastic wrap and refrigerate until ready to serve. (Peanuts can be salted or unsalted.)

DELUXE PEANUT BUTTER CUPS

6 tablespoons confectioners' sugar
1/4 cup sour cream
2 tablespoons whipping cream
1/4 teaspoon vanilla

3/4 cup chunky peanut butter
1 1/4 pounds semisweet chocolate, chopped
3/4 cup dry roasted peanuts, unsalted, halved

Mix sugar, sour cream, whipping cream and vanilla. Stir in peanut butter. Cover and refrigerate until well chilled. (Can be prepared 1 day ahead). Place 36 foil mini-muffin cups (2 inches in diameter) on two cookie sheets. Melt chocolate in top of double boiler, stirring until smooth. Drop 1 teaspoon chocolate into each muffin cup. Rotating each cup, spread chocolate 3/4-inch up insides of cups with small palette knife. Refrigerate until chocolate is set, about 20 minutes. Drop 1 rounded teaspoon peanut butter mixture into each cup. Flatten slightly with back of spoon. Remelt chocolate in top of double boiler over simmering water. Spoon enough chocolate (about 1 teaspoon) into each cup to cover filling completely. Sprinkle each cup with several peanut halves. Dip fork into remaining melted chocolate. Carefully drizzle over cups to create decorative pattern. Refrigerate until chocolate is set, about 20 minutes. Store in airtight tins. Can be prepared up to 4 days ahead and refrigerated. Makes 36 cups.

CHOCOLATE CHIP PEPPERMINT KISSES

2 egg whites
1/8 teaspoon cream of tartar
1/2 cup sugar

6 ounces chocolate chips
1/4 teaspoon peppermint extract

Beat egg whites until foamy. Add cream of tartar. Beat until whites stand in peaks, but are still moist. Add sugar, 2 tablespoons at a time, beating thoroughly after each addition. Fold in chocolate chips and peppermint extract. Drop from teaspoon onto ungreased brown paper. Bake at 300 degrees for 25 minutes. Remove from paper while still warm. Makes 3 dozen.

Vi Kimbrell

INDEX